The Island of Lundy

The Island of Lundy

A.F. LANGHAM

SUTTON PUBLISHING

First published in 1994 by
Alan Sutton Publishing Limited, an imprint of Sutton Publishing Limited
Phoenix Mill · Thrupp · Stroud · Gloucestershire · GL5 2BU

Reprinted in 2001, 2002, 2004

British Library Cataloguing in Publication Data
A catalogue record for this book is available from the British Library.

ISBN 0 7509 0661 8

Cover illustration: a view of the island of Lundy

Maps and diagrams by Mike Komarnyckyj.
Typeset in 10/13 Plantin Light.
Typesetting and origination by
Sutton Publishing Limited.
Printed in Great Britain by
J.H. Haynes & Co. Ltd, Sparkford.

For Joanna
and for
Emily, Elizabeth and Jonathan

CONTENTS

Acknowledgements

I am very grateful to a large number of people, most of whom are listed in the text and in the Preface, for their help in producing this book.

I am also grateful to those friends who have given permission for me to reproduce their photographs and to Colin Taylor for the use of his excellent map of Lundy.

Over the years I have received invaluable assistance from many of the islanders and from the Landmark Trust, by whose generosity the island is kept open and made accessible to the public.

Preface

This book, the result of over forty years of part-time study and research, grew from *Lundy, Bristol Channel* which my former wife and I published in 1959. Our work, reshaped to conform to the Islands Series of David & Charles, was published as *Lundy* in 1970, with a second edition in 1984. The wealth of new information that has come to light since then and the many changes that have taken place on the island have necessitated a complete redrafting of the original manuscript.

Many kind friends have offered advice and passed on new information but especial mention must be made of the late Felix Gade, longtime agent on the island; of Mr K.S. Gardner and Professor Charles Thomas for insights into Lundy's past; and to the late Mr M.R. Bouquet for advice on maritime matters. I was particularly fortunate to have had the Lundy papers of the late Mr A.E. Blackwell, former Curator of the North Devon Athenaeum, of the late Miss Eileen Heaven, and of the late Dr A.T.J. Dollar passed on to me. I must also record my appreciation of the staff at the British Library and the Public Record Office for their help and interest.

In the chapters on history I have used the term 'Norman' to include Plantagenets and other French-speaking invaders from northern France. Certain speculations about the history of the church on Lundy, of the Giants' Graves, of Beacon Hill, and of Madoc have been included – these are all merely speculation and the future will prove them true or false. They have not been widely published before and deserve inclusion.

To avoid unnecessary repetition the references in the Notes to prime sources are abbreviated (e.g. Chanter, Loyd, etc.) with the full details of these sources listed in the Select Bibliography.

In consequence of the increasingly complex study of the natural history of the island together with the wealth of recent publications of Lundy specialities, the chapters dealing with Lundy's mail service and stamps, archaeology, flora and fauna have been recently rewritten to give merely an outline of the speciality they describe while giving details of where fuller information can be found.

TONY LANGHAM
Reigate, 1994

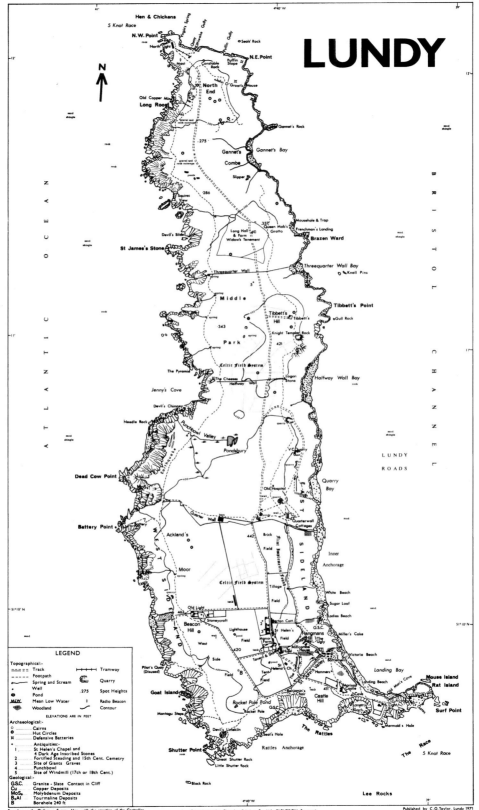

LUNDY

Hen & Chickens

5 Knot Race

N.W. Point

North Light

N.E. Point

Mast

Constable Rock

Puffin Slope

Seal's Rock

Groat's House

North End

Old Copper Mines

Long Roost

Gannet's Rock

.275

Gannet's Bay

Gannet's Combe

Slipper Pt

Squires View

.286

Mousehole & Trap

Frenchman's Landing

Queen Mab's Grotto

.337

Long Hall & Farm
Widow's Tenement

Devil's Slide

Brazen Ward

St James's Stone

Threequarter Wall Bay

Threequarter Wall

Knoll Pins

Middle

5

Tibbett's Point

Tibbett's Hill

Tibbett's

Gull Rock

.343

Knight Templar Rock

Park

421

Celtic Field System

The Pyramid

The Cheeses

Halfway Wall

Logan Stone

Halfway Wall Bay

Jenny's Cove

Devil's Chimney

Needle Rock

Punchbowl Valley

Pondsbury

VC Quarry

LUNDY ROADS

Dead Cow Point

Quarry Bay

Battery Point

Quarterwall Cottages

Quarter Wall

Ackland's

Brick Field

442

Flint Implements found

Inner Anchorage

Moor

White Beach

Sugar Loaf

Celtic Field System

Tillage Field

Ladies Beach

Old Light

E A S T   S I D E L A N D

Beacon Hill

Stoneycroft

Lighthouse

Barton Cott.

G.S.C.

St Helen's Field

Hangmans

The Ugly

Miller's Cake

West Side

Manor Farm

Millcombe

.420

Tavern

St Mary's Ch.

Victoria Beach

Pilot's Quay (Disused)

Hanmers

Landing Bay

Field

Tent Field

Field

411

Battlements

Mouse Island

Rat Island

Goat Island

Benjamin's Chair

Castle Hill

Marisco Castle

Landing Beach

Man's Cove

Mermaid's Hole

Surf Point

Rocket Pole Pond

G.S.C.

Rocket Pole

Montagu Steps

Devil's Limekiln

Seal's Hole

The Rattles

Shutter Point

Great Shutter Rock

Little Shutter Rock

Rattles Anchorage

The Race

5 Knot Race

Black Rock

Lee Rocks

LEGEND

Topographical:-

====	Track	┣━━━┫	Tramway
-----	Footpath		Quarry
	Spring and Stream		
•	Well	.275	Spot Heights
	Pond		
M.L.W.	Mean Low Water	┃	Radio Beacon
	Woodland		Contour

ELEVATIONS ARE IN FEET

Archaeological:-

o .... Cairns
⊗ .... Hut Circles
⌂ .... Defensive Batteries
• .... Antiquities:-
1 .... St Helen's Chapel and
         4 Dark Age Inscribed Stones
2 .... Fortified Steading and 15th Cent. Cemetery
3 .... Site of Giants Graves
4 .... Punchbowl
5 .... Site of Windmill (17th or 18th Cent.)

Geological:-

G.S.C. .... Granite - Slate Contact in Cliff
Cu .... Copper Deposits
MoS₂ .... Molybdenum Deposits
B₃Al .... Tourmaline Deposits
B .... Borehole 240 ft

A T L A N T I C   O C E A N

B R I S T O L   C H A N N E L

W E S T   S I D E L A N D

Based upon the Ordnance Survey Map with the sanction of the Controller of H.M. Stationery Office, Crown Copyright Reserved.

Printed by the Clevedon Printing Co., Ltd., CLEVEDON, Somerset.

Published by C.G. Taylor, Lundy 1971

Chapter One

EARLY HISTORY

During the glacial fluctuations of the ice ages, Lundy was alternately a sea-girt isle or a rocky tor at the mouth of the Severn Estuary. Recent research has shown that the last glaciation actually encroached on to Lundy's plateau, depositing moraine and grinding down the tops of the coastal crags so that the large valley systems of Gannet's Combe and Millcombe were eventually formed by the draining melt-water.[1]

In the early post-glacial age with sea-level some 35 m below the present, Lundy appears to have been some ten times its present size. Further icemelt raised sea-level so that by 8000 BP 'sea-levels were 20 m below the present with the island still four times its present size. At 6500 BP in the later Mesolithic, a sea-level of about 10 m below the present gave the island an additional surface area twice its current size. Even at the beginning of the Bronze Age, a period during which a series of communities were established on the island, sea-levels were 3 m below the present. . . . Only during the middle and upper Paleolithic, a period of human occupation yet to be discovered on the island, might Lundy have appeared as a promontory connected with the mainland.'[2]

The oldest evidence of man on Lundy was discovered in 1932[3] when a large number of small megalithic-worked flints and wasteflakes were found in the Tillage and Brick Fields. Although poor in quality and made from local beach pebble flint, probably brought there by glacial action, the collection included crude forms of microliths, microburins and bipolar cores produced by a nomadic group whose diet depended on fish and seabirds.

About 3500 BC men of a more advanced culture from the mainland of Europe arrived in Britain and brought with them a knowledge of agriculture and skill in the working of stone. They were also advanced enough to produce distinctive pottery and to trade over considerable distances. The hut circles and pigmy flints of Lundy are thought to date from this Neolithic period, although firm dating is not possible.

Yet another influx of settlers arrived in southern England c. 2000 BC whose culture – based on an ability to work metal (first bronze and later iron) – evolved into the Celtic period which was to last over a thousand years. Traces are still evident on Lundy of the pattern of farming from c. 1000 BC until well into the Christian Era.

There were three main centres of settlement, although traces of huts and fields are present over almost all the island. The earliest is a settlement of Late Bronze Age

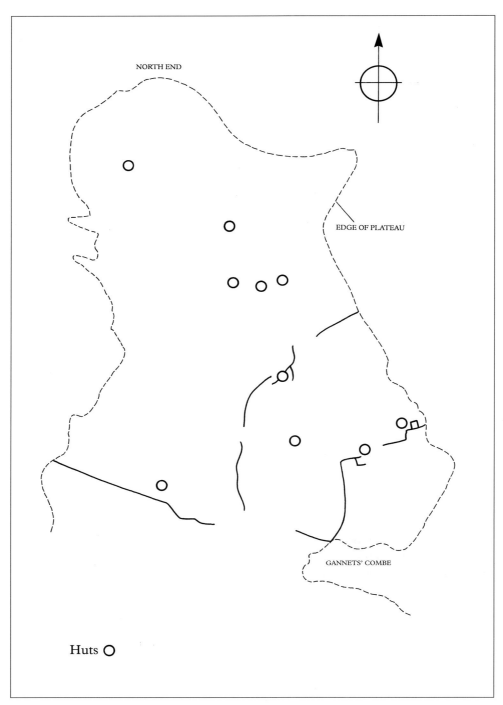

NORTH END

EDGE OF PLATEAU

GANNETS' COMBE

Huts ◯

Gannets' Combe Settlement

type, occupying the plateau north of Gannets' Combe. Here a low wall encloses a dozen stone huts, some in a good state of preservation. The huts are of two types, one about 3 m in diameter conjoined with rectangular chambers, the other about 10 m across. A further group of huts south-east of the combe has occasional outliers as far south as Threequarter Wall.

The second settlement was between Threequarter Wall and Halfway Wall where low grass banks, the ploughed-out traces of Celtic field systems, are associated with hut sites.

The third area is south of Quarter Wall where ploughed-over grass banks again define old fields, with circular mounds showing the sites of former huts. These Celtic field systems appear to have remained virtually unchanged on Acklands Moor until the mid-nineteenth century.

As early as 450 BC Carthaginian traders had established links with the silver miners of the Bristol Channel coast and by AD 150 the channel had become an international trade route. So struck was the Egyptian geographer Ptolemy by the similarity of the passage between Hartland and Lundy to that of the seaway between Gibraltar and Africa – the Pillars of Hercules – that he named Hartland Point as Heraclis Promontory on his map of the world.

Pre-Christian Iron Age pottery has been found on the island, but with the invasion of Britain by Claudius in AD 43 the old Iron Age society was replaced gradually by a more sophisticated economy. In the south-west the native Celtic traditions lingered longest to emerge eventually in the fifth and sixth centuries as a sub-Roman culture.

On Lundy no firm evidence of Romanization has yet been discovered and the few sherds of Roman pottery in Bristol Museum which may have come from the island are inadequately labelled. There do, however, appear to be two Roman literary references to Lundy. The first, by the Roman geographer Solinus, describes an island off the Devon/Cornwall coast which both Richmond and Frere identify as Lundy, though perhaps a stronger case can be made for the description to apply to Scilly. The second reference refers to the time when Britain was still under the Romans and states: 'There was said to be a specially holy race of men on Lundy Island, who refused trade and had visions of the future. To the Greeks and Romans holiness meant the refusal to trade for money.'[4]

Following the collapse of imperial control over Britain, the eastern lowland zone was quickly invested by 'Saxons, Angles and Jutes', though in the west the Celtic communities were influenced more by Irish Christianity. Settlement sites of this period on Lundy are not clearly identifiable, although a few scraps of imported Mediterranean pottery from this period have been found just north of the present village and the early Christian 'undeveloped' cemetery on Beacon Hill dates from this time. The site was investigated in 1968 and 1969 and shown to stand

within an extensive field system with associated huts belonging to the later centuries BC and the earliest centuries AD; some pottery may indicate use into

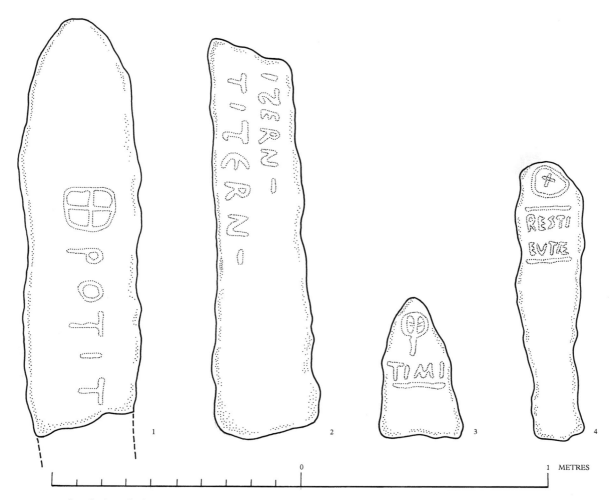

Lundy inscribed stones (not made from new impressions)

the fourth century. The area of the cemetery enclosure itself previously included at least one hut and overlies one field lynchet . . . the original structure was a bank, perhaps with a single line of boulders; presumably its original shape was oval.[5]

There is a squarish flat-topped cairn, or Leacht, which is presumably a special grave – perhaps that of a saint or the founder of the Christian community there – a mass of unmarked graves and a collection of nineteenth- and twentieth-century marked stones in the vicinity of a ruined chapel which itself is probably medieval. The most important feature, historically, is the group of four early Christian memorial stones which alone would make the site unique.

Suggested sitings of early memorial stones against the south wall of St Helen's chapel cemetery, Lundy

Two of the stones have horizontal inscriptions but all are cut in Roman capitals. They read:

1. + POTITI (later sixth century) of Potitus (?St Patrick's grandfather)
2. . . . IGERNI . . . I.TIGERNI (AD 600–650) (?Vort)igerni Fili Tigerni
3. OPTIMI (*c.* AD 490–500) the memorial of Optimus
4. RESTI EUTA (*c.* AD 500) a Celtic name

Geoffrey Ashe highlights the importance of Lundy in Celtic mythology:

In Welsh it has an uncanny character and is supposed to be Annwn or rather a place where mysterious realms can be entered. Various hills and islands are points of access to it. The most important hill is the Tor at Glastonbury, the

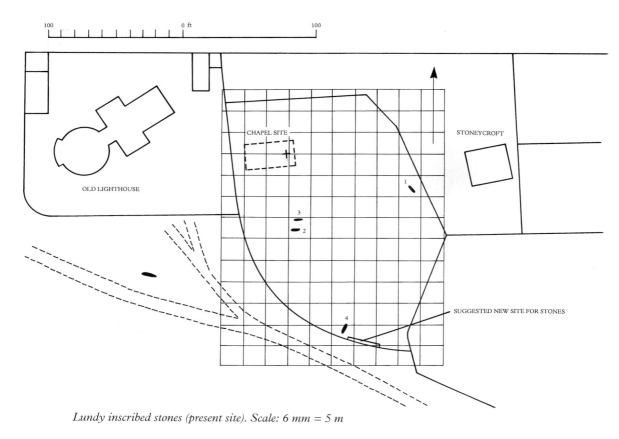

Lundy inscribed stones (present site). Scale: 6 mm = 5 m

most important island is Lundy. . . . Annwn's inhabitants have human form but are not strictly human. They are immortals – fairyfolk or demons according to one's point of view. Some are Gods thinly disguised. Living humans can enter Annwn, and so are spirits of the dead, but it is neither a heaven or hell in the Christian sense. To a certain extent it resembles Avalon. . . .[6]

This magical property may account for the legend of St Govan (who flourished in the fifth century) and who was being pursued by pirates from Lundy when a cliff-face on the coast of South Wales opened up to reveal a fissure which sheltered and hid him.

Many of the islands off the west coast of Britain, including Lundy, were known to the Celts as 'Isles of the Dead'. They were regarded as holy islands which formed gateways to the next world and to which the illustrious dead were ferried, there to be buried with solemn rite amid the spirits of their forefathers.

An old Welsh name for Lundy was Ynys Wair, or Weir, meaning the Island of Gwair or Gweir – the name of a mythical person who was apparently imprisoned in some sort of otherworld place.[7]

The four Dark Age inscribed stones

The reality of this period has been shown by Anne Robertson who, writing in 1974 on the coin hoards of the Bristol Channel, reveals that the period of the fourth to fifth centuries was a time of frantic raiding by the Irish on both sides of the Bristol Channel, ensuring that life on Lundy at that time was perilous.

The Celtic Britons of the west were driven into Cornwall by the Anglo-Saxon King Egbert about the year AD 805. At the same time Viking raiders in their longboats were harrying the British coast in a pincer-like movement southwards by way of the Irish Sea and northwards from their settlements on the coast of continental Europe. Being seafarers and meeting no naval opposition 'they were able to make their bases on islands off the coast, or in the mouths of rivers without fear of attack'.[8] The earliest Viking raids in the Bristol Channel were on a small scale in AD 795 against South Wales; in AD 835 or 843 raids were made against the north Somerset coast; and in AD 851 along the estuary of the Taw.[9]

An attack in 854 or 846 suggests that the marauders were Vikings from Ireland, and in 878 a chieftain named Hubba left South Wales and crossed to North Devon at the head of some twelve hundred men. He attacked Cynuit[10] and suffered a defeat during which he himself was slain. The Hubbastone at Bloody Corner near Appledore is said to mark the scene of this action, and it has been further suggested that the Giants' Graves on Lundy are those of Hubba and his men, but there is no evidence whatever to support this nor any record of Hubba having been of unusual height.

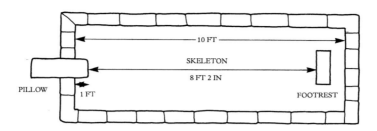

a: conjectural sketch (1925) of 1860 discovery

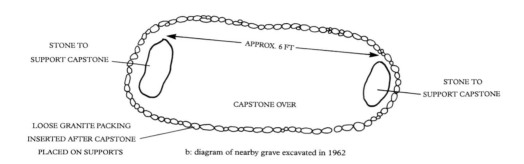

b: diagram of nearby grave excavated in 1962

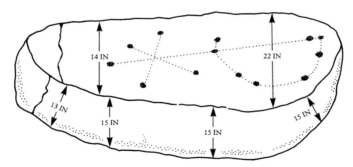

c: giant's stone (capstone of 1860 grave) with conjecture of Chi-Rho symbol, from linking surface 'cups'

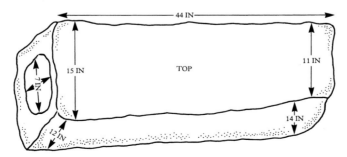

d: giant's pillow, found inside 1860 grave

The Giants' Graves

At the time of their discovery these Giants' Graves on Lundy caused great excitement and speculation. W.H. Heaven, the owner, was convinced they were Viking, but detailed work by K.S. Gardner and others since 1960 has shown this site to be no more than a late medieval cemetery.

The first graves were discovered by accident in 1856. In 1928 Dr W.S. Bristowe excavated a further grave, and in 1932 Dr Dollar and T. Lethbridge found more. The number of bodies found in the immediate area totals twenty-five. While digging, Bristowe unearthed a French coin which was later dated to AD 1380, a find which fits well with all the other evidence to date the site between the fourteenth and seventeenth centuries. The Giants' Graves are supposed to have contained skeletons 8 ft in length. The associated discovery of some glass beads has been used to date the burials, although the earliest reports seem to suggest that the beads were not actually in the graves and Bristol Museum, where the beads are now held, dates them to the ninth century AD.

A little to the west of the graves is a low rectangular enclosure which may prove to be an associated chapel[11] and the entire complex just to the west of the island's High Street, in a field known as Bulls' Paradise, seems to be the settlement and fortification in use until the thirteenth century at least. Regarding burials, it should be remembered that until the nineteenth century, victims of shipwreck could not be buried in consecrated ground unless they were known to be Christians.

There are many other records of Viking forays along the Bristol Channel coasts between 878 and 997 and these invaders who crossed to and fro so many times must have been closely familiar with Lundy. The island is mentioned in the famous Orkneyinga Saga[12] and the passage which dates between 1139 and 1148 relates to Svein Asleifson, Ragnvald Kali the Earl of Orkney and Robert the Englishman (who is possibly Robert FitzHamon, though he died as early as 1107).

Svein Asleifson arrived on the coast of England in mid-winter, a refugee from the ashes of his home. Bishop William the Old sent Svein to the Hebrides to care for a chief named Holdboldi and while there Svein made Harald and Rognvald joint Earls of the Isles. He borrowed two ships from Rognvald and sailed down the east coast of Scotland. During a winter spent on his estate in Caithness one 'Robert, an Englishman' brought him an appeal for aid from Holdboldi who had been driven out of his land in the Hebrides by a Welshman, who bore the name of Hold. Svein was always ready to help a friend especially if there was to be a fight and so early in summer he again borrowed two ships from Rognvald.

After searching down the coast of Scotland for Hold the Welshman, Svein came upon his track in the Isle of Man where Hold had killed a local Chieftain. Svein found the widow to be both wealthy and fair, promised to avenge her wrongs and promptly became the lady's second husband. The honeymoon was brief, for Svein was soon at sea again in the company now of Holdboldi. Together they scoured the western seaboard gathering a good haul in the process of seeking Hold. Not till the end of the summer did they locate him in a stronghold on Lundy. It was too late then; the Welshman after a short siege was saved by winter weather. The attackers went back to spend the winter in the Isle of Man.

Svein for his part left his bride when spring arrived and made ready for another joint expedition. His false ally, however, excused himself and sailed away. Holdboldi had secretly arranged with Hold to make common cause against Svein. But Svein had two good Orkney ships and had a good season on a raiding cruise of his own. Then, for a second time, Svein wintered in the Isle of Man but it was then that the misguided Holdboldi tried, and failed, to assassinate Svein. But in failing, Holdboldi had a shrewd idea of what might be in store for him so he fled hot-foot to the shelter of Hold's fortress on Lundy.

Svein preferred not to tackle Lundy again. He left Man for good and sailed north to the Orkneys.[13]

Writing of this time when Lundy was plainly in the hands of a Welsh Freeman, E. St John Brooks says: 'I think there is a good deal of evidence for a connection with Wales rather than with England for some considerable time after the Conquest.' He cites three important facts. First, there is no mention of Lundy in 'Domesday Book'

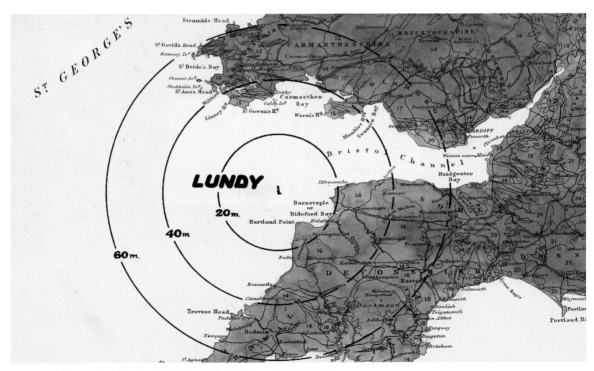

A map showing Lundy in the Bristol Channel (J.Dollar)

of 1086, showing that the island had not yet passed into Norman hands; second, the original island church was dedicated to St Elen, a Welsh saint; and, third, the earliest name given to the island in the Pipe Rolls is Ely, which is probably a shortened form of Eliensis, meaning 'of St Elen' or Hely, which is exactly parallel to the early forms of the name of the Welsh river Ely at Cardiff, which is Celtic.[14]

The Normans had arrived in North Devon as early as 1068, as in the summer of that year the eldest sons of King Harold (who had been killed at the Battle of Hastings) led a force of sixty-four ships from Ireland into the mouth of the Taw where they were defeated by the Norman, Count Brian de Penthièvre.[15]

The first Norman family to take the title of the island were the De Newmarchs, presumably at the very end of the eleventh century, and the first mention of the Marisco family in connection with Lundy occurs in 1154, while in 1166 they are recorded as holding the island from Henry de Newmarch for a fifth part of a knight's fee.

A few years earlier in 1163 as Henry II's forces again moved against the North Wales Kingdom of Gwynedd, 'an emissarie of the Prince of Gwynet landed at Lund to seek aide against Henrie of Englande'. The emissary is unnamed but may well have been the Welshman Prince Madoc himself, who is supposed to have used Lundy as a base and to have sailed from there, westwards, about the year 1170.

'Madoc, with his brother Riryd, Lord of Clochran in Ireland, prevailed upon so many [Welshmen] to accompany them as to fill seven ships and sailing from the isle of Lundy, they took an eternal leave of Wales.'[16] However, it seems unlikely that the Mariscos, who were at this time loyal Normans, would have allowed Lundy to be used in this way by Welshmen fleeing from Henry II, and indeed Professor Gwyn A. Williams in his book *Madoc, the Making of a Myth* (1979) discounts associations with Lundy and doubts Madoc's very existence.

Chapter Two

THE DE MARISCOS

With the arrival of the Normans in the West Country, Lundy assumed a new importance and for the next two centuries the family who were to become most closely associated with it were the Mariscos. Although spelt in many ways, of which 'de Marisco' or 'de Mariscis' is the Latinized form, the surname occurs also as Marreys, Mareir, or even Marsh and might derive from the marshy area of north Somerset between the Rivers Axe and Parrett, where the family settled.

A forebear may have come with the Conqueror[1] though it is known for certain that in AD 1100 one of the thirty-five illegitimate children of King Henry I was named William de Marisco.[2] This birth occurred at a time when the concept of primogeniture (right of eldest son to inherit) was developing to avoid the endless splitting of estates, and with it came the increasing importance of legitimacy which finally led to the concept of male dominance and the consequent loss of status for women. The full inference to be drawn from the AD 1100 birth and its first mention of the Marisco family in England is discussed below.

The Mariscos are first mentioned on Lundy during the reign of Stephen but on acceding in 1155 Henry II commanded the return of all lands that had been granted away (and this included Lundy) during his predecessor's reign. The Mariscos failed to comply and remained in possession. For political reasons and to establish his credibility, authority and conformity Henry made several generous gifts to the popular Order of the Knights Templars. Although Lundy was among these gifts it was still not surrendered by the Mariscos, who were fined for retaining possession. In 1194, and again in 1195, William de Marisco is recorded as owing a fine of 300 marks for retaining custody of Lundy.[3] Two years later in 1197 William was fighting for the king in France as he then received 100 marks 'to pay the Walensian infantry . . . for their services, and to the same William, their Constable, 3 marks for his services. As to the same [i.e. William] £4 for the service of twenty cavalry each with two horses by gift through the writ of the Archbishop of Canterbury.'[4]

When King John acceded to the throne in 1199 he confirmed the grant of Lundy to the Templars[5] and then stipulated that they should pay '50 marks and a palfrey for having lands in Somerset which were the wages of Nicholas de Kiville as long as William de Marisco shall hold island of Lunde [sic] against the King's will and theirs'.[6] The Mariscos clearly maintained their hold on Lundy as in the following year the Templars stated that 'they ought to have seisin of their Island whence they were disseised unjustly'.[7] A record of 1202 states that the Templars were in debt for their holding of Marisco lands in Somerset while William de Marisco held the 'Island of Lundely'; and also that William still owed 120 of the 300 marks which he had been fined.[8] The same year the Sheriff of Devon made a return of 40 marks which he had received for the defence of the ports against William de Marisco,[9] from which it is apparent that William had been using Lundy as a base for piracy against the North Devon coast and traders. In view of this, and of his continued presence on Lundy, it is difficult to understand a grant made to him by the king in 1204 of the Manor of Braunton[10] and of his appointment to be in charge of some of the royal galleys. The king's quarrel with the Church may have adversely affected the Templars' position, as an order of 1204 granted to 'the Brethren of the Temple to have yearly at the Exchequer £10 granted to them until the King shall have assigned to them £10 worth of land, or until they have right against William de Marisco of the Isle of Lunde'.[11]

In July 1216 King Alexander II of Scotland marched through England to Dover where he awaited Louis, son of the king of France. Many of the English barons sided with Louis against King John and William de Marisco must have been among their number as he was one of the prisoners captured by the English after a battle with the French fleet, off Sandwich on the Kent coast, in July 1217. Meanwhile Henry III had come to the throne and when peace was concluded on 17 September 1217 all prisoners were 'absolved and freed'.[12]

On 7 November 1217 Hugh de Vivonne was advised: 'Know that William de Marisco has satisfied us as to his loyalty, and therefore we bid you restore, without any delay, the Island of Lundy, belonging to the aforesaid William, and William's wife with his four sons and two daughters captured on the island.'[13]

In the Pipe Roll of 1219 William is charged: 'xj li et iiij s. pro habenda insula de Ely Lundeie.' This fine of £11 4s for retaining possession is less interesting than the scribe's entry of Ely as the name of the island. This was subsequently cancelled and the name Lundeie inserted.

In the following year, with William still in occupation, the Templars were given 100s 'in lieu and full recompense for it'. By 1222 William was sufficiently trusted to be allowed to move to Lundy the stone-throwing machines called mangonels which he had on his lands at Camley.[14]

William de Marisco died peacefully in 1225 and was succeeded by his son Jordan. At this time William's brother Geoffrey was Justiciar of Ireland where he lived with his son, also named William, who until 1235 appears to have led a quiet and respectable life.

Trouble, however, was obviously brewing as the Patent Roll of 18 Henry III (i.e. 1235) records: 'An order from Henry the Third, to the Earls, Barons, Knights and others of Devon, to take care of the coast towards Lundy, where the King's enemies keep', adding 'that unless you provide for it, the King has ordered Henry de Tracy,

MARISCO FAMILY TREE

Kings are underlined; illegitimate offspring are indicated by hatched lines.

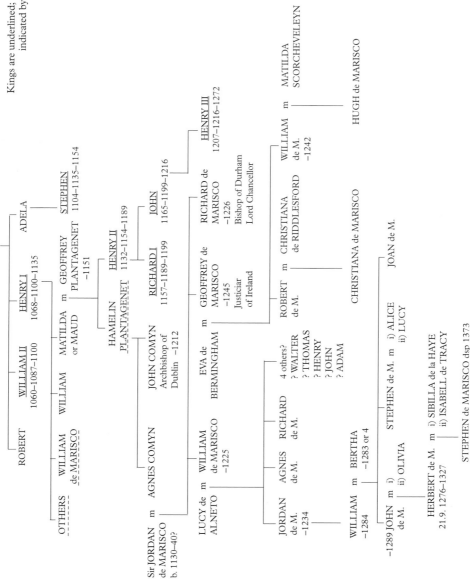

Reginald de Valletort, Philip de Bellomont and Galfrid Dinant, that at your expense, with the advice of the Sheriff of Devon they keep the peace in those parts – 7th Feb. – Ordered the four knights above mentioned, that if the men of the county will not do it, the King will order it to be guarded at their expense by those four knights'.

The marshal of the king's lands in Ireland, Earl Richard, was on very good terms with Geoffrey de Marisco; they were both great Irish landowners and their governmental duties presumably brought them together. However, Earl Richard rebelled against Henry III and was eventually killed – a bitter blow to Geoffrey de Marisco who had tried to remain loyal to the king during the marshal's rebellion. Following the defeat of the rebellion, both Geoffrey and his son William were fined 3,000 marks and three of their relatives were also fined and imprisoned. Geoffrey and William were not freed until late in 1234, long after all the other associates of the dead marshal. Even following their release they were not free of suspicion, as the king confiscated three of their Irish castles against their future fidelity.

When a new justiciar, Maurice Fitzgerald, was appointed, Geoffrey and his son came to London, most probably in an attempt to vindicate themselves and to plead their cause with the king. It was while in London that they came upon Henry Clement, a clerk, who had been sent as a messenger to the king by the new justiciar. Relations between the Mariscos and Henry Clement were already strained as William had already accused Henry Clement of putting obstacles in the way of his affairs at Court and of using his influence to avert the royal favour. Clement was boasting that he had been the 'cause of the death of Earl Richard the Marshall' who was a 'cruel enemy of the King and Kingdom'.[15] A group of William's friends had threatened Henry Clement at Rochester, and since his arrival in London 'a boy in buttons', a messenger of William's, had called daily at the houses near the Palace of Westminster to ask where Henry Clement was and where he would lodge.

At midnight on Sunday 13 May 1235, sixteen men arrived on horseback at the house where Henry Clement was lodging; six of them sought out and murdered him. Suspicion immediately fell on William de Marisco, and all those associated with him fled. William, with his household and friends, fled westwards and it was rightly suspected that they were making for Lundy. Another group of associates went to East Anglia, while Geoffrey de Marisco took sanctuary at Clerkenwell. The king outlawed William, and the new marshal of Ireland was made to swear that he would not receive William or his associates on his lands. William must have reached Lundy soon after leaving London whereupon the rightful owner of the island, William the son of Jordan,[16] was anxious to dissociate himself from his fugitive cousin. That he achieved this is clear from a letter sent by the king on 9 June 1235 saying: 'Grant to William, son of Jordan de Mariscis, that he may safely come out of his Island of Lundy with his men, come to England and stay there and retire from there; Grant to him also that Merchants may safely go to and from his said island as they used to do and mandate accordingly all bailiffs.' On this same day Geoffrey de Marisco was allowed to leave the Hospital of St John at Clerkenwell in safety, with all his men except those charged with Henry Clement's death. William, son of

Geoffrey, and his wife, Matilda, were deprived of their lands in Ireland,[17] but whether she was with him on Lundy is not certain.

On Lundy, William turned to piracy and to resisting the king in whatever way he could. In 1237 Henry III was obliged to prepare ships against 'certain evildoers, to wit, William de Marisco and his brother[18] and their accomplices of the land of the King of Scotland' who 'had put to sea with Galleys and were preying on Merchants and others crossing from Ireland to England'. At this time the king was on the point of war with his brother-in-law Alexander II of Scotland, with whom William had made some sort of alliance.

On one of the abovementioned forays, William de Marisco and his crew, desperate to avoid imminent capture, were given sanctuary by Abbot John de la Ware at Margam Abbey on the South Wales coast. This unwise but Christian act was not forgiven until 28 August 1242, a month after William de Marisco's death, when the abbot of Margam was pardoned for his indiscretion and received into the king's grace.[19]

Meanwhile, the king did not press the siege of Lundy until after an attempt had been made on his life in 1238 by a man who confessed that he was an agent of William, son of Geoffrey de Marisco. On 8 September the king, holding court at Woodstock, was confronted by an intruder who, pretending to be insane, called out: 'Resign thy Kingdom to me', and added that he bore the sign of royalty on his shoulder. The king was not disturbed by what he considered to be the ravings of a madman, but that night this very man, armed with a knife, entered the king's bedroom intending to murder him. The king, however, was elsewhere; the alarm was raised and the intruder overpowered. After his confession he was torn limb from limb at Coventry.

Efforts to capture William and his followers were now intensified:

> William de Marisco . . . having attached to himself many outlaws and malefactors, subsisted by a piracy of goods, more especially of wine and provisions, making frequent sudden eruptions on the adjacent lands, spoiling and injuring the Realm by land and sea, and native as well as foreign merchants in various ways. . . . [W]hen many nobles of England and Ireland had learnt more fully how the said William and his followers could not be surprised except by stratagem, they apprised the King that the securing of this malefactor must be affected not by violence, but by policy.

On 2 January 1242 an order appointed 'Walter de Bathonia, Sheriff of Devon, to keep the coast of Devon from the incursions of the King's enemies staying in the island of Lunday'.

On 7 February a final order was given for the capture of William. William Bardolf, a Norfolk baron, chose two knights and twelve sergeants to accompany him. One of these knights, Richard de Chilham, was granted a loan of 20 marks on 26 May 'to get himself equipment'.[20] The enterprise was a complete success.

According to Matthew Paris, 'William was betrayed by one of his men whom he had detained on the island against his will. The rocks protecting the place could only be scaled at one point and William imprudently set this man to guard the weak point. It was a misty day and William was sitting at meat when the King's men came.' Despite possible treachery, landings made under cover of mist would have been invisible from the plateau.

The captives were taken to Bristol and subsequently to London where William de Marisco was imprisoned with five others in the Tower, while the rest of the band were held in the Newgate and Flete Prisons. 'The Constables were ordered to put them in irons and in strong places.' On the 14 July the Constable of the Tower, Richard de Bovill, delivered William de Marisco, Aimerai de Beaufeu, Reginald de Marisco, Robert de Montibus and William's chamberlain (Richard) for trial.

> On the Eve of St James, on receipt of the Royal Warrant, the said William and sixteen accomplices taken with him were legally convicted and sentenced to death with peculiar ignominy by the King's express command. Nevertheless, the said William, after Sentence had been passed on him, and when on the eve of suffering death, so long as he yet lived, constantly affirmed, invoking the judgement of God, that he was free from and utterly guiltless of the crime of High Treason charged against him and the same of the death of the before-mentioned clerk [Henry Clement] and that his only motive for withdrawing to the island had been by avoiding to turn aside the anger of the King, which by whatever judicial expiation, or other humiliation, it had always been his first wish to appease; but when he had fled to the island, and called some friends to his assistance, he was driven, as he had said, to support his wretched existence on necessities snatched from every quarter. Pouring out his soul then before God in confession, he acknowledged his sin to J. de St. Giles, one of the order of preaching friars, not betrayed into expressions of malice in his own excuse, but rather accusing himself. And thus with soothing words of consolation the discreet preacher and confessor dismissed him in peace, persuading him to sustain his approaching death as an evidence of penitence.

He died on 25 July 1242 'being first dragged from Westminster to the Tower and thence to the . . . Gibbet, when he had there breathed out his wretched soul, he was suspended on a hook, and when stiff in death was lowered, disembowelled, his bowels burnt on the spot, and his wretched body divided into quarters which were sent to the four principal cities in the Kingdom, by what pitiable spectacle to strike terror into all beholders'.[21]

Matilda, William's widow, was detained at Gloucester until June 1243 and was unable to regain possession of any of her Irish property until 1247. William's father Geoffrey, on regaining his freedom in 1235, had been allowed to return to his possessions in Ireland though he remained there for only three years, travelling thence to Scotland and finally to France, where he died in July 1245. His body was returned to Ireland and buried at the Church of St John of Any, Co. Limerick. The whereabouts and position of the owner of Lundy (William, son of Jordan de Marisco) during these events is not known.

There are so many contradictions and unanswered questions in the history of the Marisco family and Lundy that make it difficult to understand some events. The first member of the family to incur the king's displeasure was Jordan, the nature of whose misdemeanour is not stated. Although the Mariscos held Lundy against the wishes of the king, and despite the attempts of the Knights Templar to take rightful possession of the place, they were granted the manor of Braunton in 1204. Similarly, William de Marisco, who had been captured among the French in 1217, was soon afterwards allowed to return to Lundy and even, in 1222, to refortify it.

If the words of the would-be assassin of Henry III at Woodstock are considered – 'Resign thy Kingdom to me, I bear the mark of Royalty on my shoulder' – the rebels could have been claimants to the throne of England. If the William de Marisco (born about 1100) was a forebear of the Lundy Mariscos,[22] the family may well have felt that their claim to the throne was stronger than that of anyone who had reigned since the death of Henry I in 1135, as after that date all the kings of England had been descended through women from the original Norman line.

Had the Mariscos been descended from royalty through a male line, albeit illegitimately (and the lion rampant on the Marisco coat of arms supports the royal connection), this would help to explain the erratic behaviour of the family. Some members would have felt their claim to be so strong that they should rebel against the reigning king, while others would be content to be loyal and to receive favours and pardons from a far-from-secure monarch who would be aware of the strength of some of the Marisco family's claims.

Chapter Three

EARLY MIDDLE AGES, 1243–1485

Following the capture of William de Marisco, Henry III at once took steps to secure control of Lundy and to ensure that the island would not again harbour his opponents. The importance which the king attached to the island must have been considerable, judging both from the frequent references to it in the Rolls at this time and also from the fact that no less a person than William de Cantilupe (the seneschal of the royal household and one of the most powerful men at Court) was sent there to report on the measures being taken to establish the king's authority.

The captive William de Marisco and his band were first lodged at Bristol where the bailiffs were ordered to allow 'the King's prisoners . . . one penny daily to live on'.[1] Three days later an order was given to the mayor and sheriffs of London holding them responsible for the safe custody of the prisoners in the 'King's gaols of Neugate and Flete'.[2] With his prisoners now in safe custody, the king set about establishing a garrison on Lundy.

On 23 June an order was made giving 'to Henry de Traci £100 to carry to the Sheriff of Devon for the living of the Knights, Sergeants and Mariners appointed to keep the Island of Lunday for the King'.[3] On the same day the Sheriff of Devon was ordered to 'tow to Aufrincumb the unfinished galley which William de Marisco began to make in the said island and there to finish it so that it may be ready to be fitted out when the King shall order, the cost to be credited by the view and testimony of lawful men', and to pay the sum of 23s 4d to Roger Giffard 'being arrears of five marks which the King ordered to be given to him for his expense in going to storm the said island'.[4] A further order was given to the sheriff

> that he should go, together with Henry de Tracy and Galfridus de Dynan to the Isle of Lunday and on the advice of these same people and of William de Rummare, the Constable of the said island, should see that the wages of those who will delay in guardianship of the island can be measured, until William de Cantilupe is able to come to that place and arrange more fully about the guardianship of the aforesaid island. Thus however such guardianship should remain to protect that island which should be guarded with care and without danger to the King until the arrival of the aforesaid William de Cantilupe

about August 11th. But for those who must delay meanwhile in the aforesaid island, he should arrange to have their own wages through the right and testimony of Henry III as it has been ordained through them, about the £100 which he sent to the Sheriff by the same Henry [de Tracy] and which he should receive from him for that purpose.[5]

In July an order was also sent to the bailiffs at Bristol to provide a ship in which William de Cantilupe and his party would sail from there to Lundy.[6]

Meanwhile, thirteen of William de Marisco's men were still detained in the Flete Prison and in October the king ordered each 'to have one penny daily for his maintenance out of the farm of the town from this Michaelmas so long as they remain there'.[7]

Preparations for the Lundy garrison continued in earnest. In November 1242 an order was sent to repair 'the King's buildings in the island so that the King's Knights and Sergeants keeping it in winter can dwell there safely'.[8] It was probably in view of the approaching winter that it was decided to postpone the building of a permanent fort as an order 'to make a limekiln near the island of Lunday for the work of

Lundy's impregnable castle (J. Dollar)

fortifying a castle there and to dig or quarry stone there and to haul it to the works'[9] was cancelled. The king, however, did not relax his vigilance and in the following spring work on the castle was resumed.

The Sheriff of Devon was ordered in February 1243 to 'take with him a man skilfull, faithfull and discreet in mason's work to the island of Lunday, and by his counsel and that of the Constable there choose a suitable site for a good tower with a bailey-wall, to be fortified with good lime and stone; and to begin and continue the work by the counsel of the Constable, out of the issues of the sale of rabbits . . . till the tower is finished'.[10] An order of the same date provides for the wages of four mariners who were on the island,[11] and arrangements were made for lime to be taken to Lundy for the new building.[12]

The population of Lundy at this time was at least fifty as Richard de Especheleg, who was now constable, had under him 'twenty sargeants receiving 6d each daily, twenty sargeants and four mariners receiving $2^{1}/_{2}$d each daily, and one sargeant Constable of the said sargeants receiving 8d daily, all dwelling in garrison on the island'. Apart from these there were two ploughmen who were on the island to till the king's lands and two shepherds keeping the king's stock, as well as a dairymaid.[13]

In June and August two further sums were to be delivered for the completion of the 'tower' and the Sheriff of Devon was ordered to send all the rabbit skins from Lundy 'for delivery in the wardrobe of Roger the Tailor, saving to the Church of the island the tithes arising therefrom'.[14] There was, therefore, a church on Lundy at this time.

By May 1244 with the tower presumably completed and the island felt to be secure, William de Cantilupe was acquitted of his responsibilities.[15] He was succeeded by Richard de Clifford on whose behalf a boat from Bristol was ordered to 'carry his supplies and harness to the island'.[16]

During the term of Richard de Clifford's custodianship the Sheriff of Devon was ordered to 'set free the galley of Lunday, which he has in custody',[17] presumably the same one which he had been keeping at Ilfracombe. For armaments 'it is ordered to the Constable of St. Briavels to render to Richard de Clifford, Constable of Lunday, 2000 quarrels [a type of arrow] for the arming the castle of Lunday'.[18] The expense of maintaining the garrison was met in various ways; for example in 1245 it was ordered ' . . . of the Mayor and Aldermen of London that from the possessions which belonged to John Gloripet, who lately killed Martin Malherbert of London, they should render without delay to Richard de Clifford £20 for the wages of the servants who reside in the island of Lunday'.[19]

Henry de Tracy replaced Richard de Clifford on 16 July 1245 and remained in charge until 8 August 1250 when Robert de Walerond, a baron of Parliament, took over.[20] Lundy must have been a source of some revenue to the Exchequer as the king directed that the dues which should have been paid to him at Michaelmas 1250 and Easter 1251 should be spent by Robert de Walerond.[21] The guardianship of the island was next entrusted to William la Zuche who was appointed in May 1251 'during pleasure . . . to keep the isle of Lunday with the castle and mandate to

Robert de Walerond to deliver it to him by an indenture of the arms, utensils and other things therein'.

In February 1254 the king made a gift of Lundy to his eldest son, Edward, 'to be held of him and his heirs for ever',[22] but as Edward was then only fifteen years old the gift was only nominal and William la Zuche remained a keeper, being ordered in October 1254 to put 'Adam de Aston, or his proctor, in possession of the Church of St. Mary, Lundy'.[23]

There is a gap of ten years before further mention is made of Lundy in the Rolls, then in July 1264 Mauger de Sancto Albino (St Aubyn) was directed to deliver Lundy to Ralph de Wyllyngton.[24] A sidelight on the confusion of these times of civil strife is afforded by an order of 15 September 1264 for the 'commitment by the Council of the Barons of the Council to Humphrey de Bohun the younger of the island of Lunday, with the castle and other appurtenances. Mandate to Mauger de Sancto Albino to deliver it to him',[25] followed by a repetition of the commitment on 14 October but 'with mandate to Ralph de Wyllenton . . . to deliver it to him'. Wyllyngton had held the island since 12 July, and in taking up the guardianship had been required to confirm that the commitment of Lundy to his keeping gave him no rights therein. The barons had defeated the king at Lewes on 14 May and were probably anxious to ensure that Lundy was under their control; the barons held power for a further year until Prince Edward defeated de Montfort and was able to assume control of the kingdom and restore order. On 14 June 1265 Edward committed the island to the keeping of Adam Gurdon 'so that he keep it safe, and in the King's fealty until then, the King will enfeoff him of it, on condition that he renders 100 shillings a year at the Exchequer or the King will refund him his expense in keeping it'.[26]

Whichever alternative Adam Gurdon may have chosen, the arrangement did not last very long, as in the following June the king's brother, William de Valencia, Earl of Pembroke, was ordered to deliver Lundy to the king's son, Edmond (Crouchback), Earl of Chester, Lancaster and Leicester 'as other keepers have had it'.[27]

In the second year of his reign, 1274, King Edward I ordered a census to be made of Lundy by twelve jurymen, who reported: 'They say that Lord Oliver de Dineham holds the manor of Hartland in capiti . . . they say that the island of Lundy is the escheat of the Lord King through the death of William de Marisco, outlaw, and the Lord Oliver holds the island "per Bayiam"[28] of King Henry, father of the King Edward who rules now, [though] they do not know with what warrant.' To their description of the island they add: 'In summer, even in time of peace, it is necessary to have fourteen servants and a Constable to watch the defences of the island, and in winter ten servants.'[29] Oliver de Dynan would seem to have been holding the island without authority, and following the report of the jurymen he was ordered to deliver 'to Geoffrey de Shauketon the island of Lundeye, which the King has committed to him during pleasure. Order all tenants to be intendent to him as Keeper.'[30]

The following day the Sheriff of Devon was ordered to 'cause Master Geoffrey de

Shauketon, King's clerk, whom the King is sending to the island of Lundeye to extend all the lands within the island, to have ten marks for his expenses'.[31] ('Extend', in its legal sense, means to value or assess.) The bailiff of the island was commanded to provide a jury from the island to help him.[32] Following this, Lundy was leased to Oliver de Dynan at a rent of 20s a year from 9 July 1275.[33]

De Dynan seems to have sublet to tenant farmers, as a legal document of 1279 relating to Lundy together with other holdings exists between 'Richard of the island' (father) and Richard his son, which recognizes that although the lands concerned belong to Richard the son, Richard of the island may hold them during his lifetime on payment of one rose annually on 24 June.[34]

By 1281 Sir William de Marisco (son of Jordan de Marisco) had apparently convinced the king of his title to Lundy, and that the rebellious behaviour of his father's cousin, who had lived on but not owned the island, was in no way connected with his right of ownership. Lundy was duly granted to 'William and his heirs by the service of the tenth part of the fee of one Knight'.[35]

On his death in 1284, William de Marisco was succeeded by his son John, who in turn held the island until his death five years later in 1289, when it passed to his heir, Herbert.

Herbert was only thirteen years old and a minor, so the king granted 'the custody of Lundy to Rotheric, a yeoman of Prince Edward'[36] on 3 February 1290. John de Marisco's widow, however, possibly anxious to prevent the island reverting to the Crown, claimed the entire possession as her dower. The precise course of events thereafter is unclear as there were conflicting claims to the island. In 1291 'Roderic de Weylite came before the King . . . and sought to replevy[37] his land in Lundy, which was taken into the King's hands for his default against Olive, late the wife of John de Marisco'. The final result was that in 1300 Olivia de Marisco gained possession of the island.[38] When she died on Lundy in 1321 Herbert de Marisco, her son, sought to establish his right to the island and appeared 'at an assize of novel disseizin' at Exeter on Friday 6 March 1321 and 'recovered the island from Sir John de Wyllyngton, of the same family as the former Governor of that name, and the Justices issued their precept to put Herbert in re-seizin'.[39] Why Sir John de Wyllyngton should have had possession is not clear but as he was pro-Lancastrian the king, ever anxious that Lundy should not fall into unfriendly hands, seized all the Wyllyngton lands. A writ was issued to 'Richard de Rodeney, keeper of the lands which belong to Thomas, Earl of Lancaster, and other rebels, and of the forfeited lands in Counties Devon and Cornwall' to find the 'extent of the lands of John de Wylyntone in Womberleigh, Beauford, Honeyshagh, Stoke and Londay Island'.[40]

Not only was the king at war with the Scots, who attacked Lundy in 1321, but he was also facing internal rebellion. Following the defeat at Pontefract of the Earl of Lancaster, the king recalled his banished favourites, the Despencers, and in June 1322 made a 'gift for good services rendered and to be rendered by Hugh de Despencer the Younger, to the said Hugh and Eleanor his wife, of the Isle of Lunday, late of John de Wylington, late an enemy and rebel of the King by whose forfeiture the said isle came to the King's hands; of the corn, hay, grass, cattle and goods in the Island of Lunday'.[41] From this it would appear that the claims of Herbert de Marisco were overlooked, unless, of course, he too had been a rebel sympathizer.

In 1324 Roger Mortimer went to France where he formed a liaison with the king's estranged wife, Isabella, and in an attempt two years later to overthrow the king, they invaded England.

The king fled with Hugh de Despencer the Younger and some others to Chepstow where they embarked and sailed westwards. After beating up and down the Severn for about a week, adverse winds forced them to land near Cardiff from where they progressed on land to Margam where they rested during 3 and 4 November 1326. On the 3rd the king 'granted letters of protection for one year to John Joseph, master of the king's ship "Goodyer of Kaerdif" and seven mariners of the same ship, namely, John Bursy; Richard de Shlo[Sully?]; John Dinevras; William Davy; Nicholas Aufey; John Moriz; and John Payn.' It seems probable that the king planned to sail in this ship from Aberavon to Lundy, where he would rest and await developments before, if necessary, sailing to retirement in Ireland.

On 5 November the king arrived in Neath and after conferring unsuccessfully with Welsh princes, moved eastwards only to be captured at Llantrisant. The Despencers were put to death and Edward II was taken to Berkeley Castle where, after his deposition on 7 January 1327, he was brutally murdered.

Westcote, in a little poem, describes the king's flight:

> To Londi, which in Sabrin's mouth doth stand,
> Carried with hope (still hoping to find ease)
> Imagining it were his native land,
> England itself; Severn, the narrow seas,
> With this conceit (poor soul!) himself doth please.
> And sith his rule is over-ruled by men
> On birds and beasts he'll King it o'er again
> Tis treble death a freezing death to feel,
> For him on whom the sun hath ever shone;
> Who hath been kneeled unto, can hardly kneel,
> Nor hardly beg what once hath been his own.
> A fearful thing to tumble from a throne.
> Feign would he be King of a little isle,
> All were his empire bounded by a mile.[42]

Meanwhile at the end of 1326 Herbert de Marisco had died, having been deprived of the possession of Lundy[43] first by his mother, secondly by Sir John de Wyllyngton and lastly by Hugh de Despencer!

Prince Edward became guardian of the realm after his father had been captured, and he appointed Otto de Bodrigan as Keeper of Lundy. De Bodrigan took over from William de Kerdeston and was paid £10 for the custody of the island.[44]

Once Edward acceded to the throne as Edward III he reversed the sentence of forfeiture which had been passed on Sir John de Wyllyngton and made a 'mandate to Otto de Bodrigan, in pursuance of a statute of the present Parliament to deliver to John de Wylington his island of Lundy, with all its liberties etc which escheated to the late King by forfeiture . . . and was committed to the said Otto by grant under the Privy Seal used by the present King while Guardian of the Realm in his father's absence'.[45] A week later the Sheriff of Devon was ordered to receive 'all the King's victuals' in Lundy and to sell them as quickly as possible.[46]

An interesting document of 26 April 1331 concerns 'the proposed exchange between James, Earl of Ormonde and Stephen de Marisco of the manor of Weyperons on the one side and the isle of Lundy and other lands of Stephen in England on the other'.[47] Although this deed was not completed, it does show that Stephen, son of Herbert de Marisco, considered the island to be his despite Edward III's confirmation of Sir John de Wyllyngton's ownership.

Either the ownership of the island was disputed, or the island may have been divided, or it may have been subleased, but in any case it remained in Sir John de Wyllyngton's hand from whom it passed in fee simple to his son Ralph. Ralph sold the island in 1332 to William de Montacute, 1st Earl of Salisbury and this sale was confirmed by the king.[48]

Salisbury set about resolving any disputes concerning the ownership by establishing his sole right through a series of 'Fines' or legal documents.

> At Westminster . . . [6 October 1332] and afterwards [20 January 1332–3]. . . . Between William de Monte Acuto, claimant, and Ralph de Wylington, deforciant; as to the Castle of Lunday & 10 messuages, 10 ploughlands, 10 acres of meadow, 10,000 acres of heath, 60s rent in Lunday and the advowson of the Church of Lunday. Plea of covenant was summoned. Ralph acknowledged the castle, tenements and advowson for ever. Moreover Ralph undertook for himself and his heirs that they would warrant the Castle, tenements and advowson to William and his heirs against all men for ever. For this William gave Ralph £200.

This was endorsed with the rider: 'Stephen de Mareys, son and heir of Herbert de Mareys, put in his claim.'[49] Similar 'fines' were made later, one on 25 June 1333 concerned Hugh de Despencer who, in a document worded identically to that above, renounced his claims and received 1,000 marks of silver from Salisbury, while a further document of 6 October 1334 contains a renouncement by Stephen de Marisco of his claims in return for a payment of £300.

William de Montacute died in 1344 and as his son and heir was still a minor, the king took him and his inheritance into his own hand. William's wife Katherine claimed a third part of Lundy as her dower against 'John Lotterell, Knight'.[50] By what title or for how long the Luttrells held Lundy is not clear, although the inquisition following the death of Lord John de Wyllyngton in 1337 found that Sir

John de Luttrell held Lundy of him 'by the tenure of military service'. This is difficult to equate with the purchase of Lundy by William de Montacute in 1332 unless Luttrell transferred his dues to the new owner at the time of purchase. The post-mortem inquisition of John Luttrell following his death in 1337–8 found him still holding the island. As Katherine de Montacute had dower of all her husband's possessions and yet claimed only one third of Lundy against John Luttrell it may well have been that the Luttrells had claim to only part of the island. The entire question was resolved in 1349 when Katherine died and her son, having come of age in that year, gave homage to Edward III as the rightful heir to Lundy.

When in 1350 the daughter of this 2nd Earl of Salisbury, Elizabeth de Montacute, married Sir Guy de Bryan she brought Lundy as part of her marriage dowry. Sir Guy was still in possession of the island on his death in 1390 but as his only son had predeceased him his two granddaughters, Philippa and Elizabeth, became the co-heirs. Lundy was apportioned to Elizabeth but during her minority was in the protection of the king who in April 1391 committed it to Philippa's husband 'John Devereux, chivaler, Steward of the King's Household . . . to hold the same from Easter last until the lawful age of Philippa and Elizabeth'.[51]

The island was valued at £10 at this time. During the guardianship of John Devereux the island was raided by poachers who took 'hares, conies, pheasants and partridges' where upon the king commissioned the Sheriff of Devon and three others 'to enquire what evil-doers had entered and hunted without licence in the King's free warren in the isle of Londay'.[52]

On the death of John Devereux the king granted Lundy to his half-brother John de Holand, Earl of Huntingdon, free of rent so long as the king held it during the minority of the heirs of Guy de Bryan.[53] Elizabeth de Bryan had married Robert Lovell (a second cousin of John de Holand) and when she came of age in 1400, Lundy and the rest of her inheritance was granted to her.[54]

For most of the next three hundred years, Lundy was passed down from one family to another through marriage, and for much of this time the seas around the island were the haunt of pirates whose attentions probably explain the sparsely populated or even uninhabited state of the island at this time. The Crown kept an anxious eye on the situation and from time to time admonished the absentee owners. On the death of Elizabeth Lovell the island passed to her daughter Maud, who died in 1436, and thence to Maud's son Humphrey, Earl of Arundel, who died two years later at the age of nine. The inheritance then passed to Humphrey's half-sister Avice, who had married James Butler, 5th Earl of Ormonde and Earl of Wiltshire. Avice died in July 1457 whereupon her husband succeeded as the owner of Lundy until, on the accession of Edward IV in 1461, he was beheaded and his lands declared forfeit.

'The King's uncle, William Neville, Earl of Kent and Lord of Faucomberg' was awarded Lundy by the new king,[55] but when Neville died without heirs five months later the king transferred the ownership to his brother 'Prince George, Duke of Clarence, as from Michaelmas 1462'.[56] This grant was confirmed in 1465 and 1474 but the island reverted to the king in 1478 when the Duke of Clarence was convicted of treason and died, according to tradition, in a butt of malmsey.

These owners were almost certainly absentees, as in 1464 and again in 1484 in the terms of truces with the Scots 'the Lordship of Lorn in Scotland and the Isle of Lundy in the River Severn, are exempted from the truce'. This was because Lundy 'was a receptacle for pirates for whose acts the English Kings could not be answerable.'[57]

On the Scottish side it is likely that the Lorn estate was exempted because of an unresolved and uncontrollable clan dispute which was the romantic and legal Scottish sensation of 1463. Sir John Stewart of Lorn had three legitimate daughters of his wife, and one fine illegitimate son of his adored mistress. The three daughters married three Campbell brothers, the clan enemies of the Stewarts for generations, who now planned to partition the Stewart lands on the death of Sir John. However, Lady Stewart died first, releasing Sir John to marry his mistress and legitimize his bastard son Dugald who, now being of age, could inherit the lordship of Lorn. The wedding guests assembled at the kirk where suddenly a MacDougall lackey of the Campbells stabbed and mortally wounded the bridegroom. The priest, however, was just able to complete the marriage vows as Sir John died at the altar. Dugald Stewart inherited and became a just and well-loved laird while his brothers-in-law had to be content with the ancestral Campbell lands in Argyll.[58]

In 1479 a grant was made to John Wykes 'Gentilman' for life and 'for his good service to the King in England, Ireland and Wales and beyond the seas and in recompense for £155. 6. 8d due to him from the King, of the Island of Londey, with all the lands, fishings, fowlings, huntings, and other commodities, profits and emoluments by land and by water in the sea for a space of three miles round the island, late of George, late Duke of Clarence and in the King's hands by his forfeiture'.[59] The fate of John Wykes is not known, but in 1488 Lundy was restored to the Ormonde family in the person of the 7th Earl, Thomas Butler, who was brother of, and heir to, the beheaded 5th Earl.

Chapter Four

LATE MIDDLE AGES, 1485–1636

Thomas Butler, the 7th Earl of Ormonde, held Lundy for twenty-seven years until his death in 1515[1] when it passed to his eldest daughter Anne, who had married Sir James St Leger of Annery.

When Anne died in 1532 the island, then valued at 33s 4d a year, passed to her only son George. An incident two years later suggests that the island was still uninhabited as an appeal was made by Spain 'on behalf of Don Pedro de la Borda, Vizino de las San Sebastian, and Pero Minez de Malles, whose caravel after trading at Miruforda [Bideford] and Erpol [?Appledore] was taken by an English ship and the crew put ashore on Londay Isle that they might perish of hunger. They were taken off by a Norman ship and came to Biusuata [?Bridgwater] where they appealed to a Justice.'[2]

'Sir John Dudley was ordered to patrol the water about Lundy to look for pirates, especially French'[3] in 1537, but a gang of French pirates under their captain, La Valle, seized Lundy in 1542 and waylaid the Bristol traders. The fishermen of Clovelly mounted an expedition against the pirates, burned their ships and killed or made prisoners of the entire gang.[4] The record reads:

> An other shipp was taken in the West countrey, furnished with banyshed men of Fraunce, which robbed dyverse of His Majesties subgiettes, and perforce entred a smal ysle of His Majesties in those parties, and wold have kept it, but that the contrey nere unto it rose, and with small vessells entered upon the isle, and fyrst toke the most parte of the men, and aftre toke the shipp, whiche laye in the rode before it.[5]

A few years later Lord Seymour, High Admiral of England, was charged with, among other things, trying to take Lundy 'being aided with shippes and conspiring at all evil eventes with priates, [so that] he might at all tymes have a sure and saufe refuge, if anything for his demerites should have been attempted against him'.[6] He was executed on the block on Tower Hill in 1549 having made no answer to the charges levied against him, six of which concerned his abuse of power as Lord High Admiral and his close cooperation with the pirates who lurked in the waters around Scilly.

When King Henry VIII acquired the monastic estates at the time of the Dissolution of the Monasteries, the 'Rectory of the Isle of Lundy' was attached to Cleeve Abbey in Somerset under which details are given of 'Account of a certain sum of money received from Hugh, Priest, farmer of the rectory of the Isle of Lundy: Nothing received because it is all put down in the account of the Minister of that year.'[7] The minister's account to which this refers reads:

Monasterium de Clyva. Old Clyve. . . . Farm of tithes and oblations and other profits of the rectory of the isle of Lunda. 15/- of the farm of the greater and lesser tithes and oblations and the barton land there together with all the other profits of the rector of the island aforesaid as payable to Dom Hugh Priest for the term of 60 years, by indenture dated 25 yr Henry VIII [1534] payable at the feast of St Michael the Archangel next following as appears more clearly in the indenture aforesaid. Total 15/-.[8]

During the completion of a peace treaty with the Scots in 1559 an interesting mention is made of Lundy. Bishop Turnstall reported to Queen Elizabeth I that he had received 'her commission . . . to conclude a peace with the Scots. . . . The isle of Lundy being excluded in the treaty on the part of England, and the Lordship of Lorne on that of Scotland, he requests further instructions, these being without precedent. The men who best know her chronicles should be consulted herein, lest unawares she gives away part of her Crown.'[9] The queen's reply was 'as regards the suggested omission of the Isle of Lundy and the Lordship of Lorne, she will not alter the ancient order of treaties'.[10]

Sir George St Leger was succeeded by his son, Sir John, 'a drunken spendthrift', who lost money and was obliged to sell his inheritance. Grenville came to his aid, but being a businessman needed good landed security. By 1577 Grenville had lent £800 which with a further debt of £200 owed to Hugh Jones, a London mercer (for which debt Grenville made himself responsible), meant that Sir John St Leger granted away the fee simple of the island. The St Legers, on repaying the debt, were to re-enter into possession of the island. But they never did.[11]

Sir John St Leger was desperate and, interestingly, one Edward Phaer, a counterfeiter being held in the Tower, confessed 'that he had stayed in London with Sir Warham St. Leger and then with his cousin in Devon, Sir John St. Leger, and that he was to be given an island to work on [no doubt this meant Lundy] and that he had dealt with Mr. Greenfield in Devon'. Further, Phaer reported that these gentlemen had sought him out for the purpose.[12]

This business must have taken place before 1577 while the St Legers were still outright owners, though 'Mr Greenfield' sounds strangely like a mishearing of, or an alias for, Grenville. Sir John St Leger's motive was almost certainly financial and not religious and the loyalist Protestant Grenvilles would not have been party to any Catholic insurrection.

Fortunately, Sir John St Leger's daughter Mary married Sir Richard Grenville who, in 1585 on the eve of leaving for his voyage to the New World, put his affairs in order and appointed trustees to administer his estates. These trustees were Raleigh, Sir Arthur Basset and others and the estates included 'The Manor and Island of Lundy'. All were to be held 'to the use of his wife after his death so long as she remained unmarried in recompense of the jointure she might claim. . . . After her death or second marriage . . . the estate is to go to the use of Bernard, his son and heir.'[13]

Meanwhile the rising volume of traffic using the Bristol Channel had attracted increasing attention from pirates. Three of the better known who used the island were Robert Hickes of Saltash, who was there between 1576 and 1578; Captain John Piers of Padstow who was there in the 1560s and '70s; and John Challice, who was there sometime between 1574 and 1581;[14] but whether these three encamped on the island or merely sheltered in its lee is not clear.

Despite the movement from English coasts towards Ireland which followed the capture of no fewer than forty-three pirate ships off Dorset and the execution of seven of their more flamboyant captains in 1583, the risks posed by Catholic sympathizers, foreigners and pirates led Captain Christopher Carleill in 1584 to set about the capture of all pirates operating in Irish and adjacent waters. To do this Carleill enlisted the help of captured and repentant pirates and during the summer his ship lay off Lundy 'in wait for a man-of-war – the name given to vessels engaged in piracy. He captured Captain Lewis's bark, set Lewis ashore, then with all the crew still aboard her, sailed into Cork Harbour with his prey.'[15]

By 1586 the Spanish army under Parma had conquered Antwerp and was poised to invade England, aiming there 'to seize one of the Western Harbours'. Accordingly instructions were sent 'to the head constables and others' by the three Deputy Lieutenants of Devon, namely Sir William Courtenay, Sir Ralph Dennis and Sir John Gilbert ordering that there be set up 'In every place of arrival within the Hundred a small beacon, a low by the waterside to be made and one greater upon the highest hill next adjoining, as hath been accustomed. The same beacons to be watched by day and night, three by night and one by day. Not to be fired but by the advice of the Lieutenant, the next Justice, or some other named by the Lieutenant. . . .'[16] This would seem to be the origin of Lundy's Beacon Hill, as the name does not appear earlier.

However, the island was still not secure and by 1587 the authorities at Barnstaple felt obliged to launch an attack on the pirates who were still sheltering there. The expedition recorded their expenses as follows:

> Paid towarde the settynge fourth of divers men from the Towne to apprehend div's Rovers and piratte at Londey by my lord of Bathes appoyment – vs. vd. [5s 5d]. . . . And paid to vj [6] watch men for watchynge the prysoners that were taken at Londey and put in the Kayhall of this Towne xi js. jd. [12s 1d] And for a watch potte and for Candle light for the same prisoners . . . xjd [11d] And for meate and drinke for the same prisoners ijs [2s]. . . . And paid

for cleansynge and makynge cleane of the Kayhall upon the dep'ture of the p'soners . . . iiijd [4*d*].[17]

This action was clearly effective as in the following year Sir Richard Grenville wrote: 'Thus the 22 of April 1588 we put over the barre at Biddeford . . . and the same night we came to an anker under the Isle of Lundy where some of our company went on land. After we had roade there about the space of three howers we wayed anker againe and all that night we bare along the coast of Cornewall.'[18]

Sir Richard Grenville died in 1591 and was succeeded by his son Barnard. Barnard apparently did little to maintain security on Lundy as in 1594 an Englishman on the island was captured by Spaniards. This brought the following rebuke from the queen, who wrote in 1596: 'Whereas if you neglect that place her Majestie shall have cause to take the Island wholly into her own handes and to make her owne proffitt of it for the defence of the same.'[19] An earlier passage in the same letter speaks 'of the danger your selfe hath particular proofe of late, when a Gentleman was taken and carried awaie out of that island by the Enemie.'[20]

In 1597 one William Astell revealed the danger posed by Spain and its attempts to re-establish the Roman Catholic observance. In a confession dated 22 February 1597[21] he states:

> I was taken the 14 of July last within 18 leagues of Scilly and carried from thence to Farrall where as then the Spanish fleet lay, being in number 130 or thereabouts. The said fleet departed from the Groyne on the 8 of October last, with 10,000 men for the land and that was the most bound for Falmouth, and their practice was that after their arrival in Falmouth the *Lantotha* should stay there with half of the Army, and the *Countie Palma*, Captain Elyett an Englishman being his guide, should with the other half in small flyboats and pinnaces have gone for Plymouth. But the storm taking them at East North East 20 leagues off Scilly put them back. There was cast away in that storm the great *St. Bartholomew* with 100,000 ducats. 16 or 18 men saved; there was divers flyboats lost which were not much regarded, but a great levauntisco with much treasure and men, I know not correctly how much. . . .

This was obviously a large invasion fleet and the pilot, Capt. Elyett, was most probably a Catholic mercenary with local knowledge. Indeed, the *Armada Pilots Survey of the English Coastline, October 1597* states: 'Isle of Lundy – In the sea four leagues from Barnstaple to an island called Lundy, it is a good anchorage, there are on land a dozen inhabitants and some cattle.'[22]

Following the storm the fleet was reinforced 'by 7 sail and a few Italians', and the confession continues:

> Capt. Elyett departed toward the Court of Spain about the beginning of January last to seek licence of the King for the coming to take the Isle of

Londey minding to keep it with a 100 Spaniards and 40 English. His pretence was that he would bring with him a flyboat which should bring all his provision of victuals and munition, which flyboat, after his arrival, he meant presently to send back. He meant likewise to bring with him 3 pinnaces about 12 tons apiece; 2 of them should be rigged and furnished, and the other he meant to bring in quarters to keep upon the land until he had great need. With these pinnaces he meant to have troubled the river of Severn and, as occasion should be offered, with one of them to have sent news into Spain.[23]

William Astell's confession continued the following day when he refers to two pinnaces – one under William Love and the other under Capt. Eaten. These were both obviously Catholic Englishmen and it is highly probable that this Capt. Eaten is the Capt. Esten who was dislodged from Lundy ten years later, and that William Astell is a misreading of 'one Ansley' who was involved in Sir Robert Basset's scheme which now unfolds.

During the closing years of the sixteenth century, with minds turning to the impending death of Queen Elizabeth I, the thoughts of those landed families who had never forsaken the old religion turned on the prospect of a Catholic succession.

Sir Robert Basset of Heanton Punchardon, near Barnstaple, was born in 1574 and 'pretended some right to the Crown' on the death of Queen Elizabeth. His claim was through both an illegitimate and a female line as his father's mother, Frances Plantagenet, was the daughter of Arthur Plantagenet, Viscount Lisle, who was the illegitimate offspring of King Edward IV and the Lady Elizabeth Lucy, between whom there had been 'a real marriage contract'.[24]

Basset already had an interest in Lundy as he had undertaken to buy from Robert Arundell (who was in the process of giving up his fourth part of the lease of the island's grazing) 'so manie beasts & cattell & other goods then remaynynge & beynge upon the said Iland which were the said Robert Arundell's as did amount unto the some of £12 of lawfull money of England'. Arundell apparently delivered only £9 worth of cattle and then died, whereupon Basset petitioned the queen for redress against Anne Arundell, Robert's widow, who claimed she knew nothing of the matter.[25]

'Like many West Country gentlemen [Basset] owned a ship (the *Lions Claw*) and was deeply involved, with various associates, in privateering ventures, some of which were barely distinguishable from piracy.'[26]

The evidence of Basset's conversion to Catholicism comes from a letter which William Pole, of Shute, a Devonshire gentleman wrote to his uncle, Sir John Popham, on 18.1.1600. Pole was Basset's brother-in-law; their wives were sisters, the daughters of a local Judge, Sir William Periam. Popham, also a West Country man, was Lord Chief Justice and had become notorious as a derector and repressor of recusancy. In his letter Pole reminds his uncle that he has already, some two years ago, written to warn him that Basset was being 'corrupted and seduced to Popery'. This places Basset's conversation in or about 1598 and is compatible with his authorship of the *Life of More* which he might well have written at such a time.[27]

The seducer appears to have been the Dominican Nicholas Hill, excited as were other members of his order by the radical fantasies of an ideal state then being conjectured, of which Sir Thomas More's Utopia was one.

'Hill,' Pole went on, 'has been to see a Jesuit imprisoned in Newgate, and I fear the sequel thereof will be evil, if it be not prevented, for though Sir Robert Basset standeth not curious in any religion (with sorrow I write), yet lately he hath practiced his frauds with popery and hath confessed privately that Sir William Courtenay and himself have combined themselves that way, and it is known that these kind of people prepare themselves for innovation'. In fact, said Pole, Basset had confessed to him a particular design in hand. Immediately he planned to travel abroad with Hill. Meanwhile, he had 'resolved to have the isle of Lundy, and there to place a malcontent fellow, one Ansley, a Somersetshire man'.[28] Sir William Courtenay 'was already deeply suspect'; Cecil's agents had reported that he was in touch with the Spaniards, who expected him to cooperate with them if they should land in the West Country.[29]

But it was to be three years before Basset carried out his plan. In November 1601 'one of his associates, for whom he had stood surety, had seized a ship belonging to some French merchants of St Jean de Luz. This was sheer piracy and when the matter was brought to court, Sir Robert was adjudged liable to pay £15,000. This heavy financial blow caused him to risk all on a lunatic political venture. Basset's proximity to Lundy, his claim to a quarter of it, his problems of debt, his conversion to Catholicism, perhaps even lingering dreams of Utopia but above all his claim to the throne persuaded him to flee to the island and hold it as a beachhead for the Catholic invasion that he expected.

For over a year he seems to have waited there in vain and been ignored. The Crown had more urgent, simmering rebellion in the north to confound while the Spaniards were more interested in the coast of the English Channel. The death of Queen Elizabeth was the signal for Basset to flee and head for Rome to make his case. Accordingly in July 1603 he 'took shipping at Appledore in the Port of Barnstaple' and sailed to La Rochelle.

He seems to have been quickly disillusioned, for in a letter to his brother from Pisa in September 1603 he writes: 'My last letter I wrote was from Marseilles which did specify my constant resolution to prosecute my settled intentions wherewith in my former [letter] I acquainted you. Finding how they are like to succeed I wish with all my heart that I were at Lundy in as poor case as I came from thence, where I would gladly spend my days in an obscure hermitage.'[30]

Basset must have remained in Rome during 1604 but by May 1605 was writing to King James I hoping to clear 'your displeasure and suspicion of my rash miscarriage, which by my follies incurred in so high a degree . . . etc'. Basset also expressed the desire to live in Brussels or the Low Countries 'to be nearer England and to gain your mercy'. Lord Salisbury received a letter from Brussels dated 4 May 1606 mentioning one 'Signor Augusto' ('King of England') and going on to say that Sir Robert Basset had arrived and was going 'in haste to the Nuncio with whom he said he had very earnest business'.

But nothing came of Basset's plans. After years of requests, and in view of generous financial bequests, the king eventually felt able in 1611 to grant a pardon to Basset on condition that he reported quarterly to the Bishop of Exeter for correct religious instruction and that otherwise he remained in his house at Heanton – a property that must have been spared when all his other possessions had been confiscated in 1606.[31] Basset remained at Heanton, and there he died in 1631.

Although Basset's attempt at ownership was over, Capt. Eston (or Eaton) was still in the area and appears to have fallen in with one Capt. Thomas Salkeld to make Lundy their base for piracy.

Although complaints had been made at Barnstaple in 1608 about the pirates operating from Lundy, a deposition made by William Younge of Pembroke on 17 March 1610 finally stung the authorities into action. William Younge stated that

Capt. (Thos.) Salkeld captured him and his bark (laden with coals, goods and passengers, from Trembath and bound for Ireland) in Milford Haven on the 6th April 1609, carried them afterwards to Lundy Island, where he set the vessel adrift on the rocks, and she was totally lost. On the same day he [Salkeld] went ashore at Milford Haven and killed 8 beeves, 30 young lambs and many wethers, conveying them all on board his ship. On the 13th of the same month he landed at Dale a town at the entrance to Milford Haven, spoiled the inhabitants of their goods and set their houses on fire! At the same time he took from the quay a bark belonging to an inhabitant of Dale, laden with iron, oil and beer and set her adrift and she was dashed to pieces on the adjacent rocks. On the 20th March he took a Mr. George Eskott's bark which was bound for France and made him and his men prisoners; the same fate attended the vessel of one John Bennet of Appledore. Both these vessels Salkeld, after taking out such portion of their cargoes as he thought fit, together with their sails, abandoned to the wild impulse of the waves and they were shattered to fragments on the rocks of Lundy. On the 23rd [April] 1609 he landed on Lundy with his men, with colours displayed, in defiance of the King of England, wished His Majesty's heart were on the point of his sword, and proclaimed himself King of Lundy; and on the 25th March, being Sunday morning, he obliged his prisoners to carry stones for the purpose of forming a quay for a port in his newly acquired territory. He divided them into three separate companies, lest they should attempt any refractory movements. One portion he sent to an isle south of Lundy and then he marched to the north of the island four miles distant. They were not to communicate with each other on pain of death. In the evening of the same Sunday a Flemish ship of 200 tons burthen, from Rochelle, laden with salt and bound for Bristol, came into the road of Lundy. Salkeld sent his longboat off to her, instructing the crew to say that she belonged to a King's ship, and to offer to supply her with a pilot. A storm arose in the night and the ship was constrained to make sail, carrying with her a few of Salkeld's men. A Weymouth vessel, which he had captured the same day, also escaped under cover of the storm leaving, however, two of the crew in Salkeld's power. On the 26th he called his men and prisoners together and threatened those who would not abjure their King and Country and receive him as their Sovereign, with execution on a gallows which he had in readiness. He caused the heads of some of his captives to be shaved, in token of slavery, and set them to building walls for a fort and constructing a platform for cannon to command the road. He brought three pieces of cast-iron ordnance on shore and a cannon, styled in the warlike language of the day, a 'murtherer', to be planted on the Fort and on an old ruinous castle adjacent, but honest George Escott of Bridgwater defeated, by a coup-de-main, the measures of this daring and infatuated ruffian. Escott had been confined by Salkeld in a little house too badde for dogs to live in. There he concerted with some of his fellow-captives the recovery of liberty. Issuing forth with his companions through a hole in the dilapidated hovel, Escott, who alone was armed having a poinard in his hand, and noe more, did enter his [Salkeld's] fort vyolently through his couch of guarde, and there did discern Salkeld's confederates who were rebels, traitors and pirates, and some he toke and some he put to flight; then all the company by one consent made Escott their Commander for the King. Then presently Salkeld fled away with Escott's bark and goods; and if this enterprise had not took effect, all had surely died for this Salkeld did mean to have kept the island during his life.[32]

(In passing it is worth noticing that by dividing his prisoners into three groups – one on Rat Island, one at the North End, and the third presumably between them – together with mention of the gallows he had in readiness, that these gallows may have been erected on Hangman's Hill in the south, and at either Gannets' Combe (known as Gallows' Combe on all maps until 1835) or on nearby Tibbett's Hill (a probable corruption of Gibbet Hill) in the northern part of the island.)

Only three days after William Younge's deposition of the deplorable situation at Lundy, a commission was issued to the Earl of Nottingham, Lord High Admiral, on 20 March 1610 authorizing the Earl of Bath as Lord Lieutenant of Devon, together with the Mayor and Aldermen of Barnstaple, to send an expedition against the pirates. The conditions, that any goods or ships captured from the pirates were to be retained in return for the expenses of the expedition, were obviously contended as the gentlemen took two years to decide the correct interpretation of the commission. Thus 'Capt. Eston and Capt. Salkeld built their lair on Lundy Island from which they sallied out, while Lord Warden and Lord Admiral were wrangling as to which should have their ships and goods when they were caught.'[33]

When the expedition did eventually set sail on 31 August 1612 a total of sixty-eight men were aboard the ship *John of Braunton* and the barque *Mayflower*. After a chase to Milford Haven the vessels returned to Barnstaple with four prisoners, John Seath alias Finde, Thomas Perryman, Thomas Smyth and John Hove, who were later taken to Exeter jail. The king ordered that ' . . . in consideration of the good service done unto us of late by our trusty and well-beloved George Escott . . . [We] do give and grant unto him an annuity or pension of 1s 6d of lawful money of England. . . . '[34]

Whether the neglect of Lundy was the cause or the result of the presence of pirates is not clear, but Barnard Grenville had sufficient control to be able to offer sanctuary there to his cousin, Sir Lewis Stukely.

Stukely had been knighted by James I on the latter's notorious ride to London in 1603, but in 1618 in his capacity of Vice Admiral of Devon had the unhappy task of arresting his cousin Sir Walter Raleigh. Raleigh was immensely popular and the anger which the public could not vent on the king was turned instead on Stukely. When he complained of the scorn with which he was treated in all quarters, James I replied: 'On my soul, if I should hange all that speak ill of thee, all the trees in the country would not suffice.'[35] As if this were not enough Stukely was accused in January 1618/19 of clipping coin and a royal pardon could not prevent his becoming a social outcast. He went to Lundy where he died in 1620, allegedly of insanity and as a pirate, though there is no evidence for this.

In 1625 it was reported that three Turkish pirates had seized Lundy with its inhabitants and had threatened to burn Ilfracombe. Although this was denied by Capt. Charles Harris of HMS *Phoenix*,[36] the government inquiry which followed took evidence from Nicholas Cullen that 'the Turks continued at Lundy a fortnight. I saw the Turkish ship lying in the road off Lundy.'[37] No more is heard of the Turks, but on 26 April 1628 it was reported that 'Four French ships took about 26 sail of ships in Severn and other parts of the coast and took also the Isle of Lundy and rifled it and so left the shore.'[38]

Although Sir Barnard Grenville did not die until 1636 he seems to have passed the island as a wedding gift to his son Sir Bevil Grenville in 1619. In June 1630 Sir Bevil received a letter from his close friend Sir John Elliot, the Vice Admiral of Devon, 'to sound him on behalf of Sir H. Bouchier who he believes will be drawn into a fair price for the island'.[39]

In declining the offer Sir Bevil replied that 'he had been contemplating making improvments including such fortifications as might prove an efficient defence against the pirates who infest the coast'. Elliot at once foresaw the danger that Sir Bevil might displease the government if he carried out his intention to fortify, and there followed a long correspondence in which Sir Bevil ultimately accepted Elliot's advice to abandon any ideas of fortification.

During the summer of 1631 Sir Bevil took advantage of the fine weather to begin to build a pier and to erect some sort of fort to protect his island from pirates. In a letter to his father he writes: 'I am going thither this week to see my great works finished, which I hope will be within this month', and later in another letter to his father: 'I have already made a Kay and harbour there at great cost, which the island ever wanted before whereby an industrious man . . . set on a course of fishing . . . may as I think easily gain £500 a year by it.'[40]

However, there are many reports and references from 1630 to 1634 of piracies at Lundy. In 1632 the notorious Capt. John Nutt made Lundy one of his headquarters, styled himself 'Admiral Nutt' and left his 'Vice Admiral' Smith in charge of the island. Nutt was caught and tried, though he eventually managed to obtain a release, while Smith fled from Lundy to avoid capture. However, Smith is reported to have returned in the following year.[41]

On 16 July 1633 'a great outrage [was] committed by a Spanish man-of-war of Biscay who . . . landed eighty men at the island of Lundy, where, after some small resistance, they killed one man and bound the rest, and surprised and took the island which they rifled and took thence all the best provisions they found worth carrying away, and so departed to sea again. . . . The Biscayer was a vessel of 150 tons with about 120 men, Captain Meggor being captain. They had lately robbed a French bark. Mark Pollard was the name of the Lundy man killed.'[42]

Following this outrage the government commissioned Capt. John Pennington in command of HMS *Vanguard* to end the piracies. He was given absolute powers by the Secretary of State on 9 September 1633 and reported five days later that Capt. Meggor (Le Maigre?) was in fact 'a Frenchman in a ship of 60 tons with five or six small pieces and that he had lain these 14 days at an island called Chosse, near St. Malo'.[43]

Despite the naval presence a report of 28 January 1633/4 mentions 'that there are two pirates about Lundy which stay there to rob the barks which go from Bristol to Ireland and Wales',[44] and the following month the 'merchants who trade in small barks . . . were very fearful of Captain Brundiville [Pronoville] seeing he is now grown desperate, and has put himself in a small vessel or clinker. . . . He was one of them that chased about Lundy.'[45]

Algerine pirates were reported to be using the island as a 'Harbour and Shelter' in 1635 and to 'commit spoil there'.[46]

Despite the pirates Lundy appears to have remained attractive to other parties. The motive behind the offer by Thomas Arundell, a distant relation of the Grenvilles, to buy the island in 1636 for £3,000[47] may have been occasioned by the need to do something about the pirates; it may have had some religious connection as there was still hope of a Catholic succession; or it may have related to the growing conflict between king and Parliament which now began to overshadow all else.

Chapter Five

THE CIVIL WAR

Throughout the many years of struggle between king and Parliament, Sir Bevil Grenville devoted himself loyally to the royalist cause even to the extent of mortgaging his manor of Bideford including Lundy for £3,000 to help raise the £20,000 needed to keep his 300 men under arms.[1] When Bevil died in action, the king assumed control of the island and quickly installed there a loyalist governor, one Thomas Bushell.

Bushell must have had considerable charm and eloquence as he had attracted the favour of both King James I and of Lord Chancellor Bacon, from whom he had learned the principles of mining.

In 1635 Bushell negotiated the transfer of the lease of the Cardiganshire silver-lead mines from Lady Myddelton and about the same time he took a lease of the Devonshire mines from the Mines Royal Society (the Crown agents from 1530 until 1689 of all ore-producing mines). In 1637 Charles I granted Bushell permission to open a mint at Aberystwyth Castle which was to be able to supply the king with coin and precious metal during the Civil War. The king had confirmed the Welsh and North Devon leases in 1642 so that Bushell, with his known love of islands and his realization from his sea journeys between Wales and Devon of the value to him of Lundy, must have been well pleased to have been chosen as royalist governor.

As the king's cause collapsed in the west during the autumn of 1645, Bushell retired to Lundy taking with him his Welsh minting equipment and bullion and, using guns recovered from a shipwreck in Bude Bay, refortified and probably remodelled the castle and built several coastal fortifications of which Brazen Ward is today the best preserved example.[2]

Secure with his 'garrison' Bushell continued to mint coin for the king[3] and continued to hold out long after the rest of the country had capitulated, so that Lundy became one of the last royalist outposts to fall.

Meanwhile Lord Saye and Sele had negotiated with Parliament for the purchase of Lundy but Bushell, whose continued presence there became an embarrassment to the new government which was unable or unwilling to overcome him by force, was reluctant to relinquish his hold. He argued that he had been entrusted with it by the king and would not part with it except on the same authority, also that it was most useful to him in connection with his Welsh and Combe Martin mines; he was far

Bushell's Lundy Groat, 1646 (shown larger than actual size) (B. Sherwood)

from his many creditors and he seems to have been genuinely fond of the island itself. His attitude was made plain as early as 16 July 1644 when the parliamentary frigate *Crescent*, under the command of Capt. Thomas Drew, arrived at Lundy and ordered its surrender. 'The same day Richard Cocke replied refusing to surrender the island.'[4] Cock was 'Bushell's Lieutenant' and remained on Lundy until the eventual surrender.

In January 1645/6 the government decided that Bushell should be invited to surrender the island on terms, and the Governor of Swansea Castle, Philip Jones, accordingly wrote to Bushell suggesting that by surrendering at once he would best be able to make terms with Parliament and regain possession of his mines. 'Sir,' the letter read, 'omit not this opportunity, the summer is now drawing on and then you may well imagine your conditions will be lower and your terms (if any) harder.'

Bushell rejected this offer and on 19 February wrote to two friends: ' . . . If you can treat with my Lord Say for this Isle of Lundy; which place, although in itself is desolate and stormy, and hath nought to invite an inhabitant, except one of my temper who therefore loves it . . . as also in regard it lies convenient for our mines at Combe Martin: . . . that if anything I have in Oxfordshire may better please him, than this remote rock, let his honour make his own conditions.' Nothing came of this proposal.

Two months later, on 20 April Capt. Crowther, Vice Admiral of the Seas, anchored in Lundy roadstead and ordered Bushell to surrender to the rightful owner, but Bushell again replied that he could not do so without the king's consent.[5]

Three days later Sir Thomas Fairfax sent a copy of the Order of the Committee of Both Kingdoms dated 12 January 1646 calling for the surrender of Lundy, in return for which Bushell was to be given back his silver mines.[6] Fairfax offered safe conduct to Bushell or one of his men to go ashore to negotiate. To this Bushell sent a representative with a reply which 'prayed for patience while he preserved his fidelity to his King and tried to discharge his debts'.[7]

Everywhere the Royalists were in retreat. Sir Richard Grenville, the younger brother of Sir Bevil, was being held prisoner on St Michael's Mount by Prince Charles after a turbulent fighting career on both sides during the war. As the Royalists retreated westwards, orders were given for Sir Richard to be transferred to either of the royalist-held islands of Jersey or Lundy 'where he would continue to be held prisoner until further orders were given'.[8] Bushell makes no mention of this and as Sir Richard soon appears in France the choice must have been Jersey.

Meanwhile Bushell wrote to the king seeking permission to surrender:

May it please your Majesty, – The enclosed I have received from my Lord Say's servant, who is Governor of Swanzey, which I conceive was sent by his Lordship's direction, wherein he invites me to the surrender of this Isle, being his Lordship's known purchase; in the perusal of which I was not at all startled at the threats therein, but must confess myself moved at the obligations it minds me of, with which I formally acquainted your Majesty in the presence of my Lord of Dorset, since which Captain Crowther, Vice Admiral of these seas, summoned me to surrender this place. And not long after Sir Thomas Fairfax sent a drummer with his letter and an Order from the Committee of Both Kingdoms, wherein they proposed their assistance in restoring me to my interest in the silver mines if that I would deliver up this island to my Lord Say. Your Majesty well knoweth how I have maintained Lundy at no other contribution but my own, and how cheerfully I have exposed my friends and my own credit for your service, as well as exhausted them in the discovery of the Mines Royall; besides the place in itself is useless except in some advantage it may yield to me. If your sacred Majesty would be pleased to vouchsafe me leave to express my gratitude to my Lord Say by my quiet and free surrendering it, which I hope your goodness will not deny me, but if otherwise your Majesty shall require my longer stay here, be confident, Sir, I shall sacrifice both life and fortune before the loyalty of Your obedient, humble servant, Thomas Bushell. Lundy 14th May 1646.

White awaiting the king's reply, Bushell was kept under pressure. Some of his servants were arrested on the mainland, Capt. Crowther sent another summons, the Committee of Both Kingdoms served another notice and finally Lord Saye and Sele wrote to say that the king had ordered the remaining royalist strongholds to surrender. At the same time Bushell was summoned by the Committee of Devon. These events provoked Bushell to write to Saye and Sele protesting that since he had 'been careful to preserve your Honour's Isle at my own charge, without doing the least injury to any . . .', he should at least have his estates restored and an act of oblivion for his servants.[9]

The king finally replied:

> Bushell, We have perused your Letter, in which We finde thy care to Answer thy trust We at first reposed in thee; now since the place is unconsiderable in it self, and yet may be of great advantages unto you, in respect of your Mines, We do hereby give you leave to use your discretion in it, with this Caution, that you do take example from Our selves, and be not over-credilous of vain promises, which hath made Us great, only in our sufferings, and will not discharge your debts.
>
> From Newcastle 14 July 1646

On receiving this letter Bushell felt free to negotiate terms to his best advantage. In a reply to the Committee of Both Kingdoms he mentioned 'his several losses by Sea and land, and his great charges in fortification thereof' and set out three conditions for surrender, namely

1. the restoration of his estate, goods, mines and mints to be confirmed by Parliament;
2. 100 tons of his lead and 100 tons of potters ore to be brought from Wales to Bideford in order to discharge his debts and to aid in the restoration of the mines at Combe Martin;
3. a pardon for his servants and miners at Combe Martin.

While awaiting the committee's reply Bushell wrote a long letter to his friend Ingram on 24 September explaining that he had confidently hoped to 'balance the breach' between king and Parliament and to give his reason for staying on Lundy as 'my affection for solitude, the pressing of my miners at Commartin, and also to prevent an ill inhabitant which should have prejudiced the King's cause, the Countries traffik, and surprized the honourable owner from his purchase right'.[10]

Bushell's motives for holding on to Lundy may all have been secondary to his hope that Lundy could serve as a refuge/staging post for Charles I if the monarch should so desire (remembering Edward II's plans). Such thoughts would have faded after Charles was captured.

Supplies on Lundy must have run very low – the barque *Fortune* was able to extract an inflated price for provisions it sold to Bushell, whose plight led to whispers that he had had to resort to piracy. This was quite out of character and Bushell was able to reassure Lord Saye in a testimonial signed by sixty-one worthies of North Devon that during his residence on Lundy 'so far from injuring anyone, [Bushell] had been of great service to them in keeping it out of the hands of Pirates'.[11]

About this time Lord Saye wrote to Bushell offering £3,000 which would seem to be to enable Bushell to clear the royalist mortgage, which had been incurred by Sir Bevil Grenville.

Parliament finally published a bill on 9 July 1647, which was ratified the following day by Lords and Commons which accepted paragraphs 1) and 3) of Bushell's requests.

Bushell travelled to London and signed the treaty on 10 September 1647, but having failed to receive the lead and ore mentioned in his paragraph 2) was not in a position to repay his creditors. The creditors were waiting for him. No sooner had he arrived in London than he was arrested at the instigation of Mr Mordant Snellock who declared that 'Captain' Bushell had owed him £150 for the last seven years. This was quickly smoothed over and Bushell's release secured after receipt of a letter from Fairfax.

It was not until 24 February 1648 that the island and the garrison of twenty-two men were finally surrendered to Lord Saye and Sele's son, Major Richard Fiennes, who described the occasion:

> Both me and my souldiers met him [Bushell] at the Kay of Crovelly . . . where we were forced to stay fifteen dayes for a winde, before we could arrive into the Road of Lundy; And his Lieutenant having notice that it was us by their Governor Mr. Bushels shooting off a pistoll, gave us at our landing a salutation with all his Guns, and a volle of shot, as an entertainment of friendship, and free welcome, which made me so confident of his former profest fidelity in surrendering the same, that both my selfe and my men marcht through his guard unto the Castle, commanding his own men to remain in another house, lest the ignorance of some men on both sides might beget a difference through exchange of language, and mis-understanding of the truth: but as soone as they had understood the King's consent for a surrender to the right Owner, and the Conditions made on their behalfe by their Governor, Mr Bushell . . . the morning tide following they tooke shippe for Ilford Combe . . . having demanded of his Lieutenant Mr. Richard Cock what store of provision was left in the island, he replyed with a deep protestation, that for six monthes before Mr Bushell went over to treat with your Excellency . . . they nor their Governor had not eaten a bit of bread in six monthes nor scarce drank a barrell of bear in two yeares, alleaging the occasion was the Governor's known losses by land and sea. . . .[12]

The letter ends:

A List of those men's names which I found on the Island.

Tho. Bushell Esq. Governor	Tho. Brayley
Mr. Rich. Cock Lieut. Gover.	Henry Battee
Capt. Edward Owen	James Bouden

Major Rich. Pomeroy	Samuel Shortridge
Lieute. Oliver Bouck	Jo. Wheeler
Rich. Kynsam	Jo. Thorne
William Gilbert ⎫	Geo. Gilbert
John Scott ⎬ Gunners	Rich. Harris
John Trout ⎭	William Matheage
William Skiner	Rich. Chinge
Daniel Hanger	Fra. Hobbs

On landing at Ilfracombe, Bushell and his men proceeded to the mine at Combe Martin where for the next year or so schemes were afoot for renewing and extending the workings.

Lundy passed to Lord Saye and Sele who felt that as both an aristocrat and a supporter of Parliament he was in a suitable position to try to effect a reconciliation between the king and his captors. But following the execution of Charles I on 30 January 1649 Saye and Sele retired from public life and withdrew to the island soon afterwards – the exact date is not known but he was there in 1651[13] – and it is probable that he wrote two books while there.[14]

The Commonwealth Navy sheltered at Lundy while pursuing Prince Rupert in June 1649,[15] although pirates were still active in the area. In 1650 Lord Saye and Sele received a letter from one William Hinton 'aboard the *Royal Delight*' a royalist privateer, which had seized a ship carrying supplies to Lundy. Hinton writes: 'My Lord, Not far from that preety Island, whereof your Lordship is petty Prince, it was my fortune last evening to fetch up a small vessel . . . laden with some provisions of your Garrison I could wish it had been of some considerable value because . . . so notoriously famous is your Lordship, for your activity against your Liege Lord the King's Majesty of ever blessed memory; yet as little as it was, it did me good to seiz upon it by virtue of my Commission from His Majesty that now is. . . .'[16]

Normal trading patterns seem to have returned by 1651 as the *Elizabeth* of Flushing put in at Lundy for two days and picked up a pilot there.[17] But in the following year the barque *Gift* of St Ives, sailing from her home port to Ireland, was driven by a storm towards Lundy and was captured by a French man of war. The Frenchman 'forced her to ride farther into Londye Roade where they remained at anchor all that night, and the next morning . . . they wayed anker. . . .'[18]

Parliament was fully aware of the danger that Lundy might fall into the hands of one not wholly sympathetic to their cause, especially as by this time Lord Saye was suspected of royalist sympathies and had acquired the nickname of 'Old Subtlety' from his ability to sense the trend of popular feeling. Parliament accordingly decided to send 'Four files of Musketeers under the command of some fit person, who shall take a convenient portion of ammunition with him.'[19] Communication with the island was safeguarded by a warrant 'protecting from impress the company of a bark belonging to Lundy Isle',[20] and which lists the name of the master and four men.

The chosen 'fit person' was probably Sir John Ricketts who was there in January

1658/9 entrusted with the protection of the island. Saye and Sele remained on Lundy until just after Cromwell's death in 1658. Capt. James Young was lying at anchor at Lundy when news arrived of the dissolution of the old Parliament and the vote for Restoration. Young records that the island 'had only a pretty strong house like a castle, wherein lived a gentleman that retired from England on account of loyalty',[21] but on learning the news this 'gentleman', Saye and Sele, was quickly back at the centre of power where he took his seat in the House of Lords in 1660, became a member of the Privy Council, and was soon appointed Lord Privy Seal.

He died in 1662 and despite the local legend that he was buried on Lundy, was interred at Broughton Castle.

Meanwhile Bushell, ever adept at presenting his case in a good light, petitioned the new king for, among other things, reimbursement of the money he had spent on fortifying Lundy: 'I was at great charge of maintaining Lundy Garrison and building the Castle, which amounted to £5,570.' He further entered a claim for the pay of 104 men, a number considerably more than that of his garrison at the time of surrender, but a figure which may have included those employed in the Lundy mint, or in the Welsh or Devon mines.

Bushell's claim was supported by John Grenville, Earl of Bath, to whom the island had reverted, who said, 'touching my knowledge of his Services and Deportment in the time he Commanded the Isle of Lundy . . . never person behaved himself more like a Gent . . . for he not only built the Castle from the ground at his own charge fit for any Noble Person to inhabit, but also recovered several great guns whereby he defended the Isle against all invasion, it being attempted to have been stormed with twenty Saile of Ships at one time.'[22]

Bushell died in 1674, aged eighty, and was buried in Westminster Abbey. He had made a will but on examination was found to have died £120,000 in debt!

Chapter Six

FROM 1665 TO 1754

At the Restoration Lundy was returned to the Grenville family in the person of Sir Bevil Grenville's son, John, newly created Earl of Bath.

In 1667 three French privateers, who had been 'skulking under the island of Lundy' where they seized six barks bound for Barnstaple, sent the crew of one ashore to obtain a ransom for their master. Shooting went on for three or four days, and a report of the incident was sent to the Admiralty by the Admiralty officer in charge of the district. In this he stated that the island was slenderly guarded and that it had been possible for four or five men to land and reach the houses before they were noticed, and 'if the Dutch should take the island it would block up the Severn, and a dozen good men could secure it from the world. Every Englishman should be instrumental to the security of his nation.'[1]

With the accession of William and Mary in 1688 the Dutch suddenly became allies, and the crew of a French pirate ship, taking advantage of this by pretending their vessel to be a Dutchman, anchored off Lundy and came ashore to seek fresh milk for their captain, who was ill. This request was repeated for several days until finally the crew reported the death of their captain and sought permission to bury him in the island cemetery in the presence of all the islanders. This was agreed to, and after the coffin had been carried into the chapel, the islanders were asked to wait outside before being readmitted. The 'Dutchmen' meanwhile had armed themselves from the contents of the coffin, as there was no corpse, and made all the islanders prisoner. Then they seized 'fifty horses, three hundred goats, five hundred sheep and some bullocks, threw the goats and sheep into the sea and stripped the islanders of everything valuable, even to their clothes, and spoiled and destroyed everything, and then, satiated with plunder and mischief, they threw the guns over the cliffs, and left the island in a most destitute and disconsolate condition'.[2]

Although this ruse dates back to at least AD 860 when it was used by the Vikings in Italy, there is strong evidence that it did in fact take place on Lundy. Grose's 1776 account shows that the story is not his own but one given to him by a gentleman who visited the island in 1775. The whole tale is in quotation marks. The paragraph about the French is introduced by a reference to John Sharp, who was living on the island in 1744 and was then aged ninety-six; his father had gone there with Lord Saye and Sele who was there between 1647 and 1660, and as John Sharp himself had resided on the island for fifty years, he must have gone there about 1694. As the French attack took place in the reign of William III (1688–1702), John Sharp must have been there when it took place or have gone there very soon afterwards.

Aware that Lundy was frequented by privateers, a petition was put forward by one Richard Fulford in 1698 asking to be made a customs officer on Lundy, saying it was 'a place where considerable quantities of goods were run', but this was rejected by the commissioners who felt it was a place 'hardly inhabited or habitable'.[3]

The frigate bringing Captain Kidd and other notorious pirates who had been captured in New England made its first landfall at Lundy in 1700 where it anchored to await further instructions.[4] The House of Lords edition of *Hansard* for December 1703 shows HMS *Rye* and HMS *Penzance* 'cruising between Lundy and Milford', while the advice boat *Express* was 'cruising between Barnstaple and Lundy'. Despite these moves, that privateers remained active is evidenced by this comment of 1709: 'A Thomas Jones who having some money left to him quit the Guards and settled on Lundy only to have been ruined by the French privateers.'[5]

A few days after the death of John Grenville in 1701 his son and heir, Charles, was killed when the pistol he was cleaning went off accidentally. Although rumour spread that the death was not accidental but had been caused by the discovery of the extent of his father's debts, Charles's son William Henry, then aged nine, succeeded as the 3rd Earl of Bath. His death without issue in 1711 allowed the island to pass to the descendants of Charles's sister Jane. She had married Sir John Leveson Gower so their son John Leveson, Lord Gower, became the new owner. Lord John Gower was 'a prize worrier' and immediately sought to lease out his unexpected inheritance.

The lease was taken up by Mr Morgan on 17 March 1715 to be followed around 1721 by Richard Scores but because 'so many illegal practices were taking place' he was forced to leave, either before or soon after Barnstaple Customs officers seized a large consignment of tobacco and spirits on the island. The crew of the preventive boat which made this 1723 discovery rowed out to the island – quite a formidable feat – and left one of the crew behind for two days to guard the seized cargo while the boat returned to port to arrange a suitable vessel to collect it.[6]

Scores's departure left Lundy uninhabited, and entirely neglected by the proprietors.[7]

An incident recorded about 1740 shows that Lundy was used as a waiting point for pilots. A ship homeward bound for a month and three days from New England sighted the land, whereupon the captain 'found it to be indeed Lundy Island . . . then they crowded all the sail they could for Lundy. When they came nearer, they perceived several ships lying at anchor there, and made a signal for a Pilot; soon after comes off a Pilot of Clovelly who was there upon the island waiting to pilot ships up to Bristol. The Captain welcomed him on board, and agreed to seven guineas to bring him to Bristol.'[8]

Fear of a French invasion with use of Lundy as a base led to a petition by the merchants of Bristol dated 26 March 1743 asking that the island 'be annexed to the Crown and a garrison of about 40 men kept there with some cannon and other military stores, the trade in this channel may be greatly protected and the French and other privateers prevented from committing the like depredations for the future and the smugglers will also be hindered from the landing of uncustomed or prohibited goods thereon as formerly'.[9] No action came of this.

Piracy and privateering gave way slowly to the less difficult occupation of smuggling, against which Customs sloops, stationed at Ilfracombe and Cardiff since 1698, had been active. As early as the beginning of the eighteenth century the Collector of Customs at Ilfracombe declared that most of the Bristol Channel pilot cutters were running contraband 'and that the *Lundy Pilot, Hero,* and *Bristol Galley* did nothing else'.[10]

In 1748 Lord Gower (with the agreement of Lord Carteret, who was a fellow descendant of Sir Richard Grenville, and who retained some interest in the island) leased Lundy to Thomas Benson for £60 a year. Benson came from a prominent family of Bideford merchants and had in 1743 inherited a fortune of £40,000, a fleet of a dozen vessels, together with Knapp House, a property near Bideford, whose river frontage extended almost to Appledore town and included a quay some 200 ft long and 25 ft broad. Benson, a colourful character, had been made Sheriff of Devon in 1746 at which time he presented a large silver punchbowl to the mayor and corporation of Barnstaple. When it was politely pointed out that there was no ladle, Benson immediately supplied one inscribed: 'He that gave the Bowl gave the ladle.'[11]

Unfortunately, Benson was far from perfect. In 1740 his ship *Grace*, under the command of Capt. Hammett, had incurred Customs dues and penalties of £922 for the illegal importation of tobacco and in the following year two more of his ships, the *Nightingale* and *Britannia*, were served with writs. The *Nightingale* was the subject of two writs: for £1,153 on 25,000 lb of tobacco, and for £1,660 on another 36,000 lb. The *Britannia* ws served with no fewer than six writs totalling £4,505 on 99,000 lb of tobacco. In all Benson stood to forfeit £8,319 and, perhaps far worse, to lose his reputation as a merchant. He decided to contest these claims knowing that this would take time and so ease any fine.

In 1747 Benson was elected Member of Parliament for Barnstaple and soon after gained the government contract to transport convicts overseas. At this time Bideford and Barnstaple were the main ports for the importation of tobacco, a trade which totalled 1 million lb a year, and convicts would prove a useful return cargo to Virginia. However, on securing the lease of Lundy in the following year Benson chose to land his convicts there – whether this had been his original purpose in leasing the island is not clear, but the convicts were put to good use in farming and building, and for some years all went well.

His method was quite simple – his ships arrived home with details of their cargo set out on bills of lading. This cargo would have to be cleared at Bideford or Barnstaple, but by swearing that it was for export and not for home use it would be exempt from Customs duty. The ship would then set sail, ostensibly for a foreign port, but in reality for Lundy, where the tobacco was offloaded. The convicts would carry the hogsheads up the cliff and then divide the contents into smaller packages which could then be more easily smuggled back to the mainland through the smaller unwatched ports such as Clovelly or into remote coves on the North Devon coast.

Meanwhile Benson, wearing his legitimate hat, informed the collector at Barnstaple, who in turn wrote to the Board of Customs on 21 September 1751, that he (Benson) intended to send

> to the said island sundry kinds of provisions as also four or six hogsheads of tobacco offering to give us a Coast Bond on our sending over an officer to certificate the landing so that the said Bond may be discharged thereby, we are at present at very great loss how to act in this case and therefore humbly beg your Honour's particular directions for our government, together with directions how to act in respect of goods carried to or brought from the said island without dispatches apprehending that this will constantly be done as no officers reside thereon. We hear some people are already sent to Lundy and that nos. of inhabitants will soon be on the island, it being computed that the whole island is upwards of 1500 acres so that sundry kinds of necessarys will constantly be sent and wanted thither, and the produce of the island also brought hither from time to time, particularly wool, sheep, bullocks &c and as we cannot find that this island is within the limits of any Port we are greatly perplexed how to act. We therefore pray your Honour's speedy directions herein, and am etc. . . .[12]

On 11 October 1751 Benson's ship *Vine*, under the command of Capt. John Clibell, cleared the Customs at Barnstaple with sixty hogsheads of tobacco, bound for Morlaix. The ship put in at Milford Haven supposedly waiting for orders. The Customs there became suspicious and threatened to seize ship and cargo, and so the *Vine* set sail. Three days later she was at Barry, empty, and ready to load coal. No ship could possibly have sailed from Milford to Morlaix, discharged her cargo and returned to Barry within three days. The Customs visited Lundy, and found a number of staves from hogsheads, and traces of tobacco.[13]

The Custom Board in London decided to act. They

> served writs on Benson for several cargoes of tobacco that his vessels had loaded for export. These writs were, in effect, for repayment of the Customs duties that had been remitted to Benson. The Board were making the assumption that the tobacco had been smuggled back onto the mainland. The figures were quite staggering – nearly 200,000 pounds of tobacco amounting to over £8,300 in duty, and there is no doubt that this was merely the tip of the iceberg as far as Benson's smuggling operations were concerned. Benson

decided to test the legality of the writs in the Courts – indeed on the face of it he appeared to have a reasonable case as there was very little evidence to support the Board's allegations.[14]

However, Benson was fined £5,000 and deprived of his office.

Meanwhile the convicts whom Benson had undertaken to transport to America were working as slaves on Lundy. Visitors in 1752 noted that they were housed in the castle, and the walls of Benson's Cave below the castle are deeply inscribed by no fewer than thirty-eight pairs of initials, all in the eighteenth-century script and some with eighteenth-century dates. When compared with the known names of felons sentenced by the Exeter Quarter Sessions to transportation, it appears that Benson, having obtained the £20 transatlantic transportation fee for each prisoner, landed an entire shipload in 1749 and another in 1752.[15]

From the literature it is known that in the summer of 1752 there were at least twenty-three convicts at work on the island, but that seven or eight escaped that summer, rowing towards the mainland.

Either as an attempt to disarm his critics or in a gesture of overconfidence Benson allowed a party of three houseguests including his nephew Thomas Stafford and Sir Thomas Gunson the Sheriff of Somerset, who were staying at Knapp in July 1752, to visit the island. There they were met by Benson's staff including an Irishman Jeremiah Magra (?McGraw), a man called Andrews, Captain Marshal of Barnstaple, and an apprentice named Richard Ashton who supervised the work of the convicts, together with Ann Stoar, a North Devon girl working on the island as a servant.

At the time of the visit the convicts numbered thirteen men and three females and they were seen at work. Afterwards one of the visitors noted:

The Island at this time was in no state of improvement; the houses miserably bad; one on each side of the platform; that on the right was inhabited by Mr Benson and his friends; the other by servants. The old Fort was occupied by the convicts, whom he had sent there some time before, and employed in making a wall across the island; they were locked up every night when they returned from their labour. And about a week before we landed seven or eight of them took the longboat belonging to the island, and made their escape to Hartland and were never heard of afterwards. Wildfowl, it being the breeding season, were exceeding plenty, and a vast number of rabbits; we employed ourselves every day in pursuit of them. The island at that time was overgrown with ferns and heath which made it almost impossible to go over to the extreme of the island. Had it not been for the supply of rabbits and young sea-gulls our table would have been but poorly furnished; rats being so plenty that they destroyed every night what was left of our repast by day. Lobsters were tolerably plenty, and some other fish we caught. Mr Benson carried over some deer and goats, which increased, and were very wild and difficult to get at.

The path to the house was so narrow and steep that it was scarcely possible for a horse to ascend it. The inhabitants, by the assistance of a rope, climbed up a rock in which were steps cut out to place their feet, up to a Cave or magazine, where Mr Benson lodged his goods, and which was occasionally locked up. . . . There happened to come into the road, one evening, near twenty sail of vessels, which induced us to turn out early next morning to see them weigh their anchors, and sail. The colours were hoisted on the fort, and they all, as they passed Rat Island returned the compliment, excepting one vessel, which provoked Mr Benson to fire at her himself, with ball, though we used every argument in our power to prevent him, urging 'the impropriety of it, as it might be noticed; and for our own ends, as ammunition grew scarce, for our diversion in shooting'.

He replied that the island was his, and every vessel that passed it and did not pay him the same compliment as was paid to the King's forts, he would fire on her. . . . He often said that the sending the convicts to Lundy, was the same as sending them to America; they were transported from England, it mattered not where it was, so as they were out of the Kingdom.[16]

As Benson failed to pay the original fine the Sheriff of Devon was forced to levy it, and in lieu of payments he seized tobacco and other goods which were hidden on the island. These were not sufficient to clear the fines which now totalled £7,872 and so Benson's Bideford estates were seized by the government early in 1753.

Meanwhile Benson had perpetrated the greatest outrage of all. He heavily insured the cargo of one of his ships, the *Nightingale*, which set sail on 28 July 1752 for America, but after light airs, and under darkness, crept back to Lundy where on 31 July 1752 it unloaded and hid its cargo of convicts, pewter, linen and salt. The following day it set sail and some miles west of the island the master, Capt. Lancey, set fire to the ship and abandoned it. The crew were rescued and landed at Bideford where Lancey and his two mates and boatswain declared before the notary public (whose name was Narcissus Hatherly) that the ship had caught fire accidentally. However, another member of the crew told a convincing story to the contrary and so Capt. Lancey and his shipmates were detained while inquiries were made.

The Board of Commissioners of Customs wrote to the collector at Barnstaple on 26 September 1752:

Gentlemen – The Commrs having received information from a gentleman in Sth. Wales that a new trade is carried on at the Island of Lundy and that many ships bound outwards from Barnstaple Bay unloaded there and that the cargoes are afterwards returned to that country in other vessels. That a platform with guns is erected and shot fired to bring ships too for to give an account who and what they are, but the men in them are not suffered to land and it is apprehended unless an immediate stop be put to it, the island will become a magazine for smuglers [*sic*]. You are to make a strict inquiry into

Beach Cannon

what is above sett forth & report a state of the case with such observations as shall occur to you upon the whole matter for the Commrs. consideration & directions.

The collector replied a few days later, on 13 October 1752:

Honble Sirs – we received Mr Secry. Wood's letter of the 26th Ulto and in obedience thereto humbly report that we have made enquiry into this affair but cannot get any perfect account or learn anything that may be depended on, the reports being various and contradictory. We are humbly of opinion that a smugling trade may be carried on there if attempted with a good deal of success as a number of small vessells may constantly hover with safety in Lundy Road and there both land and take in goods in a clandestine manner to the great detriment of the Revenue & fair trade, and we know not how it can be prevented unless the Island was by a clause in some Act fixed within the Limits of a port, without which the legality of some seizures we h[um]bly apprehend may be diputed as we are informed the island being upwards of 4 leagues from any shore & nearest to this Port. We further hbly report that applications are frequently made to us for despatches for carrying sundry sorts of goods to this island for the use (as sayd) of the inhabitants but as some of them require security, we are at great loss how to act no officer being there to certifie the landing so as to discharge the bond. The proprietor therefore complains & says the island cannot be supplied with proper necessaries & threatens the officers for refusing despatches alledging that he is deprived even of the common privileges of a subject and that the island by means thereof must become useless to his very great detriment. We therefore beg your directions herein for our government.

Lundy was a thorn in the flesh for the Customs. The collector at Cardiff believed that 'there never lived yet a man on the island of Lundy who was not connected with smuggling' and the commissioners 'felt they had a special problem with Lundy; it was not within the limits of any port, and was about 12 miles from the shore, which made the legality of any seizures doubtful. Furthermore it was very difficult to patrol as the smugglers had erected a platform with cannons to prevent the Customs vessels landing on the island. Once again the only answer seemed to be the outright purchase.'[17]

To this Benson had an answer. In 1753 he petitioned the Lords Commissioners of the Treasury on behalf of himself, the owners of Lundy, and its inhabitants that the island should be made a port and that licence be granted to Benson to build a pier. The commissioners did not fall for this ploy and instead asked Customs for a report. Customs replied in a letter dated 27 March pointing out the trouble they had had with Mr Scores in the 1720s and their worries about Benson. It was felt that as Lundy was so convenient for smuggling, that if it became a legal place to land goods it would become another Isle of Man – 'a magazine of goods for illicit trade'. They also recommended that a sloop be sent to patrol the Lundy area – and to this the Treasury agreed. Customs eventually raided Lundy in July and recovered the cargo of the *Nightingale*.

This was the end for Benson who fled to Portugal. Inquiries must have taken time as it was not until 25 February 1754 that the case opened in the Court of Admiralty, Old Bailey. There 'John Lancey and John Lloyd, First Mate, were indicted for unlawfully burning and destroying the ship *Nightingale* . . . with the intention to defraud'. From the evidence it is clear that Benson used Lancey's dependence on him to force him into an act which was quite against his conscience and character, and despite the promise of loyalty and help, Benson had fled and left Lancey to suffer the penalty of death at the age of twenty-seven. John Sinnet was released; and Lloyd was tried but acquitted.

It was afterwards said of Benson that he was 'an enemy, not of one country only, but to the world, as the pest of society and a disgrace to mankind'.[18] Somehow Benson managed to withstand the popular clamour for his extradition and trial, and it was even said that some years later he returned, incognito, to North Devon possibly in the guise of holy orders.

He settled in Portugal where he died in 1772.[19]

Chapter Seven

FROM 1754 TO 1834

Earl Gower died in 1754 at the age of sixty and as he had no heir, executors were appointed to dispose of his estate, a process which was to take them over twenty years.

During these two decades Lundy seems to have been neglected, as the only family living on the island at the time of Gower's death (probably the Andrews family referred to by Grose) who 'sell liquors to such fishermen who put on shore there',[1] had left by 1761 when the island was 'at present uninhabited'.[2]

The Andrews's departure may have been hastened by a report sent to London by the local collector detailing the seizure and search at Appledore of the collier *Nottage*, newly arrived from Swansea, on which 'two ankers of Brandy were discovered in the Master's cabin and later six small bales of tobacco and some bottles of wine were dug out of the coal'. The collector commented, 'these colliers are a great annoyance and cause continual problems. The fines for smuggling are not sufficient to put a stop to their business.'[3] Thomas Morris of the *Nottage* had been fined only £20 and did not lose his vessel.

During the summer of 1765[4] the 'Principal Merchants of the City' of Bristol considered 'A scheme for building a Lazaret [fever hospital] on the Pike [peak, summit] of Lundy, like that on Chidney Hill', but nothing came of this and the island probably remained uninhabited until 15 February 1775 when John Borlase Warren bought it from Lord Gower's executors for only £510.

Warren was a man of some talent and wealth. Although only twenty-one years old when he bought Lundy, he had served in the navy and been elected Member of Parliament for Marlow. The baronetcy which had been extinct since 1689 was revived in his favour in June 1775 and in the following year he took his MA degree at Cambridge.[5]

Although his original interest may have been 'partly by way of a place of refreshment for his crew, and partly on account of the harbour where he could occasionally lay up his vessel,[6] Sir John devoted much energy and capital to the improvement of the island. Fortunately we have three eyewitness descriptions of about this time: that of the Revd Thomas Martyn, Sir John's former tutor (see Chapter Twenty-one on cultivation); the second is Grose's; and the third is the diary of a gentleman,[7] plus the notes actually sent by Warren to his agent.

Sir John Borlase Warren (unknown)

Sir John is believed to have lived on Lundy during his ownership and according to the 'Journal of 1787' to have 'employed 40 labourers or mechanics yearly' and to have spent upwards of £6,000 on improvements which, according to Grose, included 'Surveys thereof, with intent (if practicable) of building a pier there, and once more causing it to be inhabited and cultivated'. The farmhouse – now the Old House – was probably built on the site of an earlier building and was the 'one dwelling house' mentioned by Martyn in 1775. The forty labourers who planted trees, repaired existing walls and built new ones seem to have been housed at 'Newtown', a new settlement of a few buildings at the northern end of the present-day High Street which appears on maps after this date, only to disappear after 1840 when many field boundary changes took place.

The notes taken from the Admiral's notebooks to his agent,[8] though fascinating and detailed, are not dated but seem to have been written soon after Warren's purchase in 1775. They begin:

Captain Wood to take Sir John's cutter lying at Ilfracombe to Southampton and there sell her or consign her to Mr John Gaty, builder, but she is not to be parted with under £450 and the money to be paid into the hands of Mr Charsley and when paid to him he is then to discharge every person there at Lundy except Capt. Wood, Lamb, and such others as shall be thought useful upon the island – those to be paid but not discharged. As soon as that is done, to send a proper husbandman to cultivate and improve the Land and Stock the same with 60 head of Cow Cattle and 500 sheep and more if the Land will maintain them.

A proper Farm Yard to be made and convenient building to be erected as such Farmer shall judge necessary for the carrying on the Farming and Dairy business. Captn. Wood to go to Schetland [*sic*] to invite three or four familys over to the island to live and each family to have a House and Acres of land and to have the Use of Sir John's Boats for fishing upon paying one half of the Customary profit to Sir John. The Boats to be under the direction of Captn. Wood.

On the outbreak of the War of American Independence in July 1776 Warren was 'moved to sell his yacht and part with Lundy in order to volunteer for sea service'.[9] In another notebook apparently written at this time instructions are given for the running of the island in Sir John's absence and for the building of a large house on land between the Old Hotel and the Old Light, and the building of a fort and pier. The notebook reads:

As a proper Governor is appointed, he is to correspond with Mr. M. every fortnight, as to Expenses, money in hand, store &c giving an account how the work goes on. The Architect will lay before the Trustees in plan of the House, Fort, and small pier intended to be built; the money for which will be left in their hands. The superintendency of the Buildings will belong to the Architect and the Overseer. In case anything happens, the Architect is to be applied to in order to redress it. The Governor is to inform the Trustees of anything wanting in the Island, and they are to apply the remedy as they think proper. As it will be necessary to have the island laid out into proper Farms, the doing of that I leave to my Trustees, who may be informed of any particulars relating to that by the Lieutenant Governor. As it has been thought that for the peopling of the Island in order for the occupying of the Farms, that Highlanders would be best suited to the situation and station of the place – if it should be approved of hereafter by the Trustees, when a proper estimate has been made of the expense of the Farm Houses and settling of the People &c, a further sum may be granted. It is thought that some fishermen should be introduced, as hereafter a Fishery may perhaps be put on foot, to the interest of the Proprietor and the colony. But in this and every other concern about the island, the Trustees will act as they think most proper; except that if any Plan is made for settling the Island, I would have it sent to me for my approbation and concurrence.

There is a vessel employed at £16 per month, the charge of which, if absolutely necessary will be allowed for the time being. If other vessells [*sic*] can be freighted cheaper, the Trustees will employ them as they think proper.

If Highlanders should be approved for the settlement, the Trustees may apply to Captain John Grant of Limehouse Lane Greenwich who will direct them to the best means of having them conveyed to the island. As there has been a proposal laid before Merchants of Bristol about building a larger Pier; it would be proper to apply to Mr Birch, who can give them information about that subject, and upon such information the Trustees will act as they judge best.

Mr Birch would seem to be the agent on the island as there is a further note which reads: 'The Agent Birch and the surveyor Arnold recommended by him, apparently linked together, and suspected of grievous craft, it will be proper to keep them in utter ignorance of any designs to discharge them, or at least not to employ them farther than shall be necessary.'

A most interesting insight into Sir John's plan for a fort is found in the library of Customs and Excise for this period. It reads:

8th July 1776. Hallows Hatfield, agent for Sir John Borlase Warren, Baronet maketh oath that – Two brass field pieces, three pounders with carriages, two five and a half inch mortars with beds, two hundred iron shott three pounders, one hundred iron shott nine pounders, one hundred five and a half inch shells with fuses, one cask containing one hundred and fifty shott one pounders, three chests of thirtyseven musketts, seventyfive pistols, two brass blunderbuses, twentyeight cartouche boxes, thirtysix cutlasses, thirtyeight bayonets, twelve half-pikes, twelve pole axes, one keg containing ten pounds musquet ball and eight barrels gunpowder which came here in the *Venus*, Archibald Long, Master, from London and transhipt here on board the *Lundy Packet*, Christopher Andrews Master, all which said Military Stores were landed the 21st of May last in the Island of Lundy.

The departure of Sir John Borlase Warren and his waning interest in Lundy, with its consequent lack of supervision, prompted Peter Fosse, the collector at Ilfracombe to report to London in 1781: 'We have received intelligence from undoubted authority that large quantities of tea and brandy are frequently discharged out of Armed Smugglers from France and lodged on the Island of Lundy till opportunities offer of putting the same on board Pilot Boats belonging to the Port.'[10]

Although the island may have been offered on a twenty-one year lease it was eventually sold outright on 2 February 1781 to John Cleveland of Tapeley, the MP for Barnstaple, for £1,200.[11]

Among the pilots at this time was 'Mr William Walters [who] was taken on board the *Montague* at Lundy by Captain George Brown on October 3rd 1782 and piloted His Majesty's Ship safely up to Flat Holmes. . . .'[12]

The Collector of Customs at Swansea reported to the board in London on 23 November 1782:

Enclosed we lay before your Honours an account of a seizure made on the 14th instant by Captain Dickinson of the *Lady Mackworth* Armed ship on the island of Lundy in the Bristol Channel. And we beg leave to observe to your Honours that at present there is a considerable trade carried on in the smuggling line on the said island an instance of which appears by what Captain Dickinson informs us who says that on this passage to this Port from Plymouth and Falmouth with the trade of this neighbourhood on the 14th inst about 7 o'clock in the morning being close in with the Island of Lundy he saw a small cutter off that island which he supposed to be a privateer or a smuggler and immediately gave chase but not being able to come up with her he manned and armed his boats and sent them on shore with orders to search the island as he had reason to believe the cutter had landed part of her cargo. After they had landed they made a strict search they found in the cavities of the rocks and in small huts 128 ankers [9-gallon kegs] of brandy and 4 bags of Bohea tea which have been lodged in His Majesty's Warehouse here.[13]

Apart from the pilots and the smugglers it appears that the only residents in 1783 were 'two farmers and their families',[14] showing that the model settlement of Newtown with its 'Schetland' immigrants had not flourished.

John Cleveland obviously took little interest in the place as a note dated 29 March 1785 reports: 'Knight, the smuggler, is now at Lundy Island, having been driven from Barry. The protection of his armed brig having been removed, smuggling has greatly diminished here.'[15]

The Times of 25 October 1786 reported that there was talk in Bristol 'that the Government were about to purchase the Isle of Lundy . . . for what purpose is not known, whether for building a Lazaretto, or to confine and employ felons . . .'. Five days later it reported, wrongly, that the island 'belongs to Sir John Borlase Warren, who bought it some years ago when he kept some famous sailing vessels, and intended to have settled it. Some fashionable engagements however prevented him at that time from carrying his plan into execution, and his domestic enjoyments have, perhaps, since that time, turned his thoughts from the romantic project.' This essay casts doubt on both the character and achievements on Lundy of Sir John.

There are three interesting descriptions of Lundy as it was during John Cleveland's ownership. The first, dated between 4 and 10 July 1787, was written by one of a party of visitors to the island:

We went to the house which Sir John Warren built for his own residence. . . . Sir John Warren began a quay, which was never finished. . . . You ascend into the island by a narrow path, just wide enough for a horse to get up, which leads you to a platform, where two roads meet; one conducts you to the castle . . . the other (to the house lately built by Sir John Warren) wide enough for carts, and where they land goods that are to be carried off, or brought to the island. At some small distance above the landing-place are the remains of an ancient wall, on each side of the way, supposed to be built to guard the entrance to the island, that being the only accessible point, and, it is said, that there was a chain formerly fixed there. You find on many parts of the island, where there was the least chance of landing, upwards of forty ancient structures of stone-work, some without any cement, and others strongly united with it, on which guns were planted in Queen Anne's war with the French, when the enemy greatly infested the coast of the Bristol Channel. I saw the remains of one of the guns (on a platform, facing the east) which was burst with powder a few years since; and another gun on the beach, at the landing-place, which was brought from the same battery, by order of Sir John Warren. . . . After dinner we walked to view the rocks on the western part of the island, and saw vast quantities of wild fowl, (it being the breeding season) and the method of taking them in nets, which the inhabitants use, for the advantage of their feathers. The nets are made in the form of those commonly used for taking rabbits on warrens. They are fixed on the rocks, and sometimes on the ground, on sticks, in the breeding places. Every morning and evening the natives watch their nets, and take out the birds that are entangled. They catch in a good season 1,700 or 1,800 dozen, and make 1/- per pound of their feathers. People from the neighbouring coast are hired to pluck them, at 2d. per dozen and pluck about 4 dozen per day. . . . These birds, it appears, annually foresake the island, when the young birds can fly, and are not seen again till the time returns for depositing their eggs; the natives collect these eggs, and send to the Bristol Sugar Refineries.[16] The muirrs are the most profitable twelve of them producing one pound of feathers. After being plucked they are skinned; these skins are boiled in a furnace for the oil they yield, which is used instead of candles; and the flesh is given to the hogs, who feed on it voraciously. . . . On a pleasant spot between the Chapel and the house, our traveller saw the ground Sir John Warren had marked out to build a handsome house on. . . . The walls of the Citadel are very perfect, of a square form; it is converted into modern dwellings, the turrets which were chimneys still serve the same purpose, of which there are four – one at each angle – . . . In front of the house five guns are planted [i.e. the castle] . . . The morning of Saturday, (the 7th of July) was appropriated by our Traveller and Mr Cleveland to arranging disputes among the tenants, and swearing in Mr Hole constable of the island; but in the afternoon, they laid the foundations for illuminating the island, and the surrounding element. In the afternoon we took a walk to the Chapel, and the Beacon-Hill, to determine which was the highest spot, for erecting a lighthouse, the Merchants of Bristol having offered to build one at their own expense, if Mr Cleveland was agreeable, and had appointed to meet him that week on the island, to fix on a proper spot. On examining the ground, we thought the Beacon-Hill, the highest and most proper spot for the purpose. . . . On Sunday the 8th . . . prayers were read by the Rev. Mr Cutcliffe, and a sermon preached by Mr Smith, to a congregation of 22 persons. . . . On our return [from the North End] I saw the remains of a windmill. The North part is now incapable of being improved, from Mr Benson's setting the heath and ferns on fire, while he was in possession, so that the earth continued burning for some days, till it came to the bare rock, and now nothing vegetable grows on it.[17]

The second record of this period is given by Grose who says that 'In 1794 there were seven houses on the island and twenty-three inhabitants.' The buildings, apart from the castle and chapel, were 'a house near St. Helens Well where a brewhouse is now building, a watch-tower at the landing place and another at the North End. There are two walls of moor stone running across the island; one called South Wall, dividing the South from the Middle island, the other called Half-way Wall dividing the north from the Middle island and placed about halfway between the South and North ends. Many ruins of old walls are to be seen, which were fences to inclosures, and plainly prove a great part of the island to have been once cultivated.'

Alarmed by the threat of invasion by French revolutionaries the military undertook a review of their defences in the west of England and in 'Letters sent and Received by the Barrack Master of the Cavalry Barracks at Barnstaple 1794/1807' a letter of 1795 gives a third description of the island following an inspection there of 'any buildings there that may be appropriated to the service of Government'. It reads: 'You have, enclosed, the plan and dimensions of all the buildings on the island of Lundy. . . . There are several forts on the island, six small and one large cannon. The number of men, women and children on the island does not exceed twenty . . . [the island] and is now let at £70 per ann. The tenant has about five years to expire of his term. It is a very healthy place.'[18]

The threat was real, and following the failure of the French to land an army of 12,000 in Bantry Bay in December 1796 in support of the Irish peasantry who were on the point of revolt, the French sought alternative British targets.

Three months later, in February 1797, William S. Tate, an Irish-born American in the service of France, planned an attack on Bristol which was to be burnt by a landing-party that would withdraw immediately. A force of 600 regulars and 800 convicts dressed in captured English uniforms that had been dyed black embarked in the frigates *Resistance, Constance* and *Vengeance* which together with the lugger *Vautour* set sail on 18 February. 'By midday on the 20th they were off Lundy waiting for a change in the tide to get up to Bristol. Two small ships from Ilfracombe were captured and sunk.'[19] After heading eastwards they realized that they could not reach Bristol before daylight, so changing their plans, headed north-westwards for South Wales. A ship from St Ives reported spotting four foreign ships near Lundy between 10 a.m. and 4 p.m. on the 21st, and it was on the 22nd that the force landed near Fishguard.

Although the four ships of the invasion fleet sheltered at Lundy on the 20th, and again passed the island after the Bristol target had been abandoned in favour of South Wales, there is no record of any Frenchman landing on Lundy at this time.

It may have been this fear of French invasion or of government requisition that led to the annoucement in *The Times* of 28 October 1802 that the island was to be auctioned at Garroways Coffee House, Cornhill. It was reputed to be of '2,500 acres . . . with a very considerable and profitable trade . . . of the feathers and rabbits' and to be 'now in the possession of a Tenant at Will at £215 per annum'.

The buyer was Sir Harry Vere Hunt, Bart., who during a walk in London just happened to pass the auction room where the sale was in progress. 'Attracted by the noise he entered it' to hear the auctioneer dwelling on the advantages of Lundy – that 'it never paid tax or tithe, acknowledged neither King nor Parliament nor law civil or ecclesiastical and that its Proprietor was Pope and Emperor at once in his scanty domain'. Sir Harry made a bid and the island was sold to him with effect from 17 November 1802 for only £5,270. His motive for buying is not clear – he may have been attracted by its apparent freedom from taxes, or he may have seen it as a safer property than his estates in Ireland. He certainly 'planted there a small Irish colony, and drew up for them a compendious code including a quaint law of divorce in matrimonial disputes'.[20] It is mentioned elsewhere that these Irish immigrants were housed in the castle and are remembered chiefly for having removed the remaining timbers associated with the castle, including the remains of the original barbican or West Gate that had been strengthened when King Edward II was expected to seek refuge there. One Michael Mannix was agent for both Sir Harry and later for his son, Sir Aubrey. The most likely reason for Sir Harry's purchase was his knowledge of government interest and, with his contacts in the War Ministry, hopes of a quick profit by resale. The government did eventually agree to buy it from him and in 1803 he wrote to his wife saying that he hoped the price would be £10,000. However, after the government had the island surveyed they decided it would not suit their purpose, and with the loss of his friend Lord Hobart, following a change of government in 1804, Hunt lost all hope of making a quick sale.

Lundy was leased to Mr H. Drake from March 1805 until June 1807 and the Irish settlement continued, with inevitable crises, for many years. The composition of this settlement is not known but names on a map of 1832 may be those of some of the settlers: McDonnells Moor Spring; Parson's Field; Belsey's Field; Larry's Garden; Navel's Garden; Fryer's Garden; William's Moor Spring; and Budd's Moor Spring.

Following Sir Harry's death on 11 August 1818 Lundy passed to his son, Sir Aubrey de Vere Hunt[21] who, anxious to rid himself of his late father's many debts, set about selling the island. His early choice of one John Benison as potential purchaser was ill-judged as Benison spent years trying to ensure that Lundy was both tax-free and independent.

It was during Sir Aubrey's ownership that the long-projected lighthouse was built and the presence of resident, observant officers, together with the ending of the French wars, so reduced the use of the island by smugglers that the Barnstaple collector was able to report in 1820 'with some satisfaction' . . . that the island of

Lundy is considered to be devoid of smugglers'. This confidence may have been a little premature as a later tenant, Capt. Jack Lee, had many caches for brandy 'halfway up the shale slope above the Beach' and the Heaven diaries record with shock the offers made by various French seamen to engage in smuggling.

Sir Aubrey offered the island at public auction on 8 February 1822 in the same coffee house where his father had bought it, but there were no buyers.

While Benison continued to show interest two gentlemen, John Matravers and William Stiffe 'one from co. Wilts the other from co. Somerset' visited Lundy in 1823, interested in purchase and it was to them that the island was eventually sold on 21 June 1830. Sir Aubrey is reputed to have been a gambling man and when playing cards with Matravers and Stiffe, staked the island and lost the game. The prize, or stake, was £4,500.[22]

By now the Irish seem to have disappeared as 'its only inhabitants are the inmates of a solitary farm-house and the keepers of the lighthouse'.[23] Despite being told that it 'is likely to become of more importance from the recent discovery of a valuable silver and copper mine from which the present fortunate possessors . . . will it is said realise at least 12,000L a year by the mines alone',[24] the new owners suddenly found themselves possessed of an island they did not want. They set about finding a purchaser and eventually, in 1834, found William Hudson Heaven.

Chapter Eight

FROM 1834 TO THE PRESENT

William Hudson Heaven, who bought Lundy in 1834 for £9,870, was to own the island during one of its most prosperous periods. He made Lundy his home and that of his family for over eighty years. From his childhood days in Bristol William Heaven had cherished the ambition to own an island. He inherited property in Jamaica from his godfather and Burke's *Landed Gentry* says that 'he purchased Lundy Island with the compensation received for his emancipated slaves'. He had at first considered the island of Anticosto in the St Lawrence River which was on offer for £5,000, but his advisors thought this too risky a venture and suggested instead that he should buy Lundy 'for its wild game shooting'.

Mr Heaven was well satisfied with his purchase and at once set about improvements. He appointed William Malbon at his agent and commissioned Edwin Honychurch to design the villa (now known as Millcombe) which was completed in 1836 in the valley of the same name, Mr Heaven having decided against Gannets' Combe as an alternative site. The completion of this house was a considerable achievement especially as he 'had to have all the materials for building Millcombe, as well as most of the furniture brought up by the steep and rough old beach road, dragged on sleds by donkeys, and possibly oxen'. It was about this time that Mr Heaven 'introduced horses, but considering the strain of dragging supplies too much for man and beast up the old road, approached the Elder Brethren of Trinity House to collaborate in making a new road which forks from the old one and winds up to the Battlements, they to supply engineers and labour (skilled) and to divide the cost between them, the haulage of T.H. stores, coal and oil etc, being by far the heavier usage of the road. Their advisory engineers, being of opinion the said proposed road was practically impossible, W.H.H. was his own engineer and had it constructed.'[1] As Trinity House had already built the length of road from the Battlements to the plateau, a continuous road suitable for wheeled traffic now existed from the beach to the top of the island. Mr Heaven, living as a resident lord of the manor, was on hand to make many other improvements.

In July 1840 *The Times* announced that Lundy was to be sold by auction and gave the following glowing description:

The mansion is of recent creation and embodies within it all the accommodation 'a patriotic little monarch' can desire with corresponding offices of every description. Where shall ambition find such a solace in all its lofty pretensions? Amid this scene of quiet repose and perfect independence two of the most favoured sea-bathing establishments are all but in view. An excellent farmhouse has recently been built with Kyanised[2] timber and slated roof and there are six superior cottages close by. A great part of the island is let with this farm for seven years at an exceedingly low rent but the great source of revenue is yet to be divulged; First 'the extensive fishery' without the fear of any rival, especially for herrings and lobsters, which must produce an incalculably large income. The granite throughout the island in the hands of an enterprising man will realise a fortune; the 'minerals' including silver and Copper have been discovered near the beach. The sporting over the demesne undisturbed by mortal Man is of the highest order and during the season myriads of little seabirds pay their annual visit and become tributary to the island by depositing countless of their eggs and dropping their beautiful feathers, all of which become a source of income. The Woodcock, Snipe, and Wildfowl shooting is not surpassable anywhere . . . the Government is to 'form a harbour of Refuge' and Nature seems to have pointed out its eligibility for such a God-like purpose . . . the land is adapted to create a Capital Pottery . . . the turmoil of politics will not intrude to distract the harmony of the little Monarch of the Isle; happiness, contentment and independence will be as firmly fixed as the rock on which the island is placed. Communication from Bristol and Tenby is almost daily.

Despite this eulogy the island remained unsold and in 1849 Charles Kingsley wrote to his wife describing a visit he had recently made there: '. . . We dined at the Farmhouse; dinner costing me 1s 9d and then rambled over the island. . . . O that I had been a painter for that day at least!' As this was Kingsley's only visit to Lundy, it must have been on this occasion that he gained the material and inspiration for the description of the island in *Westward Ho!*

In 1852 the cabinet considered the possible use of Lundy for the detention of criminals,[3] an idea which has not infrequently been advanced regardless of the opinions of the owner. The following year another visitor wrote: 'A considerable proportion is under cultivation and is let to tenant farmer John Lee by name, familiarly known as Captain Jack . . . at his house [the farm] visitors are entertained.'[4] But John Lee not only farmed and entertained visitors, he also indulged in smuggling for which he was convicted at the assizes and fined on 4 January 1856. Later that year the island was again advertised but no sale was completed and the Lee family remained as tenants, Capt. Jack being helped by his son Capt. Tom Lee until 1861, when all the family left.

Writing in May 1858 William Hudson Heaven said that 'only two houses are inhabited except the Lighthouse' and that the 'present population exclusive of

The children of W.H. Heaven (P. Penny)

lighthouse and visitors, is 19 or 20 including labourers all boarded at the Farm'. Exactly what the labourers were doing is not clear. They may have been making improvements to the farm or they may have been building the lower Beach Road as later in the year petitions were submitted for the island to be considered as a site for a harbour of refuge. As there are no further records of the island being offered for sale until 1906 and it was exactly between these dates that companies were established to exploit the island's granite, it appears that Mr Heaven abandoned the idea of selling in favour of commercial development.

The first enterprise to be set up was the Lundy Granite Company Ltd, registered on 18 July 1863, which flourished for five years during which time it cut and worked the quarries on the East Side. This commercial exploitation is dealt with fully in Chapter Twenty and, although the company at first met with a degree of success, the shipping of the stone presented constant difficulties. Relations between the company and Mr Heaven deteriorated, possibly aggravated by the inability of the company to farm the land as had been intended. The company was eventually wound up on 19 November 1868 and when its affairs were eventually investigated the directors of the National Bank of Ireland emerged in a way not altogether to their credit.

Meanwhile further ventures were started and on 23 December 1863 the Lundy Island Floating Breakwater Company Ltd was registered with the aim of constructing a breakwater and purchasing a steam tug vessel. This company's intention was to facilitate the shipment of granite, but after a fruitless search for the directors the company was wound up in 1882 having achieved nothing. Another company formed in 1884 was successful in its object of laying a telegraph cable from Lundy to the mainland, but the venture proved unprofitable and the service was discontinued in 1887 when the company was dissolved.

Following fears of French or Prussian aggression, a military sub-committee under Vice Admiral Phillimore advised in 1881 that 'Lundy would be important in time of war in the defence of the Bristol Channel'. It proposed that three 9 in RML (rifled, muzzle-loading) 12 ton guns, costing £7,500, should be mounted in the most suitable positions on the island to stop enemy cruisers using the anchorage there and to protect the landing beach. The range of these guns was 2.5 miles and in addition two harbour defence ships would have been stationed permanently in the Bristol Channel with four gunboats and four torpedo boats. Torpedo boats were still a novel idea but were soon to prove more effective against cruisers than shore-based guns and so the Lundy fortifications never materialized.[5]

Once the Lundy Granite Company had been wound up the island farm was again leased to tenants. Mr and Mrs Dovell were there in 1875 and 1879 and they were succeeded in 1885 by Mr Wright. He in turn was followed by Mr Ackland, a retired wholesale grocer from Barnstaple, who completed the extension to the farmhouse which had been begun by the quarry company and became the first tenant to use the building as a hotel.

William Hudson Heaven died on 4 March 1883 and was succeeded as owner by his son, the Revd Hudson Grosett Heaven, who not only administered to the spiritual needs of the islanders but also provided night school 'three or four times a week' and ran a Sunday school. His longstanding ambition was fulfilled in 1896 when work began on a new church, using stone from Quarter Wall village. The completed church was dedicated to St Helena on 7 June 1897 and in the same year Trinity House completed the new lighthouses at the North and South Ends of Lundy, whereupon the old lighthouse on Beacon Hill was abandoned.

The two new lighthouses were built with granite that had been left in the quarry workings and for a few months in 1897 the quarries were again noisy with workmen. Later that year an attempt was made to revive the quarry workings by Lundy Granite Quarries Ltd, but as only seven of the 30,000 shares were taken up in the first year the company was wound up in 1900. In December 1899 another company was floated, the Lundy Island and Mainland Quarries Ltd, but this too sold only seven shares from a total of 80,000 and so suffered the same fate as its predecessors, being wound up in 1911.

The entire island was now let on lease. Mr George Taylor became tenant farmer from 1899 and in 1902 he set about commercializing the island by appointing Mrs Pellman to run the Manor House Farm and Lunch Room. The brothers Lewis

Saunt and W.F. Saunt, who succeeded Taylor on 1 June 1908, remained on Lundy until 1918. During that time they lived in the oldest part of the Old Hotel but employed Mr A. St Claire to run the remainder of the building as a hotel.

Lundy became headline news on 30 May 1906 when the first-class battleship HMS *Montagu* was wrecked near Shutter Rock. The ship was only three years old, had cost £1,500,000 to build and was the flagship of the home fleet sailing on her first commission, She ran aground while testing new radio installations and although great effort was made to refloat her, she became a total wreck and salvage operations continued under difficult conditions until 1922.

When Lundy was offered for sale in August 1906, the Revd Dr Batson, 'an eccentric gentleman of independent means' from Watchet in Somerset, offered £30,000 for the island, under the mistaken impression that he would automatically acquire the rights of salvage and ownership of the wrecked HMS *Montagu*. The offer was accepted and Dr Batson returned to Watchet 'where he promised the Freedom of the Island to all Watchet sailors. He also bestowed Knighthoods on a couple of sea captains and his friend Henry Davey, the local grocer, who was bidden to "Rise Sir Henry, Knight of Lundy Island". Unfortunately it soon transpired that the "King" had insufficient financial backing to complete the purchase and the deal fell through.'[6]

Press speculation was rife and the Revd Mr Heaven announced that he had not heard of the proposal of a continental baron to establish a Monte Carlo there and

The Revd H.G. Heaven (P. Penny)

would not be willing to sell with the knowledge that the island 'would be turned into a gambling hell'. A subsequent proposed auction on 25 September collapsed.

Meanwhile negotiations had begun in 1904 for the establishment of a naval war signal station and so the auctioneers were able to mention that the establishment of a naval base was under consideration, though they failed to mention that the planned complement was for only four seamen. Despite the attractions of the annual rent roll of £630 and a glowing description of the beauties and advantages of the island, the highest bid fell £6,000 short of the reserve price of £25,000.

During 1908 rumours that the island had been sold were denied by the Revd Mr Heaven,[7] who remained on Lundy until he retired to Torrington in 1911. The island was offered for sale in *Country Life* of November 1912 but, as it remained unsold, it passed on Mr Heaven's death in 1916 to his nephew, Walter Heaven.

Soon after the outbreak of the First World War in 1914 the Heaven family went back to the mainland, leaving only the tenant farmer and Trinity House staff. German submarines were active in the Bristol Channel and Lundy was rumoured to have been a rendezvous. In 1815 an MP made an exaggerated estimate of the accommodation available on Lundy that could be used to intern prisoners of war. He claimed that 'the present buildings thereon could accommodate 1600 prisoners and that the old buildings formerly used as houses for quarrymen could in a few weeks be made suitable for several thousand prisoners'.[8] To this the Under Secretary of State replied that Lundy was 'not suitable'.

After less than two years' ownership Walter Charles Hudson Heaven sold the island in 1918 to Augustus Langham Christie of Tapeley Court, Instow, a descendant of the John Cleveland who had owned Lundy 130 years previously. Mr Christie's main reason 'for buying it was that he could not bear to see from his house any land that he did not own'.[9]

Mr C. Herbert May leased the island from March 1920 and on re-opening the hotel placed it under the management of Miss Sage. Mr S.T. Dennis farmed the island from 1917 until 1920 and Millcombe House although redecorated for use as a second hotel, remained unused. Mr Christie also built the slipway in the cove near the Landing Beach, intending it for use by the island vessel *Lerina*.

Eight years later the island was sold to Mr Martin Coles Harman for £16,000 plus the ingoing valuation of £9,250 which included the *Lerina*. Mr Harman, an enthusiastic naturalist and individualist, will be remembered for his introduction of Lundy coins and stamps in 1929 and also for establishing the Lundy Field Society in 1946, when he generously allowed the society to use the Old Light and outbuildings for its work. Mr Harman took a personal and sustained interest in the work of the society and at various times was responsible for the introduction of new species. By crossing horses with the forty-two New Forest ponies he imported in August 1928 he evolved a recognized distinct breed – the Lundy pony – with considerable success. His introductions of Soay sheep and deer became firmly established, though other introductions such as squirrels, swans and wallabies were sad failures.

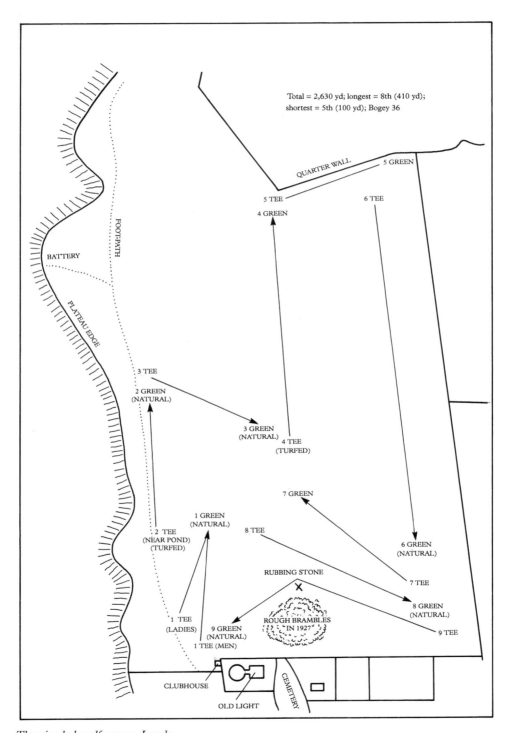

Total = 2,630 yd; longest = 8th (410 yd); shortest = 5th (100 yd); Bogey 36

QUARTER WALL

5 GREEN

5 TEE

6 TEE

4 GREEN

FOOT-PATH

BATTERY

PLATEAU EDGE

3 TEE

2 GREEN (NATURAL)

3 GREEN (NATURAL)

4 TEE (TURFED)

7 GREEN

1 GREEN (NATURAL)

8 TEE

6 GREEN (NATURAL)

2 TEE (NEAR POND) (TURFED)

RUBBING STONE

7 TEE

X

8 GREEN (NATURAL)

1 TEE (LADIES)

9 GREEN (NATURAL)

ROUGH BRAMBLES IN 1927

9 TEE

1 TEE (MEN)

CLUBHOUSE

CEMETERY

OLD LIGHT

The nine hole golf-course, Lundy

Unsuccessful too was the Lundy Golf-course. In 1926 Major Lionel Sullivan visited Lundy on a day trip and was struck by the possibilities of a course on the island. Mr Harman's interest was aroused and Major Sullivan planned a nine-hole course, capable of later extension, on Ackland's Moor. Ivor Llewellyn was employed as greenkeeper and professional and on 29 July 1927 a special steamer brought interested parties and guests. The late Mrs M.C. Harman opened the course and was one of the two amateurs who beat the two professionals in the first foursome. Membership of the Lundy Golf Club never exceeded twelve and the course was finally abandoned at the end of the 1928 season.

The steady improvements made on Lundy during Mr Harman's ownership were interrupted by national and personal financial problems in the 1930s and by the Second World War which broke out in 1939.

Until the war ended in 1945 Lundy was used as a royal naval war watching station and the Old Light was leased at £400 pa to house a detachment of six naval signallers and one officer. Unfortunately, the island suffered considerable deterioration because of the difficulties of maintenance under wartime conditions. Felix W. Gade,[10] who went to Lundy as agent in 1926, remained there during the entire war but moved into Millcombe House which was the only part of the island exempted from a lease that was granted to Mr Van Os at the end of 1940. Although this lease was taken for ten years, it was held for only fourteen months.

It was during these months in the spring of 1941 that German aircraft carried out a series of attacks on British shipping in the Bristol Channel. Following one such attack a damaged Heinkel III (IG+AL of 3/KG27) crashed on Lundy just south of Halfway Wall on the afternoon of 3 March 1941. The crew of five was captured, removed to the mainland and interned. The aircraft was burnt out. Four weeks later on 1 April 1941 another Heinkel III (IG+FL of 1/KG27), while attempting to crash-land, just failed to reach the plateau near Dead Cow Point. Two of the crew were killed on impact, but the remaining three were injured and captured. The third wartime crash occurred on 1 June 1942 when a British Whitley aircraft misjudged its altitude in thick fog and struck the island above Pilot's Quay. The main body of the aircraft, with four dead crew, fell into the sea but the tail, containing the dead rear-gunner, was wedged into the cliff-face until salvaged by the RAF. The Whitley's engines remain on the cliff-face.

Mr Harman's elder son John was killed in action in 1944 and was posthumously awarded the Victoria Cross. Five years later a memorial stone was dedicated in the old quarry on the East Side where he had played as a boy. This has henceforward been known as the V.C. Quarry

When Martin Coles Harman died suddenly in December 1954 the island passed jointly to his son Albion and his daughters, Mrs Ruth Harman-Jones and Mrs Diana Keast. Perhaps the most outstanding event during their ownership was the visit of Queen Elizabeth the Queen Mother on 11 May 1958 when, during her two hours ashore, she met all the islanders and visitors and graciously consented to sign an illuminated vellum to commemorate this first visit by royalty.

On the sudden death of Albion Harman on 23 June 1968 his one-third share of the island passed to his widow but on 1 October 1969 the three lady owners sold Lundy to the National Trust.

The purchase price of £150,000 plus £5,000 for the *Lundy Gannet* had been given by Mr Jack Hayward, and the National Trust at once leased Lundy to the Landmark Trust for a period of sixty years. Under the terms of the lease John Smith, the Chairman of the Landmark Trust, paid £1,000 per annum and most generously undertook to restore the island to a permanently viable condition.

The first visit by a reigning monarch took place on 7 August 1977 when Queen Elizabeth II, accompanied by Prince Philip, Prince Andrew and Prince Edward, paid an unofficial visit. On disembarking from the royal yacht *Britannia* at Brazen Ward the party climbed to the plateau and walked across the island past the Old Light and down the High Street and on to Millcombe House terrace where the islanders were presented to Her Majesty. After almost five hours ashore the royalty party re-embarked from the Landing Beach where all the islanders plus visitors assembled to give a rousing send-off.

In the years since 1969 the Landmark Trust had expended a vast amount of money and effort to improve Lundy. Apart from providing an 'all-island' electricity supply, gas main and water supply, it has restored the important island buildings, built others and provided excellent facilities for visitors, quite apart from financing a regular all-year shipping link.

Lundy achieved national and international notice when, in November 1986 after many years planning, the waters around the island were designated a statutory marine reserve – the first to be so declared in the United Kingdom.

Chapter Nine

FROM BEACH TO PLATEAU

Lying 23 miles west of Ilfracombe and a similar distance from Bideford Quay, but only 11½ miles from Hartland Point, Lundy stands out on a clear day like a guardian of the Bristol Channel. On a clear night its position is marked by the two lighthouse beams, which are visible over 20 miles. The island, though, is all too frequently obscured and the visibility of Lundy has given rise to the following local weather lore:

> Lundy high, it will be dry,
> Lundy low, it will be snow.
> Lundy plain, it will be rain,
> Lundy in haze, fine for days.

Most visitors appoach the island from the east and so see the more gentle coast with its steeply sloping cliffs, softened by a blanket of fern and rhododendron. The line of the plateau is broken by the silhouette of the church, of the Old Lighthouse tower near the South End, and by the Admiralty lookout on Tibbett's Hill to the north.

The Landing Bay at the south-east corner of Lundy is sheltered from the prevailing westerly winds by the towering bulk of the island itself and by Rat Island, which takes its name from its resemblance to a crouched rat. The beach which links the two, now known as Divers' Beach, is covered at high water when the passage so formed is called Hell's Gates. On Divers' Beach Mr Christie built a concrete jetty and slipway in 1920–1 at a cost of £6,000 to house the island boat *Lerina*.

The peninsula known as the Lametor, on which the South Light stands, with the adjacent crumbling saddle of shale, together overlook and shelter the main, original Landing Beach.

The unusually named Lametor and Lametry Bay date from before 1822 and, although thought to derive from the Celtic Llan-y-tor meaning 'The enclosure, or sacred precinct, on the hill', more likely derives from a Scottish farmworker (possibly one of Sir John Borlase Warren's 'Schetlanders') as Lameter is a Scottish term for lame, deformed or ugly.

Recent plans to build a deepwater jetty from the Divers' Beach have been shelved following hydrographic and financial advice, but a road was driven from the quay to the Divers' Beach in 1990. During its construction rockfalls unfortunately destroyed both the remains of the Fish Palace and also the stairs and access to the South Lighthouse. This new road, or 'Strand' at first obliterated the mouth of the Old Man's Cave, but easterly gales have subsequently scoured the Strand in places, so revealing the cave mouth. A new footpath from South Light down the cliff-face to meet the Strand road has cut through the site where wooden buidings were erected in 1896 to house the workers who were then building the lighthouse.

The inscribed stone at the foot of the ascending Beach Road was erected in 1819 by Trinity House to mark their landing place. When Mr Heaven completed his road down to this point he placed his own stone alongside for the benefit of Trinity

The marker stone at the foot of Beach Road (H. Savory)

House employees. It read: 'This island is entirely private property. There are no public roads, footpaths or rights of way whatsoever hereon.' Unfortunately, a landslip in November 1954 destroyed both this stone and the adjacent limekiln, where seaborne limestone had been burnt for fertilizer since the eighteenth century.

The way here widens on to the original sixteenth-century quay, where once stood a capstan. The quay was probably begun by Sir Richard Grenville, who was a keen builder of piers and quays in his attempt to assist trade in the Bristol Channel, although half a century later his grandson Sir Bevil Grenville is known to have completed the work in the 1580s. On this landward side the small cave is of uncertain origin and the 18-pounder cannon lying nearby is thought to have been placed hereabouts by Sir John Borlase Warren to protect the landing place, though it may have been thrown down from the castle above.

The next length of road has always been subject to damage. A buttress wall protects the landward side from falling shale and during one such fall in 1954 a 2 lb cannon ball was uncovered, later to be dated by the Tower of London as having been fired from a ship some time between 1675 and 1725. Ahead is a cottage built in 1826 by Trinity House as an oil store but known to the Heaven family as Sea View. The fishermen who eventually lived here dried their nets in an adjacent sail-loft, which had originally been built in 1870 as a boathouse.

Just beyond the cottage a steep footpath forked left to the top of the island from the wider main road. Until Mr Heaven built this wide road in 1838 the steep path was the only way to the plateau and it was described in 1637 thus: 'One way of entrance it hath into it, wherein two men can scarcely go afront together on foot; on every besides the dreadful rockes bearing out a mighty heighth, hinder all ingresse.'[1]

When the big landslip here in February 1969 carried away about 30 m of Beach Road the necessary repairs had to cut into the landward cliff, and although this destroyed the sail-loft and the first part of the old steep path, a new beginning for the route has now been cut.

Beyond the landslip, which has now been strengthened by extensive sea defences, the main road takes a gentle landward course from Salutation Point to Windy Corner. This gentle curve is bordered by ferns, wild flowers and the unique Lundy cabbage on the steep landward side, but falls away almost sheer to Victoria Beach on the seaward side. A few trees struggle to survive down this ravine, known as Lone Pine Gulch from the century-old survivor of three which lingered until 1970.

At Windy Corner the road suddenly turns inland and reveals for the first time the full expanse of the Eastern Sidings with, near the water's edge, the slate slab known as the Miller's Cake and beyond, the conical Sugar Loaf Rock which marks the junction of the slate of the south-east with the main granite body of the island. The beautiful path ahead up Millcombe Valley is one of the few places on Lundy to be sheltered by trees. It takes its name from a watermill which once stood a little way up the path on the right-hand side, just short of the three lower walled gardens. The actual mill site was transformed in the 1980s when a large septic tank was buried on the site.

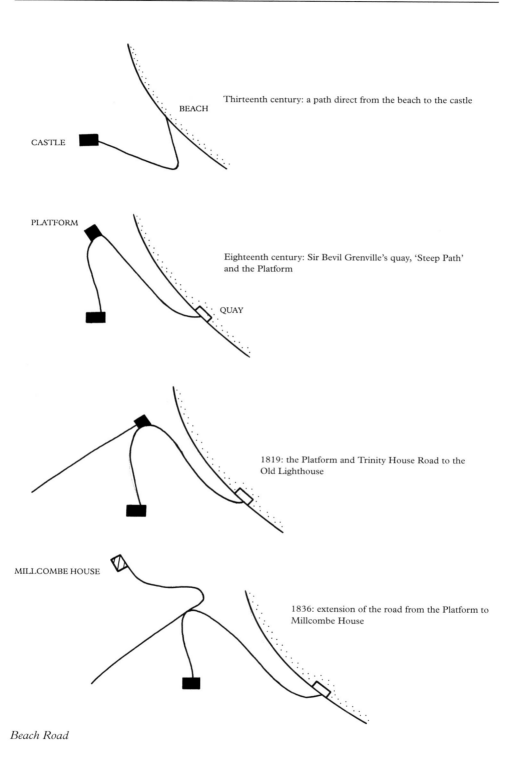

CASTLE

BEACH

Thirteenth century: a path direct from the beach to the castle

PLATFORM

QUAY

Eighteenth century: Sir Bevil Grenville's quay, 'Steep Path' and the Platform

1819: the Platform and Trinity House Road to the Old Lighthouse

MILLCOMBE HOUSE

1836: extension of the road from the Platform to Millcombe House

Beach Road

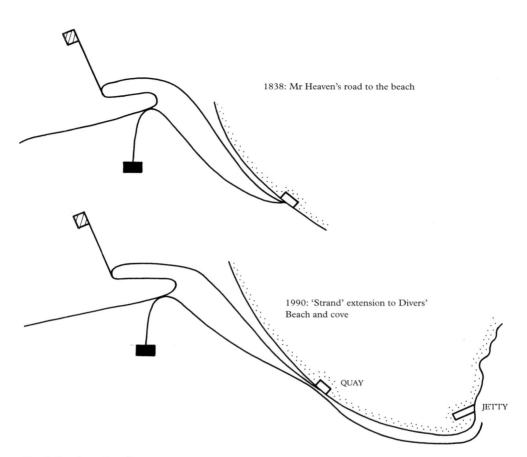

1838: Mr Heaven's road to the beach

1990: 'Strand' extension to Divers'
Beach and cove

QUAY

JETTY

Beach Road continued

The stone building opposite the lower gardens, built as a cowshed, later used as a coal store and then in 1886 for the building of a two-masted skiff, the *Heatherbell*, now houses the gas cylinders which through underground pipes supply the village above. Immediately below the building was a saw-pit but the little plateau is now the site for a teak seat.

The path leading to Millcombe House is protected by a pair of iron gates supported on gateposts which were made by splitting the 5 ton capstone which roofed the Kistvaen (see p. 107). Close by the gates was a carriage house and stable during the construction of which in 1886 some human bones were unearthed. The site became derelict in 1988 and after clearing was used partly for a reservoir that is fed from the stream running down St John's Valley. Before crossing under the road this stream also fills the original horse-trough that once served the stable. Now repaired, the horse-trough was known by the Heaven family as 'Lodore' which may have been a pun on L'eau d'or, draining as it does the outflow from Golden Well.

From near this point a footpath runs northwards along the sidings to the Quarries. Known as the Lower East Side Path, it is the lowest of the three 'shooting paths cut from St. Johns Valley to Gannets' Comb' in 1871 for Victorian hunters.

From Millcombe gates Beach Road doubles back and, still rising, reaches the Battlements where Lundy's three main roads meet.

The old steep footpath from the beach here bends sharply back on itself to continue up to the castle, while the main road which has just been described and which was built at his own expense by Mr Heaven in 1838 up from the beach, continues ahead to the plateau along the length built by Trinity House in 1819. The site takes its name from the battlemented wall 'built by William Hudson Heaven at "Peeping Corner" there being some danger of falling over the edge in trying to turn that corner when going down the road beyond a walking pace'.[2] When the 1838 road was built the bend in the old steep footpath was lowered by about 6 m and in so doing destroyed a feature known as the Platform which was further quarried in 1988.

The Platform dates from 1609 when the pirate Capt. Salkeld forced his captives into 'building walls for a Fort and constructing a Platform for cannon to command the road'.[3] The structure, some 5 m square and 4 m high stood at the hairpin bend of the steep path with a perfect view of the Landing Bay and East Side, so that guns mounted there would effectively control all entrance to the island. The 'Journal of 1787' describes 'a platform where two roads meet; one conducts you to the castle . . . the other (to the house lately built by Sir John Warren) wide enough for carts, and where they land goods that are to be carried off or brought to the island'.

The problems of access to the plateau can easily be appreciated when standing on the Battlements. The route has changed much over the centuries. Until recently the saddle of shale that faces the beach was much higher, and as late as the 1930s it was possible to walk direct from the South Lighthouse across the saddle's ridge and up some steps to the castle. The original medieval path from the beach would seem to have zig-zagged up the saddle to reach the plateau at the castle – which doubly explains the siting of the castle to act as both a watchtower and an entry point. This path would have been very narrow and very steep. In later medieval times packhorses would have come into use and the dog-legged steep footpath would have been made for them as it is wider and less steep than the old direct path to the castle.

From the Platform it seems that a new path was made leading directly inland sometime in the seventeenth century, traces of which can still be seen 1 metre or so south of the present, final road to the plateau. This final road was built in 1819 by Trinity House, who required wheeled transport to run from the Old Light, around the edge of South West Field, past Golden Well crossroads and down to the Platform/Battlements. To build this wider road Trinity House had to dig at a lower level and so had to destroy most of the Platform when they reached the dog-leg bend in the old steep path.

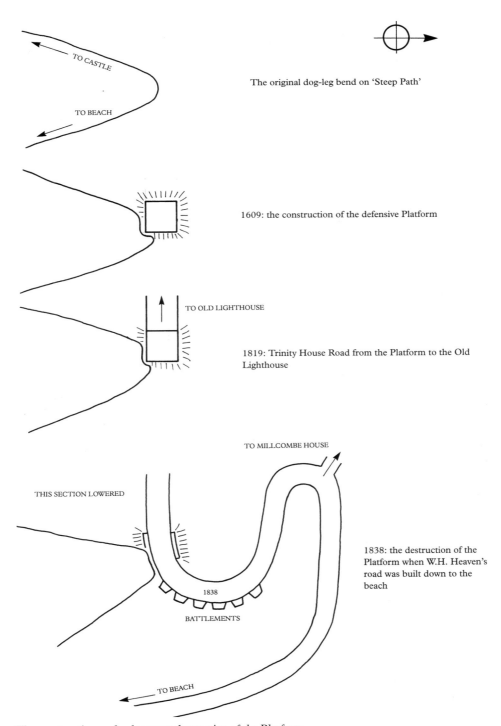

The original dog-leg bend on 'Steep Path'

1609: the construction of the defensive Platform

1819: Trinity House Road from the Platform to the Old Lighthouse

1838: the destruction of the Platform when W.H. Heaven's road was built down to the beach

The construction and subsequent destruction of the Platform

When Mr Heaven built Millcombe House he continued the Trinity House road downwards to cross St John's Valley stream before rising up to the house. Finally, to his own design he completed the present Beach Road down to the quay and beach.

From just above the Battlements the full beauty of Millcombe House can be appreciated. This classically simple building has a front terrace overlooking the gardens and bay and a range of outhouses behind. When built it had such modern features as running water and handbasins, though these were removed during Mr Christie's ownership. The house was used as the island's hotel from 1973–88.

Trees were planted to give shelter and one of the paths that radiate from the house led to the bungalow, Garden Cottage, which was built in St John's Valley in 1892 to house Mr Heaven's coachman-gardener, Mr C. Ward. The corrugated-iron building, known as Bramble Villa, was replaced in 1971 by a new wooden bungalow which until 1982 housed the island agent, but which since has been a twin holiday cottage.

The main road reaches the top of the valley at a little crossroads, where the path to the left leads to the castle, the one directly ahead leads to the south coast, and the one to the right leads to the village. On the seaward side of this last road is the battlemented wall built in 1872 to divide the top of St John's Valley from the common on which St Helena's church was later to be built.

Against the seaward side of this wall are three holiday bungalows. The oldest, the Old Schoolhouse, or Blue Bungalow, was a prefabricated corrugated-iron building

Millcombe House

erected in 1886 only a few months after the nearby corrugated-iron church (see Chapter Twenty). The schoolhouse was used for the education of the island children until the First World War, but after the island was sold in 1917 internal divisions were fitted and a small kitchen and lavatory were added. It was then used for staff or by long-lease tenants until 1976 when the Landmark Trust installed electricity and a shower to convert it into a small, warm holiday cottage.

A little to the south, again against the 1872 wall, stood a granite cattle pound which was in 1964 roofed over, extended and adapted to form two holiday bungalows – known as Big St John's and Little St John's.

The road now passes the church (which was built in 1896–7 and is fully described in Chapter Fifteen) and after crossing a cattle-grid enters what might be called the beginning of the High Street around which island life revolves.

Chapter Ten

THE MANOR FARM

The social life of the island centres around the complex which developed from the building which is now called the Old House. It seems certain that this is the building referred to in 1787 as 'the house lately built by Sir John Borlase Warren' (*North Devon Magazine*, 1824) since nowhere is there reference to a building on the site prior to this.

A drawing of 1838 shows the house with two towers, each having a single window at each of three levels and joined by a single-storey central section which had two windows and a doorway. All three sections had pitched roofs. Mrs M.C.H. Heaven in her 'Lundy Log' says that the towers contained four rooms and that the central section was a large dairy, but this may not be entirely reliable as she never saw the original herself. It is probable that the lowest of the three window levels was for cellarage, the southern one of which is still accessible, and these appear to have been used as cool rooms.

Against the south wall was a very small cottage and another abutted the north wall. Water was taken from a well under the floor of the northern room. The position of the cellar windows, together with signs of the roof level of the southern tower (which was revealed during the 1980s rebuilding) suggest that the ground level in front of this building was considerably lower at that time than it is now.

During the 1840s and '50s, Mr Heaven seems to have built up the central section of the farmhouse (to provide Rooms 19 and 20), removed the two pyramidal towers, and installed an overall roof at a lower pitch. With the establishment of the building in this form the focus of island life finally moved from the castle to what became known as 'The Farm', which not only housed the farm bailiff, manager or tenant but also afforded simple accommodation for visitors.

The *Bideford Gazette* of 14 June 1854 stated that 'Mr John Lee, the governor, provides visitors with board, lodgings, beer, porter and spirits at reasonable prices; conducts them over the island, shows them the ruins of Marisco's Castle, the remains of St. Helen's Chapel, Johnny Groat's House, Devil's Lime-kiln, and Lighthouse, and the liberty of hunting, fishing, and fowling, to visitors at the "Standard of Freedom Inn".' The exact meaning of this last phrase is lost but John Lee was certainly using the farmhouse commercially.

In 1863 the Lundy Granite Company leased most of the island and the farm and during their short tenancy they built the south wing. When the company collapsed in 1868 this new wing was not in use as it had not been completed internally. Although it abutted the farmhouse it had its own entrance – which in later years became the front door to the hotel – and there was no way through from one building to the other. The Heaven family called the south wing the New House and used it on Sundays for services or readings when Millcombe House was not available. At other times it was used as play space for the family children, who had strict instructions to keep clear of the 'stores' as 'beer and drink' were served there.

By 1871 Mr Heaven had completed the interior of this south wing to provide a drawing-room, dining-room, sitting-room and kitchen with six bedrooms (Nos. 11, 12, 14, 15, 16 and 17) above. Three years later a porch and lavatory were added near the back door of the Old House, a drain was made and an extension was begun to the dairy to cope with the mainland demand for Lundy butter. When completed the following year, 1875, this formed the central west wing of the complex.

During his tenancy of the island farm between 1885 and 1891 Mr Wright completed the work on the south wing and then used it as his own residence from 1886 complete with the first tennis court on the front lawn. Mr Wright was succeeded by Mr Ackland (1891–9), a retired Barnstaple grocer, who had clear

The Manor Farm, 1889 (F. Frith of Reigate)

plans to develop the island for tourists. He it was who first used the south wing as a hotel for which he built a lavatory and bathroom upstairs and added the main staircase. Mr Saunt, tenant from 1908–12 used the central part of the complex for himself as the 'Manor House', but enlarged the south wing's dining-room by incorporating the little sitting-room that was next to the kitchen. By 1910 the scullery, gas store and woodshed had been added, but perhaps expansion had been too rapid as the manager of the Manor Farm Hotel, as it was now called, appeared in Barnstaple bankruptcy court.

During Mr Christie's ownership from 1917 until 1925 the central building remained the 'Farmhouse' and occasional visitors were accommodated in the south wing.

Soon after Mr Harman bought the island in 1925 he breached the upstairs and downstairs walls so as to join the central Old House to the south wing in order to convert the entire building into a hotel. Three staff bedrooms (Nos. 25, 26 and 27) were added over the dairy, and the rear of the building immediately to the north of this was extended to provide a back staircase, landing, lavatory and bathroom. The single-storied wash-house that stood between the hotel and the tavern building was demolished, to be replaced by a billiard room with two extra bedrooms above (Nos. 23 and 24), providing on the ground floor a connection from hotel to tavern.

The enlarged hotel now had ten double and five single bedrooms and was supplied with electricity (at 110 volts DC) from a generator which also supplied Millcombe House and the High Street buildings. A large covered reservoir, built in 1899 and 100 m to the west of the hotel, drained water from Lighthouse Field and fed it by gravity to the large lead water tank on the hotel roof.

The Marisco Tavern & General Stores, as Mr Harman now named it, was a flagstoned comfortable room complete with piano and dartboard, with walls hung with numerous photographs and the life belts and lanterns from island shipwrecks. The bar, unique in the British Isles in not following licensing regulations, was invariably open especially whenever a visiting pleasure steamer called, while the stores sold not only essentials but also souvenirs, postcards and Lundy stamps. By the 1950s the tavern had become too small to serve both as a tavern and a store and so during 1961 the shop was transferred to the open-fronted building known as the Linhay.

When the Landmark Trust acquired the island lease in 1969 there were at first plans to rebuild the hotel, but later it was decided to abandon the building. Hotel provision was transferred to Millcombe House in 1971 and the old building was gutted. About this time island water supplies were reorganized and a large fibreglass water tank (later to be followed by three others) was erected on the 'airfield'.

However, financial constraints during the 1970s and '80s, together with a sharp fall in the number of day-trippers which followed the collapse of the steamer services, forced the abandonment of plans to convert the now-derelict hotel into a museum with accommodation. It was finally decided to demolish the Harman additions, plus most of the south wing, to reveal the original Georgian farmhouse.

The 'village' from the south, 1949

Messrs Ernest Ireland Construction Ltd were commissioned during 1982 and 1983 to undertake this work and their team of as many as thirty workers removed the billiard room with its bedrooms above, and the other Harman additions, as well as the dairy and all of the south wing apart from the old kitchen. The now revealed Georgian farmhouse, henceforth known as Old House, was divided into two dwellings, while the old kitchen with its upper rooms repaired and reroofed became Square Cottage.

The old dairy yard was levelled and grassed over but the small refrigerator room and the old radio room were retained as single-bedroom units until 1989 when they were combined into a small single-letting unit.

As part of the extensive building programme of 1982–3 the eastern part of the old tavern building, which had for years housed the barman/shopkeeper, was gutted and the wall from the old bar was breached to enlarge the floor area. The bar itself was moved to this new area while the original tavern was provided with a new kitchen to the rear and became a space where visitors could shop, eat and seek shelter. The bar and shop were fitted with shutters so that even when closed the area could remain open and accessible at all times.

Decorating the tavern are life belts and trophies from island wrecks including those from the *Taxiarchis*, *Carmine Filomena*, *Devonia*, *Cambria*, *Amstelstroom* and *Maria Kyriakides* while in the gallery is that of the *Blue Merlin*. Other items include part of the bell salvaged from the *Ethel* and the wooden plaque with a slate-inscribed outline of the island, the brass tablet below reading: 'Presented to the islanders of

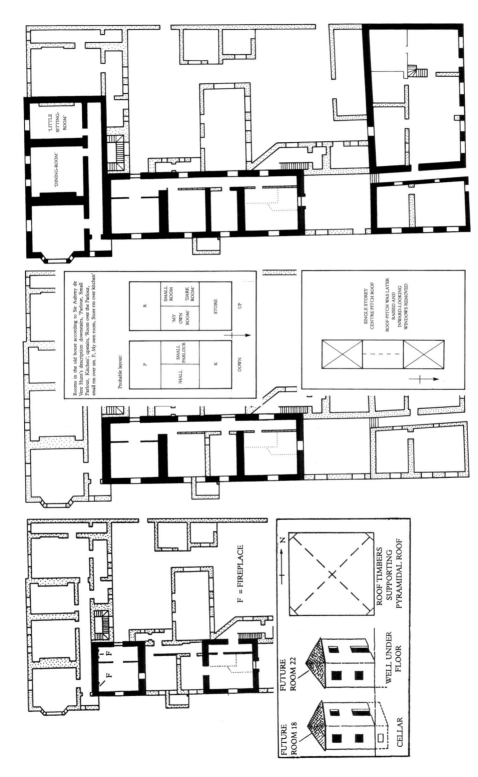

Rooms in the old house according to Sir Aubrey de
Vere Hunt's description: downstairs, 'Parlour, Small
Parlour, Kitchen'; upstairs, 'Room over the Parlour,
small rm over sm. P, My own room, Store rm over kitchen'

Probable layout:

P	R
SMALL PARLOUR	'MY OWN ROOM'	SMALL ROOM
'HALL'		'DARK ROOM'
K	STORE
DOWN	UP

SINGLE STOREY
CENTRE PITCH ROOF

ROOF PITCH WAS LATER
RAISED AND
INWARD-LOOKING
WINDOWS REMOVED

'LITTLE-
SITTING-
ROOM'

'DINING-ROOM'

F = FIREPLACE

FUTURE
ROOM 18

FUTURE
ROOM 22

WELL UNDER
FLOOR

CELLAR

ROOF TIMBERS
SUPPORTING
PYRAMIDAL ROOF

N

From left to right: the manor farmhouse in the eighteenth century; the manor farmhouse, 1822; the Manor Farm Hotel, 1868

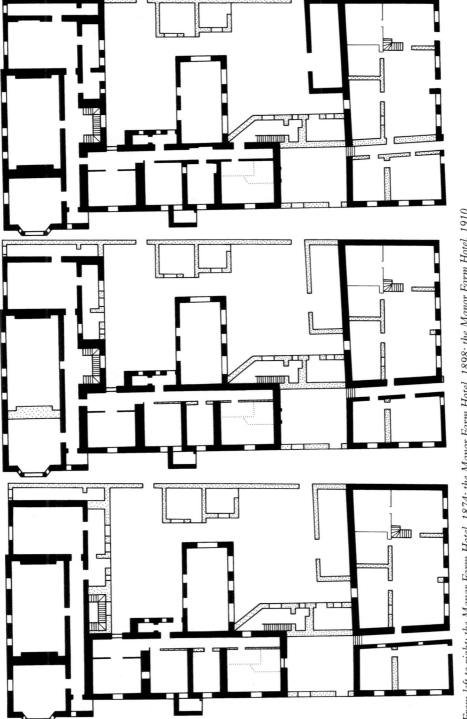

From left to right: the Manor Farm Hotel, 1874; the Manor Farm Hotel, 1898; the Manor Farm Hotel, 1910

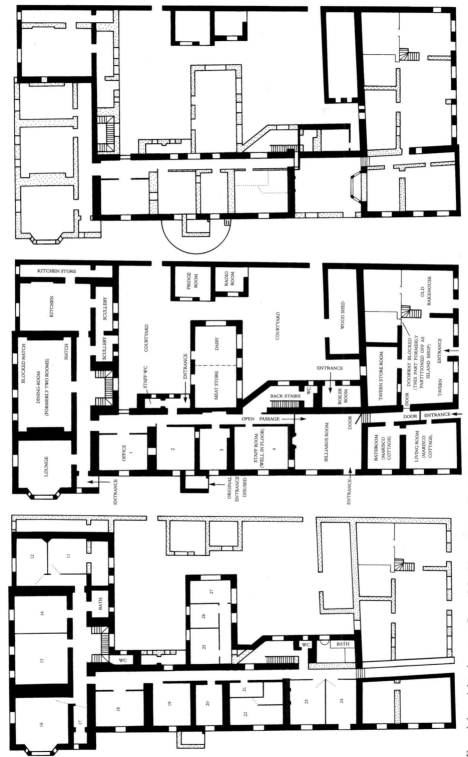

From left to right: the upper floor of the Manor Farm Hotel, 1930; the ground floor of the Manor Farm Hotel, 1930; the Manor Farm Hotel, 1983

Upper floor (left plan):

12, 11, 14, BATH, 15, 16, 17, 18, 19, 20, 21, 22, 23, 24, 25, 26, 27, WC, WC, BATH

Ground floor (middle plan):

KITCHEN STORE

KITCHEN

BLOCKED HATCH

DINING-ROOM (FORMERLY TWO ROOMS)

HATCH

LOUNGE

SCULLERY

SCULLERY

COURTYARD

STAFF WC

ENTRANCE

FRIDGE ROOM

RADIO ROOM

MEAT STORE

DAIRY

COURTYARD

WOOD SHED

OLD BAKEHOUSE

OFFICE

1

2

3

STAFF ROOM (WELL IN FLOOR)

4

BACK STAIRS

WC

BOILER ROOM

ENTRANCE

TAVERN STORE ROOM

DOORWAY BLOCKED (THIS PART FORMERLY PARTITIONED OFF AS ISLAND SHOP)

DOOR

ENTRANCE

TAVERN

OPEN PASSAGE

BILLIARDS ROOM

DOOR

DOOR

ENTRANCE

BATHROOM (MARISCO COTTAGE)

LIVING ROOM (MARISCO COTTAGE)

ENTRANCE

ENTRANCE

ORIGINAL ENTRANCE DISUSED

ENTRANCE

Lundy/ by the/ Craftsmen of Ernest Ireland for the many kindnesses and hospitality/ with thanks/16th August 1983.'

The tavern looks out on to what was the Manor Farm Hotel's garden which once boasted flowerbeds and shrubs and, from 1934, a modern lawn tennis court. This garden was surrounded by a wall built in 1870, the south-east corner of which was continued, castellated, two years later to separate the common (on which St Helena's church was later built) from St John's and Millcombe Valleys. The north-east corner of the hotel garden wall is pierced by an arched 'Gothic Gate' from where the footpath descends down Millcombe Valley to Millcombe House.

Immediately through the 'Gothic Gate', to the east, is a little 'Garden Quarry' from which slate was dug and which, when abandoned, quickly filled with water to provide a sheltered pond beloved by dragonflies. Nearby is the site of the corrugated-iron church which served the island from 1884 until 1897.

To the south of this point at the head of the valley is a completely new building, Government House, built using granite salvaged from the demolished south wing of the Old Hotel in 1982, a date recorded on its portico by the inscription: 'MCMLXXXII.' Although originally intended to be the administrator's home and office it now serves as a delightful holiday cottage.

A footpath leads from the 'Gothic Gate' behind Government House and against the battlemented wall to a small corrugated-iron holiday bungalow which Mr Heaven built as a schoolroom in 1886.

Lundy High Street, looking south

Some way down the path from Government House to Millcombe House a track diverges to the left to end at the rocky outcrop known as Hangman's Hill. The hill is surmounted by a frequently used flagpole which in Mr Harman's day always flew the special Lundy flag when he was expected.

On the seaward side of the hill is a small lookout known as the Ugly, which was built to observe shipping sheltering in the Roads. The unusual name is explained by Mrs M.C.H. Heaven who was there at the time when 'Miss A.A. Heaven had been ill and needed an outdoor convalescence [so] a small shelter was built for her in front of Millcombe House. To the family's remark that this was an eyesore she replied that it was the House Beautiful and the Ugly one was that on the hill – a hill which in the early days of the Heaven ownership was so covered with heather and heath that they called it Heath Mount.'

During the 1982–3 building work, the south wall of the Old Hotel garden was removed, and the gate which led on to the first part of the High Street was replaced by a cattle-grid.

The first part of the High Street passes the back of the Old Hotel complex on the right, while on the left is a large black building erected in the 1970s to house and service the many pieces of machinery then being introduced by the Landmark Trust. The building stands on the site of a corrugated-iron 'Lunch Room' which from 1886 until the 1940s provided refreshments and Lundy lobster teas for day visitors.

Chapter Eleven

THE EAST SIDE

Island life still centres around the complex of tavern, office and stores built by the Lundy Granite Company in 1864 and retained after the company collapse as the island store. The main road passes the back of these buildings and suddenly widens to form a little greensward outside the stores. To the west the walled former kitchen gardens have been grassed to form a picnic area joined through a new gateway to the former tea garden, where the small building which was once a brewhouse and later a kitchen now serves as a fully equipped laundry. The building to its north has become the freezer house and former pigsties in the tea garden have become a clothes-drying area. Further north stands the wooden smithy and the range of buildings called the Linhay, which houses the island shop.

West of the Linhay, but reached through the former tea garden, is a modern electric generator house and two blocks of temporary wooden buildings. In 1972 planning permission was granted to the Landmark Trust for a twenty year period to house their craftsmen and administrators in quarters which contain a medical room, a storeroom, two guest bedrooms, staff quarters and four very comfortable family units.

Opposite the Linhay stands the Rocket House, built in 1893 on a forty year lease at £3 per annum to house the life saving apparatus and to the north of this is the barn.

The barn too is a Lundy Granite Company building to which was later added a roundhouse where a horse, walking around a fixed point, could rotate a vertical post which, by means of shafts and cogs attached to a beam above, operated the machinery in the barn. This system was later replaced by a $4^{1}/_{2}$ hp oil engine until in the 1970s the building was converted into a hostel, with the roundhouse as a dormitory.

The original stables behind the barn, later used as a goathouse, have been converted into staff quarters while, further north, the Victorian slaughterhouse was rebuilt in 1985 to form a storeroom.

Opposite, on the west side of High Street, stands the Shippens, originally built in a square around a central yard. It was here during excavations for an enlargement in the 1860s that interesting archaeological discoveries were made, and although the exact site was not recorded it is believed to have been at the north-west of the present complex. The yard is now roofed over to form a garage.

A door in the north wall of the Shippens leads through to the rickyard, or mewstead, part of which houses the island dairy where the present house-cow, Daisy, usually produces fifty pints of milk daily. The rickyard also has a door in its north wall leading to the next enclosure, the Fowl Run, and these three enclosures each has a gate leading on to High Street.

Facing these three enclosures, on the east side of High Street, are the cattle pens with a row of cottages to their north. These were built about 1864 and inhabited until 1939 after which they became ruinous due to wartime neglect. In 1964–6 they were rebuilt as four charming dwellings with seaviews to the east across St Helen's Field. The well in this field, St Helen's Well, and the field name itself are modern names. The gate immediately north of the three enclosures on the west side of the High Street opens on to Bulls' Paradise, while a gate on the east side of High Street opens on to the Tillage Field.

Bulls' Paradise, lying west and north of the three enclosures described above, now houses a large cattle shelter which originally stood in the middle of the island but which was moved in 1983 to serve as a lambing centre. Archaeological excavations in Bulls' Paradise in 1969 revealed an early medieval stronghold and settlement.

The High Street ends just beyond the Tillage Field and Bulls' Paradise gates and the footpath continues northwards across the open ground which once served as the airfield.

Barton Cottages, High Street

The wall by the side of the path encloses first the Tillage Field and then the Brick Field, both of which slope gently to the plateau's eastern edge where field drainage tumbles to form a small waterfall near the Sugar Loaf Rock, where in former times ships would anchor close inshore to replenish their supplies of fresh water.

The Tillage Field was the site of part of the settlement known as Newtown, whose last traces were cleared about 1850, although the area was still so called as late as 1904.

The airfield, bounded to the north by Quarter Wall, dates from 1934 when the landing strips were marked by whitewashed boulders. Part of the wall enclosing the Brick Field had to be removed to lengthen the approach run and a windsock was fixed to an old telegraph pole near the centre of the field. Small trenches around this area date from 1940 when they were dug to deter enemy aircraft from landing.

The Quarter Wall was probably begun by Bushell, to be continued by Benson using his convict labour and completed by Sir John Borlase Warren. The area to its south was called South Farm while that to the north, originally North Farm, was sub-divided into Middle Farm and North Farm when Halfway Wall was built.

The main track progresses northwards on open ground where the effects of erosion and, latterly, modern vehicular traffic, together with the need to cross small watercourses and valleys, has turned some of the path into muddy rutted lengths. To help arrest this and to make the roadway self-draining, a party of Royal Engineers

The road north

carried out drainage and causeway work during 1979, using quarry spoil and beach pebbles as infill.

Immediately north of Quarter Wall are the foundations of twelve cottages built by the Granite Company to house employees. Having stood derelict for several years, three were dismantled and used in the building of the signal station in 1884 while the remainder were dismantled in 1896 to build St Helena's church. The block of three houses on the eastern edge of the plateau, which commands a glorious view of the Landing Bay, housed the officers of the Granite Company and although now in ruins the houses were still habitable in 1896 when they were 'at the disposal of visitors, with the sanction of Mr Heaven of course'. The southernmost of the three remained habitable until 1916.

To the north were the company's medical quarters – the Old Hospital, although ruinous by 1881, still stands whereas the surgery to its east has now disappeared to its foundations.

The main path continues ahead northwards from Quarter Wall, although a small track diverges to the east past a pond and down a marshy valley where the Lundy Field Society has a bird-trap. Beyond some stunted trees is the first of the quarries which has filled with water to become Quarry Pond. Just beyond this is a little platform on which the quarry's timecheck hut was built. It was restored in 1983 to serve as a shelter and the circular hole in the wall which once housed the timekeeper's clock has been filled by a circular slate inscribed: 'In memory of Felix

Ruins of the Quarry Hospital

W. Gade 1890–1926–1978.' (Mr Gade came to the island as agent in 1926 and lived there until his death in 1978.)

The path now descends steeply to the long terrace where it joins the path that has come from the Ugly. The terrace was built as a marshalling point where hewn stone from the main quarries was then lowered to Quarry Beach. The Lundy Field Society has another bird-trap on the terrace beyond ruined stables. Quarry Beach can be reached on foot down a narrow winding path and at sea-level the old stone-built loading jetty can still be traced.

The path through the quarries along the old tramway track is delightful, now flanked by wild flowers, honeysuckle and an occasional stunted tree. The most pleasant spot is perhaps the V.C. Quarry, so named in 1949 when a memorial stone was dedicated there to the elder son of Martin Coles Harman, John Pennington Harman, on the fifth anniversary of his posthumous award of the Victoria Cross. This was won at Kohima in Burma on 8 April 1944, when John Harman showed great heroism in destroying an enemy machine-gun post almost single-handed. The quarry had been one of his favourite playgrounds as a child and remains a most fitting site for this simple and proud memorial.

The path, now rising slowly, soon passes the last of the quarries and turns gently inland to rejoin the main East Side path. At the point where it turns inland and before it starts to rise is a new path, cut in the 1970s, which continues northwards in the shelter of the Sidings as far as Gannets' Combe.

Meanwhile the main East Side path has continued along the plateau where it is marked by granite boulders placed at intervals of 500 ft (153 m). These were placed for the convenience of coastguards walking at night or in fog from their cottages to Tibbett's Hill lookout, but it was not until each $1\frac{1}{2}$ ton boulder had been placed in position, and two of the horses that had been used to drag them from the quarries had collapsed and died, that it was discovered that the requested size had been 1 cubic foot and not 1 cubic yard!

The plateau now dips gently to the west where Pondsbury, a large freshwater lake, provides a favourite site for the island's free-ranging animals to graze and drink.

Just south of Halfway Wall can be seen the burnt-out remains of a German Heinkel bomber that crashed there on 3 March 1941.

The construction of Halfway Wall was possibly begun by Benson's convicts and completed at the beginning of the nineteenth century by a tenant farmer. It incorporates on its northern face a much older sheep-pen and ends in the east at the Logan Stone, which is a huge block of granite that once rocked.

The ground north of the wall – once known as North Farm and now devoted to sheep – rises gradually to Tibbett's Hill, just to the south of which, on the eastern edge of the plateau, is a peculiar rock formation known as the Knight Templar because of its supposed resemblance to the helmeted human profile of the order that was once associated with Lundy.

The small, robust building on the summit of Tibbett's Hill was built by the Admiralty in 1909 with an observation room on its roof from which as many as

Tibbett's coastguard station, pre-1930 (H. Jukes)

fourteen lighthouses could be seen at night. In 1971 the outside iron ladder which led to the roof, together with the observation room itself, where all removed as part of the conversion of the building into a holiday cottage. The building was enclosed by a substantial circular wall in 1989 when further improvements were made to the property.

Immediately north-east of the building are the remains of a tumulus or barrow where Loyd in 1922 'unearthed a roughly squared granite block . . . which on being raised disclosed two similar blocks, parallel to each other and at right angles to the first. Among the earth thrown out, two small pieces of flint were found.'[1]

The main path continues to the west of Tibbett's Hill and slopes gently downwards towards Threequarter Wall passing close to the feature marked as a 'Round Tower'. Chanter writes of other round towers on Lundy and conjectures that they were introduced from Ireland by the Mariscos. Loyd, however, considers this structure to be older and probably a barrow, as others are marked nearby. Chanter writes as if it stood several feet tall though it was probably robbed for stone for Threequarter Wall, which was built after he had written his account. It may in fact have been the base of a simple windmill[2] for which purpose the site is ideal, especially as this area was once ploughed and sown. Support for this explanation comes from the 'Journal of 1787': 'On our return [from the North End] I saw the remains of a windmill.'[3] Threequarter Wall, which divides the North Farm into two, was built in 1878 by Mr Thomas Wright, the tenant farmer. (After falling into disrepair it was strongly rebuilt in 1992.) It also covers an ancient settlement which is now difficult to trace as it too was probably robbed of stone to build the wall. Traces of barrows and hut circles, together with many flints, have been found here dating from the Neolithic or Early Bronze Age.[4] The area of hut circles is itself crossed by the remains of granite walls which enclose a 20 acre site known as the Widow's Tenement. The origin of the name is lost but at the centre of the site is a substantial building measuring some 15 by 6 m which excavation has revealed to be a medieval long-house. Pottery dating from the thirteenth century was found in the occupation level of the main building, which is surrounded by three less substantially built enclosures.

At the foot of the steep eastern sidings near here, and just above high-water mark are the remains of a Civil War coastal battery, the best preserved of the 'upwards of forty ancient structures of stonework' recorded around the island's coast in 1787. Its name, Brazen Ward, suggests that the guns were of brass but their fate is uncertain[5] and all that now remains is the gun platform, a small building site and defensive walling. This beautifully peaceful place was well chosen as it commands a view south to Tibbett's Point and north as far as Gannets' Rock in an area where landings are possible. The natural rock formation called the Mouse Hole and Trap is just to the north on a small projecting headland. It consists of a large square of granite tilted upon a smaller piece, just as a brick was held up by a stick in old-fashioned mousetraps. A few metres behind it is a natural hole through the rock – the mousehole!

Midway between the Mouse Hole and Trap and Brazen Ward is Queen Mab's Grotto, a sea-cave formed when sea-levels were higher than today. Seashells have been discovered on its floor but in more recent times it is thought to have been used as an ammunition store for the Brazen Ward battery.[6] The small beach just here was formerly known as Frenchman's Landing.

Beyond Widow's Tenement the main footpath skirts the head of Gannets' Combe where a wide shallow valley is formed by the union of three smaller valleys. Until at least 1835 maps name the place Gallows' Combe and it seems likely that the Heaven family quickly changed this.[7] The combe leads down through marshy land to Gannets' Bay or Cove, with the large Gannets' Rock a short distance offshore.

The Heavens placed a summer house at the point where the footpath crosses the northernmost of the Gannets' Combe valleys, but a visitor in 1894 noted that 'the house no longer stands. There is one upright wooden post in the position indicated on the [Chanter's] map, which may have been a doorpost. There is a so-called Summer House, formed of the bows of a boat, placed on the north-east point.'[8] Today there is no trace of either structure.

The peat fires which destroyed 67 acres of cover revealed the remains of an extensive ancient settlement on the rising ground north of Gannets' Combe. The site dates from the late Neolithic or Early Bronze Age and covers the whole of the plateau north of Gannets' Combe with a system of enclosing walls which contain at least eight circular hut foundations, two of which are most distinct, with prominent doorways facing to the south-east. This well-chosen site has a plentiful water supply nearby, plus an easy route to the sea, with good defensive visibility and has yielded flint tools and cores in various stages of manufacture, together with hoards of limpet shells.

The small ruinous building, measuring some 7 by 3 m with walls now less than a metre high, which stands at the northern end of the island plateau, dates from the Civil War when it was built as a watch house. In 1822 it was known as Perrin's Old House and is now known as John O'Groats since a party of Scottish sportsmen rented it in the mid-nineteenth century. Near sea-level at the northernmost point are the remains of a Civil War battery, and there is another fortification a little to its south.

Near the base of Puffin Slope, some 100 m west of the north-east fortification, a rectangular room some 4 by 5 m was uncovered in 1960. This too appears to date from the Civil War and had a rear wall some 3 m high set into the slope which supported a thrift-thatched roof. When found, the large fireplace and hearth still showed traces of ash, and the granite seat to the right of the hearth was most distinct. A further part of this defensive complex was revealed six years later when a small room measuring some 2 by 3 m was exposed about 35 m north-east of John O'Groats House about 5 m below the north-east corner of the plateau.[9]

The East and West Side paths converge a few metres short of the plateau edge where steps lead down to Lundy North Lighthouse, which has been built on the North West Point. At the foot of the steps is a short tramway which carried stores to the lighthouse from the top of a now-demolished hoist. Watching the tide race among the offshore Hen and Chickens' Rocks, it is difficult to realize that under the North West Point itself there is a tunnel some 215 m long and 10 m high, where fresh water bubbles up through the salt sea water. This 'Virgin's Spring' is almost certainly fed by water from the plateau draining through faults in the rock.

Halfway along the tramway are steps which lead down to a landing at sea-level. There is a wonderfully close view of the nesting seabirds in Kittiwake Gully from these steps and also of the Constable Rock. Risdon says the rock was so named because 'it seemeth to keep watch as a centinel [sic]' though legend has it that a Cornish giant once visited Lundy and was turned into this 10 m column of granite in return for ridding the island of its snakes and other reptiles.

Although Gannets' Combe and Gannets' Rock were once the haunt of these seabirds their last nesting site was at the North West Point. A visitor in 1894 said that 'the number of nests varies from 15 to 30 in the breeding season. They are

The Logan Stone (J. Dollar)

always placed on the N.W. point and never on the Gannet Rock. This is strange because the N.W. point is easily accessible and the rock is not.'[10] With the construction of the North Lighthouse in 1896 the last nesting sites were doomed, although the gannets continued to nest here until as late as 1903.

Even further to the north, just beyond the lighthouse, is a small lookout room with an unrivalled view. This was built for the Admiralty coastguards at the same time as the Tibbett's Hill station, but is now abandoned and derelict.

Chapter Twelve

THE WEST SIDE

The western coastline of Lundy forms a string of sweeping bays, almost all of which have a named feature at either end. Named features of all sorts abound on the West Side – the bays or coves named after shipwrecks and many of the rock formations named by pioneering cliff-climbers, while other distinctive rocks, shaped by wind and weather, have received their names from the romantic imagery of the observer.

The west coast path follows the edge of the plateau more closely than does the East Side path and so offers striking views of the Atlantic pounding the rocks below, but since the telegraph poles which linked the North and South Lighthouses and which marked the route were removed in 1977, the west coast path has become less distinct and less used.

The first sweeping bay contains the Long Roost[1] where near sea-level are the three adits driven last century in the search for copper ore. At the southern end of this bay a small stream falls down the 'Arch Zawn', a cleft leading to a little beach which overlooks Bird Island. Bird Island, so marked on a map of 1823, is the probable last breeding site on Lundy of the now extinct great auk.

Next near sea-level comes the Double-Decker Cave and, before reaching the large detached rock known as St John's Stone, another cleft and beach known as the Torrey Canyon. On the plateau here, overlooking St John's, is a point from which almost all the west coast can be seen. A favourite of the Revd H.G. Heaven, it is known as Squire's View.

The bay formed between St John's and the next large sea rock to its south, St James's Stone, was unaccountably known as Sanky Bay in 1822. It contains such features as the 'Fluted Face', St Peter's Stone, and the 'Rhomboid Rock' or 'Diamond', but most noteworthy is the smooth granite slope which runs from sea to plateau and is called the Devil's Slide.[2]

Just before the West Side path reaches Threequarter Wall, it passes close by one of the large unfinished millstones to be found on the island. This one, some 1.5 m in diameter and half a metre thick, seems to be the abandoned attempt at millstone-making by Lundy quarrymen in the 1860s.

South of Threequarter Wall the spring, which rises close to the path and to a human head-like rock called by the Victorians 'Ally Sloper' from the prominence of

Ally Sloper Rock (J. Stafford Wright)

its 'nose', falls to a little beach named Aztec Bay. The bay, bounded by St Mark's Stone at its north and St Philip's Stone at its south, contains a rock slope known as the Parthenos and other features such as Grand Falls Zawn and Langham's Cavity.

The west coast path soon reaches Halfway Wall, built across the narrowest 'waist' of the island where the western coast is indented to form Jenny's Cove. This beautiful bay (known as West Bay in 1820) now takes its name from the wreck of the *Jenny* in 1797. The rocks around here assume some unusual shapes, one near the water's edge being called The Japanese Warrior, another The Egyptian Slabs, while on the edge of the plateau are such shapes as the Two Camels' Rock, The Three Monks, and Gladstone and Disraeli! Midway in Jenny's Cove is a large flat-sided rock known as The Pyramid, which provides the most sheltered landing place on the west coast. To defend this landing place a gun platform dating from the Civil War was built at what is now the western end of Halfway Wall. The gun platform is some 5 m by 1 or 2 m, from which the Halfway Wall extends well over the western sidings. The remains of a horizontal wall near the water's edge, together with traces of a building some 50 m below the plateau, are probably contemporary with the gun platform and may be the place where one of the tenant farmers stored a small boat which he is known to have carried on his back to and from the sea. It is possible he was trying to salvage some part of the gold dust and ivory cargo carried by the *Jenny* when she sank.

The strangely rounded granite rocks near the path just south of Halfway Wall are appropriately called The Cheeses, while a few yards south and a short distance over the edge is a spring – The Butler's Pantry – that remains active during the driest of summers.

At the southern end of Jenny's Cove two rock columns rise from the sea – the Devil's Chimney and Needle Rock – between which the stream that drains Pondsbury through the Punchbowl Valley falls into the sea. The valley takes its name from the granite bowl, some 1.5 m in diameter, 30 cm deep and about 15 cm thick, that lies beside the stream just over the plateau edge. Though the original purpose and position of the bowl is not known, Gosse[3] suggested it was the font of a lost chapel, although a more likely explanation is that it is a lower millstone, there being some evidence of what may have been a watermill nearby. During Mr Heaven's ownership, the stone was 'thrown from its site by a party of workmen . . . and was shattered into three or four segments'.[4] It was repaired but broken again during the Second World War, after which it was repaired by members of the Lundy Field Society.

After crossing Punchbowl Valley the footpath is separated from the cliff edge by a series of chasms, each some 3 to 6 m wide and varying in depth from 6 to 20 m. These faults run for some 300 m in a north-easterly direction and were obviously caused by a substantial earth movement. Local tradition holds that they, together with the isolated Earthquake Rock just to the south of Jenny's Cove, first appeared after the Lisbon earthquake of 1755. Effects of this earthquake were felt elsewhere in England and so the oral tradition may well be true.

By the first knoll south of Earthquake Rock and about 5 m below the plateau are the remains of a second German bomber aircraft which, crippled, crashed just short of the plateau on 1 April 1941. Two of the crew of five were killed.

Just north of Quarter Wall, where the footpath is only a metre or two from the edge of the plateau, is a quarry, some 6 m down, where blocks of worked granite and the remains of an iron handrail can still be seen. The origin of this little quarry is not known and though it may have been one of the many trial pits dug by the Lundy Granite Company in 1860s, it is likely to have been the quarry for granite used in the construction of the Old Light, and possibly for the Battery.

Quarter Wall itself is the oldest of the island's transverse walls. Its irregular shape takes advantage of soil contours and former field boundaries and ends at its western edge overlooking a little bay which is bounded by two promontories. This bay was known as Lamb Cove in the 1820s following the wreck there of a schooner of that name and the northern promontory was humorously called The Chops from the shape of its rock formation. It is now more prosaically known as Dead Cow Point. The southern promontory is a similar buttress supporting the Battery.

The Battery, one of the most pleasant spots on the island, is reached by a steeply descending path, protected on its north side by a stone wall. The complex was built in 1862 as a fog-signal station to supplement the Old Lighthouse and was supplied with two 18-pounder guns which fired a round of blank shot every ten minutes

West Side from the north (J. Dollar)

during foggy weather. Use of the guns was abandoned in 1878 when they were replaced by guncotton rockets, but when the two new lighthouses were completed in 1897 the entire site was abandoned.

The two cottages, well sheltered from the westerly winds but now ruinous, once housed the gunners and their families – Mr and Mrs Blackmore with their six or seven children in one and Mr and Mrs Tom Lee with their three children in the other – thirteen souls in all!

The flagpole has long gone but a small flight of steps hewn through the granite leads from the cottages past three small buildings to reach the granite-walled gunhouse. The two guns were originally kept inside, the one in use was placed centrally on the grooved floor, which is sloping to reduce recoil, with its muzzle projecting through the central front window. The building had a curved corrugated-iron roof so that in the event of an explosion the roof would blow off and the blast would dissipate upwards. The roofless gunhouse is now empty but the cannons which bear the monogram 'G.R.' are mounted on either side of the building. At the turn of the century some workmen tried to throw the guns over the cliff but succeeded only in destroying the tampions.

On the plateau between the top of the Battery path and the Old Light can be seen the remains of a wall built in 1872 by Mr Heaven in an attempt to protect the area from rabbits, as it was then being brought into cultivation. The area was already known as Acklands Moor, after the eighteenth-century tenant farmer, and forms the western edge of the airfield and the site of the short-lived Lundy Golf-course. Just to the east of the path are several large upright stones in random positions, which may have prehistoric significance.

Lundy's highest point, on which the Old Lighthouse was built, first appears on maps as Beacon Hill in 1787 and almost certainly bears no connection with the nearby Christian cemetery and chapel.

Although maritime fire beacons have been known since Roman times and such beacons were occasionally served by the religious[5] there is no evidence that this was the case on Lundy and the later reference to the chapel as 'St Anne's' – a name often derived from Santan, the pagan god of holy fire[6] – seems to have been given long after the hilltop was being used for a beacon. The name Beacon Hill most likely follows the order given in 1586 (see p. 30) to establish fire beacons throughout the country, to serve as signal warnings of the Spanish invasion which was thought to be imminent.[7]

All trace of any beacon is now lost. When the first official surveyors camped within the walls of the cemetery chapel in 1804 they were not averse to robbing stone for the 'construction of their cairn'[8] and any stone hearth, such as was typically used for fire beacons, would have been obliterated completely in 1819 when the tower of the Old Light was built.

The Old Light was in use from 1819 until 1897 and was thereafter used by visitors until the Second World War when it housed a Royal Naval detachment. In 1946 Mr Martin Harman allowed it to become the headquarters of the newly formed Lundy Field Society, who used it for many years as a hostel in the care of a resident warden. One of the compound's outbuildings was converted into a laboratory as a memorial to Mr Harman after his death. The Landmark Trust undertook a major repair programme in 1982 which involved reglazing the lantern and repairs to the tower and the keeper's quarters. The outbuildings have subsequently been upgraded to provide more holiday accommodation.

The tower is fully described elsewhere but when built was the tallest light in Britain. The view on a clear day extends from Skokholm in the north-west, Bude in the south-west, and all the Bristol Channel to the east. With a turn of the head one can see Brown Willy and Rough Tor and the Cornish coast as far as Trevose to St Govan's Head and the Prescelly Mountains of Dyfed, and from the Exmoor tors beyond Bideford Bay to the grand sweep of Carmarthen Bay and the Gower Peninsula: closer to hand one has an excellent view of the island.

Within a walled enclosure to the east of the Old Light is a small stone cottage, Stoneycroft, which dates from the 1820s and was built for the use of Mr Grant, the Collector of Customs at Barnstaple who was also the agent for Trinity House. Before the days of steamships it was not unusual to build a small house for use by the agent when making his periodic visits to isolated stations as departures could be delayed by bad weather. The building had its own well in front and sewer at the back. In 1988 it ceased to be the farmer's cottage and was converted for holiday use.

Trinity House built a substantial wall around their properties and one of the small enclosed gardens behind Stoneycroft was used in the 1930s as a tennis court. The line of the Trinity House wall was continued across the island to meet the East Side path at the end of the High Street. Halfway along the length of the wall are two recent distinctive features; on the northern side are three large fibreglass tanks which act as the island water reservoir. These were installed by the Landmark Trust when island water supplies were centralized. Water is pumped electrically and automatically from many of the wells and springs in the southern part of the island to be stored in these tanks, from which the water feeds by gravity to island properties and farms.

Close by, but on the southern side of the Old Light Wall, is the aerogenerator which was erected in 1982 to provide 55 kW of electricity in wind speeds of about 25 m.p.h.

Immediately adjacent to the Trinity House properties is the Old Cemetery, described by archaeologists as the most interesting in Britain, where the foundations of the old chapel can be clearly traced.

The chapel, supposedly dedicated to St Elen, was a rectangular building to which 'was attached the oratory dedicated to St Anne'. Despite the present impression, the 'Journal of 1787' states clearly that the entrance was from the north, and adds that it was 'length about 25 feet, breadth 12 feet, doorway 4 feet, thickness of walls nearly two and a half feet'.[9] Within the bounds of the chapel are five graves of members of the Heaven family and it was while the most northerly of these graves was being dug in 1905 that the Tigernus stone was discovered. Apart from the four ancient inscribed stones there are many unmarked graves in the cemetery and it is known that several burials took place there during the nineteenth century.

From Beacon Hill, on which the Old Light stands, the land slopes gently southwards to form the large South West Field. Just a short distance south of the Old Light was an oblong enclosure dating from the early nineteenth century called originally Fryar's Garden, presumably after an island resident, but the boundary stones were removed by a tenant farmer later in the century.

A landing place at water's edge over the western cliffs at this point was originally named Pile's Quay after Capt. Pile, whose pilot skiff pioneered its use during easterly winds, while they waited on the island for incoming ships. The landing continued in use until 1910 when landslips rendered it virtually unusable. Landings were then transferred to the nearby Montagu Steps where an iron ladder from sea-level was soon installed.

The cliffs between Pilot's Quay (as the Heaven family renamed Pile's Quay) and Goat Island were the scene of an aircraft crash when, during thick fog in June 1942, a British Whitley bomber struck a little below the plateau edge resulting in the loss of all the crew.

The rocky promontory just to the south of Goat Island was the scene of the wreck of HMS *Montagu* on 30 May 1906. Salvage operations continued until 1922 using a path from the plateau to a point near the water's edge from where a suspension bridge was carried 600 ft to the ship.

At the extreme south-west point of the island is a large pyramidal rock with a

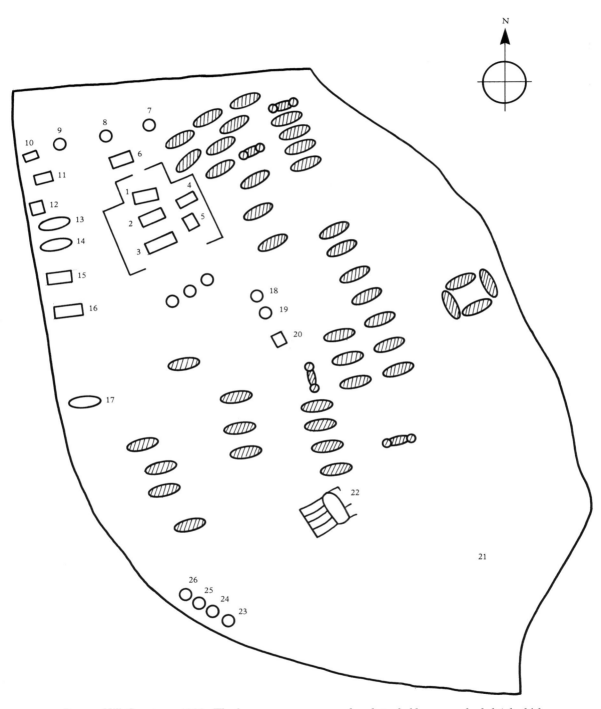

Beacon Hill Cemetery, 1982. The known graves are numbered, probable graves shaded (of which those marked ⬯ have a distinct 'head' and 'foot' stone)

Beacon Hill Cemetery. Key to Graves.
1. 'In loving memory of Amelia Ann Heaven, who fell asleep joying in the peace of God. 26th Oct. 1905. Aged 72 years.' (It is when digging this grave that the Tigernus stone was unearthed.) 2. 'In loving memory of William Hudson Heaven, owner and Lord of the manor of this island. Born 20th April 1799. Entered into rest 4th March 1883.' On the back of this headstone a copper plate reads: 'Walter Charles Hudson Heaven, born 17th November 1865, died 16th October 1929. Elder grandson of W.H.H. Owner of Lundy 1916–1918.' (When this grave was dug in 1883 'we came across the remains of a coffin with a skeleton in it about eighteen inches below the surface.' Revd H.G. Heaven article in *Western Mail*, 9 August 1906.) 3. 'In loving memory of Hudson Grosett Heaven, eldest son of Wm. Hudson Heaven, and brother of Amelia A. Heaven, Lord of the Manor of Lundy, 1883–1916. Curate in charge 1864–1886, Vicar 1886–1911. Called home February 26th 1916 in his 90th year.' 4. 'James Heaven Barrow, Curate of West Kington, Wiltshire, died on this island April 22nd 1861, Aged 25.' 5. 'Edward Stephen Heaven. Born 25th February 1837, died 23rd June 1883.' 6. The mound a few feet north of Miss A.A. Heaven's grave is the unmarked grave of Mrs Ward, wife of the gardener, who died on Lundy in April 1911. 7. 'Erected by Thomas Spearman in memory of his father, William Spearman who died Dec. 22nd 1865. Aged 52 years.' 8. Harry Styles Whitchurch (infant), 30 October 1882 (d. 26 October 1882). 9. 'Edith Irene Gade. Born Sept. 11th 1895. Died Aug. 17th 1973. Known as "Cheerful". She lived for 41 years on Lundy.' 10. 'In memory of James Young. Land Surveyor & Valuator of Perth N.B. who died here 5th Feb 1865. Aged 63 years.' 11. 'Erected by John Kyle of Glasgow in memory of Alexander his brother, who died 6th September 1864 aged 17 years. Alexander his son, who died 30th March 1865, aged 14 months.' 12. 'Here lieth the remains of Mr. Joseph A. Kennedy aged 25 years who departed this life on 25th October 1866. May his soul rest in peace. Amen.' 13. 'In memory of Felix W. Gade MC. Known as 'Giant'. Agent on Lundy 1926–1971. Died on Lundy 28th October 1978. Aged 89 years.' 14. Phoebe Poinard died 22 March 1888 (buried 26 March 1888). 15. 'This stone is erected by Captain John Lang of Appledore in affectionate remembrance of his uncle Samuel Jarman who fell over the cliff on Lundy Island Dec. 24th 1869 aged 59 years.' (The inscribed date is an error; it should read 1870.) 16. 'In loving memory of Helen Elizabeth, the beloved wife of Samuel Mayor Hast, who died on Lundy Island 31st August 1892 aged 44 years.

> I have no pain dear husband now,
> I've gone to rest on high,
> Dear Children, do not mourn for me
> I pray you cease to cry.'

17. Mr Brimacombe, d. 15 January 1895. 18. 'Martin Coles Harman. Owner of Lundy. Second son of William and Florence Harman of Chaldon in Surrey. 30th August 1885. 5th December 1954' (bronze plaque). 19. 'Amy Ruth, Wife of Martin Coles Harman. Born 13th August 1884. Died 28th July 1931.' (The inscription was originally carved on the granite stone but has now been covered over by this bronze plaque.) 20. Albion Pennington Harman, 23 June 1968. 21. Four unnamed sailors from the Hannah More (wrecked 11 January 1866). 22. Dark Ages cist grave complex (excavated 1969). 23. Potiti. 24. Tigernus. 25. Tiani. 26. Reste Evta.

There are other recorded burials, but at sites unknown:
27. 'Poor Taylor lad' fell overcliff 9 July 1871 (Heaven diaries) 28. 'Burial of Edwards' 28.6.1883 (died 23.6.1883) 29. 'When digging another grave we struck a stone on which was the inscription "Joyce Miller, died 1720"' (Revd H.G. Heaven in *Western Mail*, 9 August 1906). 30. Jones, killed while salvaging. Buried 1867 (MCHH) 31. James Swayne, died of TB. Buried in Old Churchyard (MCHH) 32. A lad from a Jersey vessel, fell while egging. Buried 11 July 1871.

sheer landward face which is now known as Great Shutter Rock from the Victorian belief that if reversed it would exactly fit the funnel-shaped cavity of the nearby Devil's Limekiln. Earlier maps refer to the rock as Shatter Point and it seems that this notorious hazard to shipping may, like other Lundy names, have been changed during the ownership of the Heavens. The Shutter was chosen as the site for the wreck of the fictitious galleon in Kingsley's novel *Westward Ho!*

Near the cliff-edge to the east of this point is the Devil's Limekiln, a massive fault about 250 ft wide at the top with almost vertical sides converging at sea-level some 300 ft below, where the sea enters through two openings. Further to the east is Seal's Hole which begins at sea-level, some 50 ft high and 20 ft wide, and runs inwards for 200 or 300 ft to end in a dark chamber estimated to be 100 ft high.

On the plateau above Seal's Hole a pole, representing a ship's mast, was erected about 1893 by the Board of Trade for the purpose of testing the rocket life-saving apparatus that had just been supplied to the island. The pole stands by a delightful pool, which has been formed in a small trial quarry, where carp can be seen swimming in the clear water and where wild flowers overhang the banks.

The footpath continues eastwards along the southern end of the plateau and soon

The Devil's Slide (unknown)

passes close by the Kistvaen, a barrow that was discovered by accident in 1851. Gosse inspected it soon afterwards and wrote: 'One of the men had noticed in a particular part of the moor that the earth returned a hollow sound. On digging, a block of granite was found a little below the surface; it was about 18 inches thick, and was estimated to weigh five tons. Its ends rested on two upright slabs, enclosing a cavity some six feet deep and as many wide . . . but for what purpose it could have been made, there was no clue to inform us . . . a fragment of pottery was the only object found. . . .'[10] The top stone was removed and split longitudinally to provide gateposts for Millcombe House. The site soon filled with water and following an accident in 1887 when a bullock fell in and was drowned, the contours of the site were eased.

From here eastwards the coast forms a large bay, known in 1853 as Rattles Landing Place[11] – probably taking its name from a pilot or ship – but now called The Rattles or Rattles Anchorage.

From the Kistvaen the footpath continues parallel to the incurving coast with the wall that encloses the Tent Field to its north. Near the narrowest part of the path a small track leads down to Benjamin's Chair, now just a flat grassy ledge revetted by walling on its seaward side. The name may derive from Benjamin Donne who was tide surveyor for the Bristol Society of Merchant Venturers and spent some time on the island around 1770. It may, however, derive from the Cornish miners who probably used the ledge as a base camp in 1853. They were investigating the area as this is where the shale which forms the south-east corner of the island joins the main body of granite. Here 'at the point of union, copper ore has been found in sufficient quantity to warrant the formation of a shaft, the erections of which were pointed out to us'.[12] In fact the quantity found was so small that the shaft was soon abandoned.[13] Four horizontal workings were made below Benjamin's Chair – three to the east and one to the west – but subsequent landslides have obliterated the paths that led to them and also obscured the mouths of the workings.

The footpath continues past Golden Well and then forms one of the crossroads at the head of St John's Valley. Directly to the east lies Castle Hill where the reservoir built on its summit in 1962 to supply water to buildings near the castle was covered the camouflaged in 1974.

While digging a few yards south of Castle Hill summit in 1936, a medieval water pipeline was unearthed which was traced from the Tent Field to the castle. It consisted of earthenware pipes, each about 30 cm long with one end shaped to interlock into the next. The pipeline's full length was lifted and reused for field drainage in the Brick Field.

Chapter Thirteen

THE ARCHAEOLOGY OF LUNDY

Interest in antiquities developed during the Victorian era and Chanter, writing of Lundy in 1877, was able to devote an entire chapter to the subject.

The systematic study which has developed into the science of archaeology is little more than a century old and as Lundy is fortunate in having been largely undisturbed or developed down the ages, it has an especial appeal to archaeologists.

A certain amount of investigation was undertaken by Loyd in the 1920s and by Dr A.T.J. Dollar and others in the 1930s, but the first detailed investigations were carried out in the early 1960s by Keith Gardner. His work[1] attracted the attention of Professor Charles Thomas and of Douglas Hague[2] and the realization of Lundy's importance led to the comprehensive archaeological survey which has been made over several years by the National Trust,[3] under the supervision of David Thackray.

The wealth of archaeological material which the survey has listed consists of no fewer than 190 sites, each of which is identified by a national grid reference with a full description and an indication of the date or period to which it belongs. Seven of the most noteworthy antiquities are listed below.

Lundy Castle

This thirteenth-century building is fully described in Chapter Fourteen. At times it has been the principal, if not the only, building on the island and the residence of the island's governor or owner. At other times it has been ruinous and robbed of stone for other building works. Between 1978 and 1982 the Landmark Trust carried out repairs to the highest standard, consolidating the keep and rebuilding the internal cottages. Further work remains to be done and promises to reveal more of Lundy's past.

Bulls' Paradise

The field immediately to the west of the High Street farm buildings is the site of what appears to have been a medieval cemetery where the Giants' Graves of 1856 were uncovered. Further burials were found in 1928 and 1932 and an archaeological dig in 1960 revealed more, bringing the total to twenty-five.

Just north of these burials the 1960 excavations discovered the foundations of a large building surrounded by a ditch. Pottery and coins pointed to a twelfth- or thirteenth-century date for this strong and commanding site, suggesting 'that it was the defended homestead of the early Mariscos' and as such would have been razed once the rebellious Mariscos were overthrown and the castle, ordered by Henry III, had been completed in 1243.

Beacon Hill Cemetery

This has been fully described in Chapter Twelve. Its archaeological importance cannot be overemphasized – the four inscribed stones alone make it archaeologically unique. The main cairn is the subject of considerable interest and may well prove to be the original resting place of a Celtic saint. There are other important graves in the cemetery apart from the several dozen mounds which are suspected to contain lesser mortals and modern graves with inscribed headstones.

Quarries

These are fully described in Chapter Twenty, but the entire quarry complex started, operated and abandoned all within five years, is a fascinating site for industrial archaeologists. The metal was salvaged, the timber has rotted and the building

Hut circles (J. D'Oyly Wright)

stones have in most cases been taken for use elsewhere on the island, although much remains on which the working pattern of the Lundy Granite Company can be conjectured.

Sadly no photographs of the Lundy enterprise are yet known, for although photography was in its infancy in the 1860s contemporary photographs of industrial workings do exist.

Widow's Tenement

A diamond shaped enclosure of approximately 17 acres with an outer fence of granite orthostats contains within it the nucleus of Widow's Tenement. Medieval site, a magnificently preserved Long-house. It is 14 m long and 4.5 m wide and has two doors opposite each other in the long north and south walls. The east end appears to have been the byre or cattle stall and the west end, which stands several feet higher, was the solar where the farmer's family would have slept. There are three enclosures attached to the Long-house, on the north-east and south-west.[4]

A hut circle and North End (F. Frith of Reigate)

The building probably housed the farmer who worked the North Farm and is named in an early nineteenth-century map which details the land holdings of Irish immigrants brought to Lundy between 1808 and 1834. After falling into disrepair it was probably robbed to provide stone for the construction of Threequarter Wall in 1878.

Brazen Ward

Brazen Ward, a Civil War battery, was constructed upon the end of a short, rocky promontory on the north-east coast of Lundy, and some 50 feet above the sea. The remains comprise the gun platform in the most commanding position, revetted on the seaward side with drystone walling, and paved below, and 40.0 m to the north are the foundations of a small rectangular building measuring 6.0 m by 3.0 m, the drystone walling being 0.7 m thick. A section put across the main chamber of this building revealed massive walls and a cobbled floor, interpreted as a possible powder store. Pottery suggests it predates the Civil War by 100 years. It may possibly be associated with Elizabeth I's warnings to the Grenvilles to defend Lundy against the Spanish.

Running south from the building and erected along the edge of a rock shelf is a substantial wall, 3.0 m high on the seaward side, and 2.0 m high internally, with a thickness of 1.0 m. The wall curves into the slope below the gun platform.

From the south side of the platform the footings of a similar drystone wall extend south-westwards across steep slopes for some 30.0 m and terminate above a gully. Behind and above this wall is the old quarry whence the stone for the construction of the battery was obtained. . . . The name 'Brazen Ward' is derived from the cannon which were mounted there. . . . Across the bay from the Main Battery [is] a stone-revetted platform. The North Battery could be one of the gun platforms recorded in the eighteenth century.[5]

Gannets' Combe Area

Before the peaty vegetation was destroyed down to the bedrock by the fires of 1933 the existence of settlements in the Gannets' Combe area was not suspected. The fire revealed no fewer than fourteen hut circles, dating from the Bronze Age, to the north of Gannets' Combe and a further five, dating probably from the Iron Age, to the south-east. Subsequent investigation has revealed traces of Iron Age field enclosures in the area between Gannets' Combe and Threequarter Wall.

Chapter Fourteen

THE CASTLE

The castle is perhaps the most interesting survival of Lundy's past history, though to call it Marisco Castle is inaccurate as it was built not by the Mariscos but by King Henry III.

Immediately after he had succeeded in regaining possession of Lundy in 1242 and executing William de Marisco, the king determined to fortify the island and so prevent it ever again falling into the hands of his enemies. Work began in the following year on the building of a 'stone fort' consisting of a small square keep, a system of outer walls and a fosse. The siting of the castle was perfect, at the top of the only path from the Landing Beach to the plateau and commanding an unsurpassable view of the east coast, the Landing Bay and the Bristol Channel. Here Lundy shows a certain similarity to other cliff-edge fortifications on sites where the seaward edge of much earlier hill forts have been eroded.

The medieval entrance to the castle and thence to the island was probably by a narrow zig-zag path from the beach which has since vanished through erosion of the shale of the saddle. The northernmost lookout, complete with observation window, commands a perfect view of the Landing Beach and overlooks traces of a steep track which is possibly the one that was 'so steep that one man could scarce pass another'.

The outer walls enclosing the bailey appear to have been pierced at two places, one north of the keep at the head of the present-day steep path from the beach and the other to the west of the keep, being some form of gatehouse giving access to the plateau.

The large ditch or fosse and the external bank flanking the North Gate site are medieval, as are the lower courses of stone to the east of the gate. One would have expected the ditch to continue towards the West Gate but a geophysical survey in 1978 revealed no evidence for this and it seems likely that 'having protected the vulnerable north approach with a formidable ditch, the medieval builders were either content that the wall alone should defend the remainder of the Bailey, or were forced to abandon more ambitious plans. Beyond the site of the West Gate, the wider perimeter is continued by the enigmatic remains of what Grose (1776) shows as a double wall. Survey suggests that this may represent the bailey wall, set into the centre of a bank, and, at some stage, robbed.'[1]

The piped water supply which leads from a spring in the Lighthouse Field and

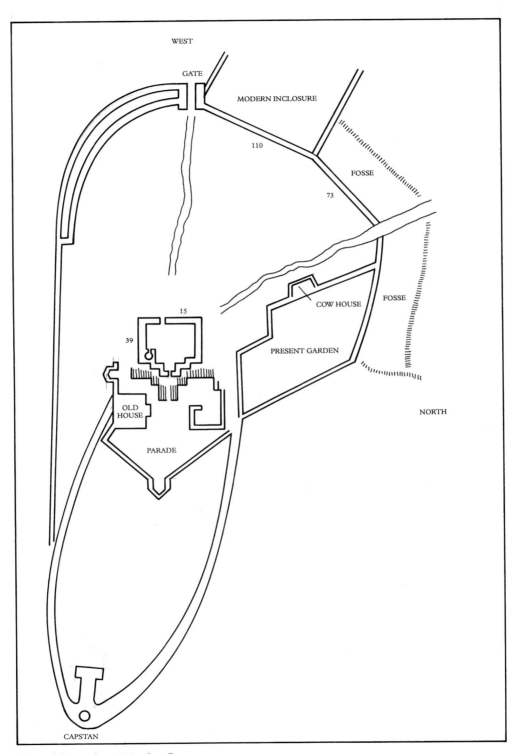

Plan of the castle, 1775, after Grose

was discovered near the summit of Castle Hill in 1936 almost certainly dates from the original building of the castle.

The keep is the oldest building on the island and until the building of the farmhouse (the core of the Old Hotel and now known as the Old House) was the principal residence. Roughly square in shape and rising sheer to the battlements, the keep retains its external appearance despite the many alterations it has undergone in its 750 years. The original building was almost certainly on two floors with walls 90 cm thick, the south-west wall being 15.5 m long, and the north-west wall 11.5 m. As the maximum floor beam was then under 9.5 m, while Lundy's minimum internal width mentioned above was 11.5 m, there must have been a crosswall, possibly pierced by arches, to support the upper floor, though all trace of this is now lost. The roof would have been pitched and either V-shaped with a central depression at the point of support by the crosswall, or more likely M-shaped having two ridges and a central valley.[2] No trace remains of original windows though the slit windows shown by Grose in 1776 might be original. The original doorway, some 2.5 m high, can still be traced in the centre of the south-east wall in front of what may have been the original forebuilding.

By the time Thomas Bushell arrived to garrison Lundy for King Charles I, the keep must have deteriorated considerably as he later submitted a claim for £5,570 for 'maintaining Lundy garrison and building the castle . . . from the ground at his own charge, fit for any noble person to inhabit'.[3] Whatever the truth of this claim Bushell certainly made considerable changes around the keep. The east bastion, shown clearly on the 1776 plan 'with two batteries on the east and south sides', is certainly Bushell's work. The wall-lines are still visible, although the south battery was not revealed until 1985. Parts of the fabric of the north-east bailey wall, perhaps including the two dilapidated square towers, may also date from the Civil War period. Immediately east of the keep the parade was stripped to bedrock in 1985 to reveal unexpected features. The 'Old House' of Grose's map may be medieval or, more probably, the result of Bushell's stewardship of the castle. 'The excavations in the "Old House" revealed traces of early 18th century occupation below the building collapse.'[4] This 'Old House' shown on the 1776 plan could well have been Bushell's own while the garrison was quartered in the keep. It has walls 74 cm thick and extends 8 m from west to east and 6.75 m north to south, with a north-facing doorway.

From the parade in front of the castle the ground slopes down steeply and two grassy paths converge at the entrance to Benson's Cave, an underground passage so named in the belief that it was used by Thomas Benson to secrete the goods he obtained by piracy and smuggling. The name is a recent one though the cement used in the cave's construction appears identical to that used in the older parts of the castle. More interesting than its actual construction or the cobbles on its floor is the question of its original purpose. The most likely explanation is that it was built by Bushell, who was a mining engineer, and whose claim to have rebuilt the castle would account for the similarity of cement. The site is ideal for a mint and store

Benson's Cave (J. Dollar)

providing both security and the space at the cave mouth to establish minting equipment. In later times the cave has served as a prison and a stable,[5] but it must have been built with concealment and security in mind. During a careful search of the cave roof in 1960 Mr C.S. Wright noted markings about halfway along, that appear to read 1747 or 1771, together with a cross. Their position is such that some staging or stored goods must have been in position. Further examination of the cave in 1965 revealed another thirty-seven inscriptions, some of the clearest reading: IS 1709, WSC 1726, WH 1750, HH 1750, IB 1751, IR 1751, and 1761 (the crossbar on the 'I' is the eighteenth-century sign for 'J'). Benson was on Lundy from 1748 until 1754 and it is known that his prisoners were 'housed in the Castle' each evening after work.

That it was used as a store is likely as Grose shows a capstan mounted at the cave mouth – whose only purpose would have been to haul goods into or out of the cave – and it is known that Benson stored his contraband in 'divers caves'.

As the shale that forms this part of the island has suffered erosion the original contours near the cave mouth must have changed. The mouth is now 1.5 m across with an opening 1.3 m high leading into a cave 19 m long, almost 2 m wide, and 4 m high. Just outside the mouth there is a recess on either side as shown in the 1776 plan. One of the recesses has a brick facing and doorway and Michael Haycraft, the mason who spent from 1977 to 1981 repairing the keep, noted that they were of unusual size, were poorly fired and contained a large amount of quartz and granite. He found similar brick deeply incorporated in parts of the keep – supporting Bushell's claim for total rebuilding – and believes them to have been fired on Lundy from clay beds which have been found in the Brick Field.

Lord Saye and Sele was the last person known to have occupied the keep but, following his departure in 1658, it appears to have been allowed to fall into disrepair. Thomas Benson who leased the island from 1748 until 1753 housed convicts in 'the Castle' and certainly used the cave which now bears his name. The convicts were employed on improvements, among other things, and may have used stone from the outer bailey wall.

With the building of the Old House which was to become the central part of the Manor Farm Hotel, the keep ceased to be the principal residence and sixty years after Grose's 1776 observation that 'five guns were placed' on the parade only 'a few old dismounted cannon . . . are yet to be seen'.[6] Grose's north-west view shows that his Old House and the lean-to were still roofed in 1775 while the keep with its east and west doorways, four corner turrets, slit windows and some crenellations was in a

Lundy Castle, 1978

poor state of repair. At this time the bailey and east bastion walls, and the west gate, or barbican, were still standing.

Sir John Borlase Warren during his short ownership from 1775 to 1781 produced some grandiose plans, and perhaps began the dismantling 'of most . . . of the walls' enclosing the bailey for the 'offices for farming' which were built about this time. These 'offices' might have included the construction of the cottages within the keep, although these may have been built a little later by Sir Vere Hunt, or his son, who settled labourers on Lundy from their Irish estates. While housed in the castle these labourers 'destroyed all the remaining woodwork, and among other things, the old entrance-gates and posts which had been placed there at the time when the Castle was prepared for the refuge of Edward II. There appears to have been a barbican or outer tower, to protect the entrance on the land site.'[7]

As there is frequent reference to the 'Fort' and the nearby 'Castle' it seems likely that the keep was known as 'the Fort', while the west gate or barbican (which probably looked more imposing) was 'the ruinous Castle'. Support for this, and confirmation of the 1820s destruction mentioned above, comes from a letter from the agent to Sir Aubrey de Vere Hunt: 'One half of the oald [sic] castle fell first Winter I came to Lundy and the other part came down last winter. . . . I assure you the entire of the timber that was in the oald castle was not worth five shilling as they all broak [sic] in the fall.'[8]

The cottages inside the castle keep were rebuilt by William Hudson Heaven in about 1850 and the west windward screen wall to protect the courtyard probably dates from this time. Three cottages were built to face the central courtyard – the north and south cottages each had two tenements while the larger east cottage which faces the entrance had only one tenement. These cottages were not used so frequently after the Granite Company left the island in 1868 as the islanders and fishermen moved into the abandoned company buildings, but they were used from time to time by islanders or to house victims of shipwreck.

The stone hut built in 1883 against the north-east wall of the keep housed the terminal of the new submarine cable. It comprised one room and a small lobby, the whole being enclosed by a retaining wall.

In 1895 a pair of semi-detached cottages were built near the keep to house Lloyd's signallers who observed shipping from a small square room built on the Castle Parade at the same time. In 1905 the Admiralty built a further pair of cottages with an attached lookout, to the west of the keep, and in 1909 the Admiralty also took over the Lloyd's cottages.[9]

Gravel for building the Lloyd's cottages was dug from a little quarry on the old steep path, where in 1902–3 the island fisherman George Thomas built a dwelling for the cost of £150. Originally called The Palace it was completely rebuilt in 1962, and is now known as Hanmers after the family who leased it in the 1930s.

When Martin Coles Harman became owner he agreed to undertake the duties of the Admiralty coastguards who then vacated the semi-detached cottages. In 1928 Mr Harman commissioned C.C. Winmill of the Society for the Protection of

Lloyd's signallers, Castle Parade (H. Jukes)

Ancient Buildings to report on the condition of the keep. Winmill's report proposing that at a cost of £1,430 the interior should be cleared, the walls strengthened and a concrete flat roof placed over the whole to form a shelter for cattle, was not implemented.

Mr Albion Harman, as part of his plan to provide holiday accommodation, converted the cable hut into Castle Cottage by raising and extending and then roofing-over the retaining wall, while at the same time converting the parade hut into a twin-bunk bedroom.

One of the first aims of the Landmark Trust was to protect the fabric of the keep, which by the 1970s was in danger of collapse and Michael Haycraft, the master mason, spent years under expert supervision carefully repairing and repointing the walls. Archaeologists from the Department of the Environment who carried out a detailed survey of the site in 1978 removed the parade hut to allow a careful study to be made of Grose's Old House.

The southernmost pair of semi-detached cottages which had been known as the Coastguard Cottages and which had been derelict since the 1940s were demolished and in 1981 two luxurious new Castle Keep Cottages were completed for holidaymakers inside the shell, on the foundations of the previous Victorian 'keep cottages'. One of these has subsequently been sub-divided to provide a total of three cottages.

Further archaeological work in 1984–5 on the Castle Parade revealed cobbled areas, what appears to be a furnace and other foundations.

When in 1989 the now ruinous and abandoned Signal Cottages were removed and the site cleared, the splendour and strength of the keep was fully revealed from the landward aspect, to compliment its striking grandeur when seen from the sea.

Chapter Fifteen

ECCLESIASTICAL HISTORY

The early history of the church on Lundy remains quite unclear despite recent archaeological work and conjecture.

The Beacon Hill site, long-recognized as of Christian importance, revealed in 1905, during the excavation for a grave within the outline of a small ruined building, an inscribed stone, the Tigernus Stone, described earlier (see pp. 4–7). With the further discovery in 1961 and 1962 of three more inscribed stones, all four of which date from the fifth to the seventh centuries, the importance of the burial site was established, an importance which further observation has supported.

After a careful reassessment of the archaeological investigations he undertook in 1969, Professor Charles Thomas believes that the Beacon Hill cemetery focused on the interment of an important individual, who he believes to have been St Nectan. The grave was subsequently opened and the remains transferred to a pre-Norman church at Stoke, Hartland where in the early tenth century a decorated stone lid of his shrine-coffin was found below the floor.[1] This important individual and the presence of the four inscribed stones would seem to date the site to a time when Celtic Christian missionaries were entering the west of England in the wake of the weakening Roman presence.

During the following centuries the island must have experienced its share of neglect or abandonment. Holy relics would have been at risk in such a place and would wisely have been taken to the mainland and finally, with the visitation, if not occupation, of Lundy by pagan Vikings during the ninth and tenth centuries, any island population would have fled or been exterminated, so ending any lingering legend passed by word of mouth. The cemetery would have lain neglected and forgotten for several centuries.

When the Mariscos arrived on Lundy they established their stronghold in the field now known as Bulls' Paradise to the west of the present High Street. Excavations there have so far failed to reveal a Christian place of worship. As Professor Charles Thomas believes 'that the likely date for the foundations of the small chapel [on Beacon Hill] was the twelfth or thirteenth century',[2] it would seem that either the Mariscos or, on their overthrow, the administration loyal to the Crown, established a place of worship on Beacon Hill.

Regarding the important question of dedication, there are no records whatsoever of Lundy's church among the Exeter Diocesan Archives,[3] and so the earliest known name is that found in the Rolls of 1244 when it is referred to as the church of St Elena[4] – which in the absence of conflicting evidence must refer to the Beacon Hill site.

Just why this name was used deserves closer inspection. The Pipe Roll of Michaelmas 1219 charges William de Marisco the sum of £11 and 4 shillings for holding the 'insula de Ely'. Most interestingly, the name 'Ely' has been subsequently scored out and replaced by 'Lundeia'.

The name Ely (for Lundy) had first appeared in 1194 when Richard I granted Lundy to William de Marisco (Pipe Roll 6 Richard I); it appears again in the Pipe Roll of the following year, and as 'Hely' in the Chancellor's Roll of 3 John (1202). E. St John Brooks notes that this may be 'an alternative or earlier name for Lundy. Or Ely may be simply a mistake and, as such, carried forward from one Pipe Roll to another.'[5] The use of Ely for Lundy, with its genitive Eliensis, could easily account for the scribe's belief that Eliensis was the genitive of Elen – St Elen – who was already the dedicatee of the nearby mainland churches at Abbotsham and Croyde.

Professor Thomas believes that the chapel whose square foundations can be traced on the Beacon Hill site dates from the twelfth or thirteenth century. The first mention in the Rolls of a church on Lundy occurs in the Liberate Rolls of 15 April 1244 when it is referred to as that of St Elena. Ten years later the Patent Rolls refer to 'St. Mary, Lunday' and by 1325 the name had become 'St. Elene'. In the absence of evidence to the contrary, therefore, the 'dedication' to Elena could well have developed from a scribe's use of 'of Ely' (i.e. 'of Lundy') and the 1254 mention of St Mary merely highlights the inaccuracies that scribes were prone to make.

By 1254 island clergy are named, as the king then ordered 'William la Zuche, Keeper of the island of Lunday, to put Adam de Aston or his proctor in possession of the Church of St. Mary, Lunday,[6] the King having granted it to him on the resignation of Henry de Wongham; and cause to be paid to him henceforth lawful tithes of fish, bird, conies and all other things which are renewed yearly in the said island'. Adam was favoured by a 'grant for life of an aery of the King's gentle falcons of the Isle of Lunday' only twelve days later.

Lundy appears to have been regarded as a distinct parish in the gift of the king or, later, the owner. Between 1325 and 1355 six rectors were appointed,[7] the frequent changes probably being a reflection of the political upheavals of the time which were followed by the ravages caused by the Black Death.[8]

On 5 June 1325 Hugh le Despencer, who owned the island from 1322 to 1326, presented the church of St Elene of Londai to Sir Walter le Bitte, who resigned on 30 November 1332. On 6 March 1333 Lord Montacute, owner of Lundy from 1332 to 1343, presented the church to Robert de Hadestoke, 'Clerke, and Rector of the Parish of Londay'. On 16 March 1338 Sir William de Tettewelle was 'collated per lapsam temporis'. He resigned in 1348. On 1 July 1350 Sir Thomas de Wynkleghe 'collated per lapse' (i.e. the patronage fell to the Bishop owing to lapse). Wynkleghe had left Lundy by 1351 and seems to have been succeeded by Sir David Kelynge who was 'collated to the Parish Church of St. Helene'.

On 14 August 1353 Sir Nicholas Comyn was collated and on his resignation Nymot Roland was collated on 3 February 1355.

The living seems to have been so poor that it was not mentioned in Pope Nicholas IV's taxation and, as it could not afford a decent maintenance for an incumbent, it ceases to be mentioned in the Register of the See until 17 July 1384 when Lundy was committed 'To Sir John Warwyke, priest, mandate to Sir William Belmeslonde, Rector of Highhampton and Vicar of Fremington to induct him'.

Although this is the last reference, there is some evidence for the continuation of the rectorship of Lundy until the Reformation, as on the Dissolution of the Monasteries Cleeve Abbey was found to hold 'the lease of the . . . Rectory of the island of Lundy valued this year [1535] as worth ten shillings annually'.[9]

It seems that this church was either destroyed or fell into disrepair, which accords well with Risdon who, writing at the end of the sixteenth century, describes the 'remains of St. Helleas Chapel . . . yet to be seen'. The cause of this decay from the time of the Dissolution must have been aggravated in the sixteenth and early seventeenth centuries when Lundy was neglected by its owners and, being virtually deserted, was prey to pirates.

A Lundy-born child, Rycharde Paymente, aged fifteen months, was baptized at Barnstaple in 1594,[10] but whether this was because the parents had left the island permanently is not clear.

It is extremely difficult to date or reconcile the burials which were discovered in 1856 and the further graves discovered in the 1920s, '30s and in 1962 a little to the east of the supposed 'Marisco stronghold' in Bulls' Paradise and the Shippen area. They appear to have been Christian with their heads to the west – who they were we may never know; they may have been outlaws or pirates, or shipwrecked mariners.

The 1856 discovery of the original Giants' Graves caused great excitement. *The Times* published the following letter from the island:

A curious circumstance has happened here since our last post-day. In digging the foundation of a wall the workmen have discovered several skeletons about two feet under the surface, one of which is that of a man of gigantic structure and probably a man of note besides, for his grave had been enclosed, whereas not one of the others had anything to mark where they had been deposited. The bones had evidently been under ground for many centuries for, on being touched and exposed nearly all of them fell to pieces. . . . Nearly all the bodies were covered with limpet shells, perhaps originally buried with the fish in them. All the burials must have taken place nearly at the same time for the skulls were lying in nearly a straight line. A stone about three feet long, roughly squared, about 18 inches through, and hollowed out at one end to a depth of about two inches like a shallow basin, contained part of the side of the skull of the large skeleton. The heads of all were laid to the west. The spot around shows traces of former habitation such as pieces of pottery, peat, ashes, etc.[11]

With the arrival of Thomas Bushell on Lundy in the 1640s, the island began a period of almost continuous habitation, with a Christian population which would have needed a church in which to worship and Bushell was the type of man who would have set about rebuilding the Beacon Hill ruin. The virtually exclusive use of the name St Anne for the Lundy church from this time – a dedication often associated with Satan, the pagan god of holy fire – could possibly have been named from the nearby hill. This hill, although not recorded as Beacon Hill until 1787, obviously did support a fire beacon at some time, most likely dating from the order of 1586 mentioned previously. Chanter's observation[12] that the cement found at the Beacon Hill chapel was similar to that found at the castle lends weight to the suggestion that Bushell may have repaired both buildings. St Anne's chapel on Beacon Hill would thus be the one used for occasional services and for the solemnization of marriages until the reign of William and Mary. There is a record of a service held there in 1787: 'On Sunday 8th [July] accordingly, prayers were read by the Rev. Mr. Cutcliffe and a sermon preached by Mr Smith to a congregation of twenty-two persons.' Although this does not specify the place of worship it goes on to describe the Beacon Hill site as '. . . an old Chapel, dedicated to St. Helen . . . some of the walls remained; the entrance, built of moorstone or spar, was from the north; its length about 25 feet, breadth 12 feet, doorway 4 feet, thickness of the walls nearly 2½ feet'.[13] The discovery of a grave below the west window of the chapel is also mentioned, as well as the 'Common burial place which surrounds the chapel'. The Ordnance Survey team led by Lt. A. Robe, R.E. who occupied the site in 1804 unfortunately completed the decay by using stone from the chapel to build a cairn. The chapel outline can still be traced and according to Chanter 'there seems to have been some ornamentation with arcades of worked stone',[14] though no trace of these was apparent even in his day.

The Lundy Granite Company had built an 'Iron Hall' on the High Street site now used as a sheep dip in which sewing and nightschool meetings were conducted. From 1864 when the Revd Hudson Grosett Heaven, the elder son of the owner, was licensed as curate in charge of the island, it was also used for two services every Sunday. When this 'Parish Iron Room' was dismantled by the insolvent Granite Company in the spring of 1868 services were transferred to the large room in the old farmhouse extension (which became Rooms 11 and 12 in the Old Manor Farm Hotel). When the company liquidators objected to this usage, services had to be conducted in the hall at Millcombe House.

This unsatisfactory situation was remedied by the generosity of a relation, Mrs Langworthy (née Sarah Heaven) who had become sole legatee of her husband's estate of over £1 million. She financed the building of a corrugated-iron church with a spire at the top of Millcombe Valley by the wall of the hotel garden. The church, which could seat eighty-two people, was dedicated on 20 August 1885 by Bishop Bickersteth who described it as a 'corrugated irony', but as it was not a permanent building it could only be dedicated and not consecrated.

On Mrs Langworthy's death the Revd Mr Heaven 'found she had bequeathed

St Helen's church, 1884–97 (unknown)

him a large legacy [and] he devoted the whole to the erection of a permanent stone church. . . . Like the ruined chapel in the graveyard on Beacon Hill as well as the little iron one this was dedicated to St. Helen . . . but there was nothing left to create a living and . . . for five years my uncle and the Diocese of Exeter combined to provide a meagre stipend for an incumbent with rent-free housing. . . .'[15]

The iron church was in use for eleven years and about 1889 a visitor noted that, each time a service was to be held, a flag was flown on the flagstaff at the castle to advise the crews of ships sheltering in the bay. The building continued in use as a meeting place after the stone church had been completed, but it was eventually dismantled – the corrugated iron being used for buildings and the timber being used for packing boxes. The foundations remain and were used in 1955 as a base for a short-lived glasshouse.

On 29 June 1895 the Revd Mr Heaven issued the following invitation:

To Builders and Contractors: Tenders required for the erection of St Helen's Church on Lundy Island. Plans and specifications lie for inspection at the offices of Messrs. Groves, Cooper and Stapleton, Bridge Chambers, Bideford. Explanations or further particulars may be obtained from John Norton Esq.

the Architect, 95, Ridgmount Gardens, London, W.C.1. Tenders, under seal, to be delivered to the address of the Architect on or before 20th July next. The undersigned does not bind himself to accept the lowest or any tender.

  Hudson Grosett Heaven, Lundy Island, June 29th 1895.[16]

Messrs Britton and Pickett of Ilfracombe were awarded the contract and progress was rapid. The foundations were laid the same year despite the unexpected discovery in September that the site chosen was on a bed of clay which extended at least 16 ft below the surface. Perhaps it was this discovery which led to the building being constructed strangely, not on the usual east–west axis.

  Many of the granite blocks used for the building came from the ruined Quarter Wall Cottages, but additional building materials were brought from Ilfracombe in the contractor's vessel *Kate* which, contrary to some reports, survived for many years after.

  The building was completed in 1896 at a cost of £4,101 5s 7d which together with the cost of the bells at £425 18s 6d and the architect's fee of £286 0s 8d made a total of £4,813 4s 9d.

St Helena's church, 1963

The church was consecrated on 7 June 1897 by Bishop Bickersteth of Exeter, supported by the rector of St Sidwells and the choir of that church, who had crossed from the mainland in the pleasure steamer *Brighton*. All 165 places in the church were filled. The crossing had been a particularly rough one and the bishop wittily acknowledged his conversion to a belief in purgatory by his experience of what it was necessary to go through to reach 'the Kingdom of Heaven'.

The Victorian Gothic-style church, now confusingly and confusedly referred to as St Helena's, has a nave, chancel, square tower, chiming clock and a peal of eight bells and though considered large today was built when the island population of more than sixty was usually complemented by the crews of stormbound sailing ships for Sunday services. The roof was originally covered with stone slates from Tetbury but these were finally replaced by grey slates in 1955. A tablet inserted in the east wall of the church reads:

> To the honour and glory of God
> and in pious memory of St. Helen
> this stone was laid
> the 5th day June 1896.

The square tower, 65 ft high with a turret up to a maximum height of 74 ft, is roofed in sheet lead and contains the clock and the bell room. In a niche on the north face of the tower is a statue of St Helena copied from the one on the high altar screen at St Albans Cathedral.

Below the face of the clock (which originally chimed) is the legend: 'Tempus Sator Aeternitati' ('Time is the sower for eternity'). The eight bells bear the following inscriptions:

1. Horam precandi iam advenisse moneo.
   (I warn that the hour has now come for prayers.)
2. Nos omnes cantamus laudes Dei.
   (We all sing the praises of God.)
3. Ut fieremus H.G.H. vicarius curavit.
   (H.G.H., the vicar, had us brought into being.)
4. Carolus Carr Societas nos fudit A.D. 1897.
   (Charles Carr & Co. made us A.D. 1897.)
5. Confuse agitatae pericla declaramus.
   (When rung confusedly we announce dangers.)
6. Retro pulsate ignes indicamus.
   (When rung backwards we signify fires.)
7. Recte sonantes gaudia pronunciamus.
   (When sounding in the right way we proclaim joys.)
8. (Tenor) Animis cedentibus dico valete.
   (I say farewell to the departing souls.)

A board on the east wall of the porch reads:

1905. Church of St. Helena, Lundy. Gloucester and Bristol Diocesan Association of change ringers. On Wednesday August 23rd, eight members of the above association, at the kind invitation of the Rev. H.G. Heaven rang a true and complete peal of Stedman Triples, 5040 changes, Tenor 15 cwt. A variation of Thurston's four part.

The Rev. H.A. Cockey	1st	W.A. Cave	5th
C.H. Tompkins	2nd	P. Came	6th
C.H. Gordon	3rd	The Rev. F.E. Robinson	7th
R.J. Wilkins	4th	The Rev. G.F. Coleridge	8th

Conducted by the Rev. F.E. Robinson, this is the first peal rung upon the bells.[17]

Their visit was almost a failure. They found that the iron bearings had suffered badly from the sea air and rendered the bells immobile. However, the party was stranded overnight by bad weather which gave them time the following morning to free the bells and so ring the complete peal.

By the end of the Second World War this corrosion had become so bad that the bells could not be rung. They were chimed at a wedding in 1954[18] but soon after were lowered to the porch where they remain, though the tenor bell was rehoisted in the tower in 1977 to mark the Silver Jubilee of Queen Elizabeth II but, being fixed in position, it can only be struck and not rung.

On the west wall of the porch is a marble tablet which was presented by members of the Heaven family. The wording, chosen by Marion C.H. Heaven, reads:

> In loving memory of Hudson Grosett Heaven,
> Priest, Lord of the Manor of Lundy who died
> in 1916 having accomplished the dream of his
> life by erecting this Church to the glory of God.

The plaque was consecrated on 19 July 1923 by the Bishop of Crediton and the bench beneath it now supports the Giant's Pillow stone found in the Giants' Graves.

On entering the nave there is a painting of the *Atlas* inscribed: 'In memory of Fokko Smit 2nd Engineer and the crew of the MV *Atlas* of Groningen wrecked near the Shutter during the night of Octr. 9/10 1942. "The Sea is His and He made it".'

The red brick walls of the nave are patterned with blue and cream coloured bricks. The font stands by the door and has a cover which was presented by Capt. Dark's family. The large rose window in the west wall was given by the James Heaven family and of the two stained glass windows one commemorates William Hudson Heaven and his wife, the parents of the donor; the other was designed, painted and given by an old family friend, the Revd H. Fleming St John.

The stone pulpit was presented by M.C.H. Heaven in memory of her parents and is inscribed: 'Thy word is a lantern unto my feet'; the screen is in memory of Lucy Sarah Heaven and was given by her brother, one of whose friends presented the lectern. The eagle was given by George Waddington, the kneelers by Cecilia Hope and the alms boxes by the groom, Christopher Watt. A bookshelf holding the prayer books has a small plaque inscribed: 'In memory of Francis Thorp, April 29th 1974.' The encaustic tiles in the chancel and sanctuary were made at Langwardine in Hertfordshire; the pillars are of Purbeck marble and the dressed stone comes from Somerset.

The reredos displays in high relief on three marble panels the Passover, Scapegoat in the Wilderness, and the Last Supper. On the east wall are two inscribed brasses: 'In aeternam Dei gloriam et in memoriam Patris Matris Fratrum Sororum hoc marmor sculptum superstites posuerunt A.D. 1897' and 'Ad majorem Dei gloriam et in memoriam dilecta Gulielmi Hudson Heaven et Ceciliae Jane uxoris eius haec fenestra donata est A.D. 1897'.

The church chalice has a broad band inscribed: 'Calicem salutaris accipiam et nomen Domini invocabo' and the paten has engraved around its border: 'Agnus Dei qui tollis peccata mundi da nobis tuam pacem', while the flagon, whose ornamental

St Helena's church plate (unknown)

border is set in amethysts, is engraved: 'Sanctus, Sanctus, Sanctus.'

When the church was complete, the land on which it stood '1,000 and 800 square yards or thereabouts' was made over to the church commissioners but the land 'was bounded on all sides by land belonging to the said Hudson Grosett Heaven' – an unusual situation that meant that technically the owner could deny access to the church. Mr Heaven hoped that the donated land would be sufficient to enable a vicarage to be built adjoining the church but this has not happened and visiting clergy often make use of the vestry, which provides primitive accommodation.

In fact the entire ecclesiastical position of Lundy in the past is obscure. The patronage of the island church was vested in Cleeve Abbey at the time of the Dissolution but it is not clear whether it then became, with the lands of Cleeve, the property of the Yelverton family or, as is more likely, it reverted to the owner of the island. William Hudson Heaven had assumed that the lord of the manor was the patron of the church. For many years the vicar of Appledore was priest in charge but in 1978 the vicar at Ilfracombe took over these duties because of the changed shipping links. More recently the island church has come under the care of a circuit of North Devon clergy.

[In 1922] the Rev. H.H. Lane was collated to the Rectory of the Parish Church of Lundy Island on the collation of Lord Bishop William Cecil, and he was duly inducted by the Archdeacon. When this got to the ears of the Registrar General in London, he challenged the legality of the Bishop's action and stated that according to the information in the hands of the Registrar General the Island had for centuries been held to be an Extra Parochial Place both for Civil and Ecclesiastical purposes, and had been so treated at the Census of 1911. . . . The Rev. Prebendary and Treasurer Chanter, who was at that time Hon. Archivist to the Diocese, was asked by the Bishop to advise him as to the island's status, in consequence of which the Bishop, Lord Cecil, declined to argue with the Registrar General and boldly stated that his action was correct. The advice which Treasurer Chanter gave was that this island has been a parish from very early times.[19]

From 13 August 1912, when the island was licensed for marriages under the Extra-parochial Places Act 1857, a parish register was begun which includes the following entries:

1864–86	Rev. H.G. Heaven, Curate.
1886–1916	Rev. H.G. Heaven, courtesy title Vicar.
	Officially Minister in Charge. Retired 1911.
1912 June 23rd	Admission of Lay Reader Walter C. Hudson Heaven.
	Resigned 24.12.1917 on sale of island [21 December 1917] and left Lundy.
1913–16	Rev. William Swatridge, Curate.

1915–21	Rev. George Scholey, Vicar of Appledore.
1918 June 23rd	Bishop of Exeter visited the island and admitted Fredk. W. Allday to the office of Lay Reader.
1919 Oct.	Church ground shortened to its present position of railed-in piece at the suggestion of A.L. Christie Esq. to Mr. F.W. Allday who noted same and reported to the authorities, Exeter.
1921	Rev. Hugh Christian Andreas Siguald Muller, Vicar of Appledore, became Curate in Charge.
1922 June 5th	'I licenced Rev. H.H. Lane in this Church pending appointment of Rector. W. Exon.'
1922 Aug. 9th	Rev. H. Lane inducted as Rector. Resigned 25.4.1924
1924–6	Mr. F.W. Allday [postmaster]. Lay Reader. Incumbency assigned to Bishop of Exeter. Net Income £75.
1942 July 1st	Resignation Rev. H. Lane, Rector, took effect.
1953	Rev. H. Muller died.
1953 Aug. 25th	Rev. R.C. Dixon instituted Vicar of Appledore and Priest in Charge of Lundy.
1953 Aug. 26th	Bishop of Exeter formerly licenced the Rev. R.C. Dixon on the island.
1972 Dec. 12th	Rev. R.C. Dixon left Appledore.
1973 March 24th	Rev. Donald L. Peyton-Jones DSC instituted Vicar of Appledore and Priest in Charge of Lundy.
1978–89	Rev. Andrew Edwards [Vicar of Ilfracombe].
1989–	Rev. W. Blakey [one of a North Devon circuit].

Chapter Sixteen

COMMUNICATIONS

Nowadays when Lundy can be reached by helicopter in seven minutes from the mainland and the island is in instant telephone contact with anywhere in the world, it is difficult to realize that before the nineteenth century there was no regular contact at all and chance visits by ships were not frequent. From the earliest times these chance visitors would barter for fresh island dairy produce or bring goods and passengers, often unexpected, from the mainland.

During the late eighteenth and early nineteenth centuries the Bristol Channel pilots, who were using Lundy as a lookout and base, began to carry mail and small items in their skiffs on a more regular basis and, once the lighthouse was completed in 1819, Trinity House began to make regular visits with their equipment, stores and staff.

Following his purchase of the island in 1834 William Hudson Heaven determined to establish his own link with the mainland. He began to charter trading vessels and the earliest record dates from 1845 when the smack *Ebenezer* (Capt. James Braund) delivered a 28 ton cargo of coal from Newport for 'Squire Heaven of Lundy'. By stranding itself on the beach on a falling tide, the cargo of coal or lime could be offloaded, allowing the vessel to sail away on the next high tide. Records show that two loads of coal were delivered annually in this way until at least 1878 whereafter, on retirement, Capt. James Braund took to fishing around the island. Meanwhile a relation of his, W. Braund of Clovelly, had contracted with Mr Heaven to carry passengers, mail and stores to the island, from at least 1853 in his fishing boat *Billy*.

By 1857 Capt. Robert Lee, known as Capt. Bill, was sailing regularly each Friday with a crew of two from Clovelly[1] under contract to both Mr Heaven and to Trinity House using his skiff, the *Ranger*,[2] a vessel later acquired by Capt. W. Bragge who continued the contracts to carry mail and passengers.

Although Mr Heaven owned 'a schoolroom yacht, the *Lady of the Isle* capable of carrying stores as cargo and passengers',[3] the only other regular visitor was the coaster that called every ten days or so to collect fish for the London market.

Capt. Bragge in the *Ranger* ended his contract with Mr Heaven at Michaelmas 1871 but continued to make the crossing by contract with Trinity House until he retired in 1877. The Trinity House contract was then taken over by Capt. Cox who sailed his smack *Chance* from Appledore 'for the benefit of its employees and for the conveying of ammunition for the fogsignal battery'. The Heaven's contract had meanwhile been given to Mr Fishwick, but when his 'fore and aft'schooner, the *Mary* was lost in February 1872, he first hired the former Bristol Channel Mission schooner *Alfred* to bring mails and supplies and then acquired a vessel, the *Lydney Trader*. By February 1873 he had chartered the *Muffy* (Capt. Marshall) but this was not an entirely satisfactory arrangement – the Heaven diaries report: 'Capt Marshall in *Muffy* came but her crew etc were tipsy and left without the mailbox.' Fortunately the diaries record about this time that the 'Skipper of Tug *Fearless*, as so often happened, called for letters.'

Finally Fishwick chartered William Dark in his trawler *Chase* and when Fishwick's contract ended Mr Heaven lost no time in appointing Capt. W. Dark, and so established a family link with the island that was to last until the death of Capt. Fred Dark in 1942.

Dark sailed regularly every Thursday from Instow and after 1879 when the *Gannet* entered service it was rarely necessary to employ any other vessel. The *Gannet* was a 40 ton pilot cutter, 46 ft long with a beam of 13 ft and a draught of 8 ft, but was admirably suited to her Lundy duties. The fare from Instow Quay was 4*s* single, 7*s* 6*d* return though Capt. Dark 'charges 30*s* for the use of his skiff on other than mail days'.[4] A black flag was hoisted on the mast attached to the hotel chimney-stack on days when the *Gannet* was coming.

Although Trinity House used the skiff *Ranger* and later the smack *Chance* to transport their staff and domestic supplies from North Devon, supplies of fuel and replacement machinery were conveyed to Lundy from the new Trinity House depot at Neyland, in Milford Haven, which opened about 1840. The 158 ton steam paddle schooner *Argus* (the second) served from 1840 (with occasional relief runs by the 67 ton Trinity cutter *Satellite* and the 60 ton *Yarmouth*). The steam paddler *Argus* (the third) was in use in the 1850s, the *Vestal* in the 1860s and the 262 ton *Beacon* in the 1870s. The *Alert* and the much larger *Siren* served until the turn of the century, and the *Vestal*, built in 1913 together with the *Siren* continued until 1925 when Neyland was closed and the depot moved to Swansea. The new 828 ton *Warden* served until the outbreak of war in 1939, to be followed after the war by the *Alert* and the *Vestal*. From 1974 the THV *Stella* and *Winston Churchill* have maintained their independent servicing of Trinity House facilities on Lundy, making ever greater use of helicopters.

On the island itself Walter Heaven had built the little sailing boat *Heatherbell* in 1886–7 and although this was intended for use around the island it did make trips during good weather to Ilfracombe, Clovelly and Bideford.

In 1911 Capt. Dark wrote to the postmaster general and requested the termination of his contract. Having spent £200 on an engine for the *Gannet*, which now required additional insurance plus a crew of three, the terms of the existing contract had become uneconomic. The GPO advertised the contract and awarded it to the lowest bidder, Capt. Hocking of Appledore whose 30 ton smack *Morning Star* was employed to carry the mails from 30 September 1911. Capt. Hocking soon

Landing stores in the cove

discovered that the service was not as easy as he had thought and on 1 March 1912 he asked to resign. Meanwhile the Bideford and Bristol Steamship Company whose 99 ton vessel *Devonia* was already trading locally, offered to carry the Lundy mails for less than that requested by Capt. Dark. The offer was accepted and from 7 March 1912 mails were carried to and from Bristol.

Throughout Victorian times, and until 1980, Lundy has been visited by excursion sailings during the summer months. The first record of such a visit is that of the *Lady Rodney* which took a party from Bideford to Lundy on 23 July 1827, but the coming of the railways so developed the seaside holiday trade that by the 1860s there were regular excursion visits to the island. Several companies competed for the trade and even the Lundy Granite Company during its short life from 1863 to 1868 ran 'a series of trips by small steamer from Instow'[5] using their steamtugs SS *Ogmore* or *Vanderbyl.*

Competition became more intense in the 1870s for this trade and operators began to offer such inducements as 'Minstrel Bands' to play en route. The *Prince of Wales* (Capt. Jackson) and the aged *Thames* (built in 1815 as the *Argyle*) ran regular excursions from Ilfracombe. Other visitors were the *Digby Grand* and the *Lord Stanley* while for many years the *Velindra* maintained a Tuesday and Friday sailing schedule during the season.

Some operators, however, were badly organized and some trippers were aggressive or drunk. The tug *Traveller* is reported to have brought '200 roughs from Barnstaple' while the *Princess Royal* with a cargo of excursionists was forbidden to land. No criticism was levied against the *Flying Cloud*, the *Lady Margaret* or the *Neath Abbey* but matters were getting out of hand and following an incident on the Landing Beach when Mr Heaven was abused, an 1897 newspaper reported that 'Pocketts splendid steamship *Brighton . . .* is the only steamer allowed to land passengers on Lundy, the proprietor of the island making this limitation in order to prevent wanton damage'.

The ban was soon lifted as Lundy needed the visitors but by the outbreak of the First World War in 1914 Messrs P. and A. Campbell were becoming the dominant company in the Bristol Channel.

During the First World War all civilian sailings ceased and an Admiralty trawler, the *Robert Davidson*, maintained a link between Lundy and Ilfracombe.

With the end of the war in 1918 the excursion steamers resumed their sailings and for the next twenty years operated an intensive summer service to Lundy. P. and A. Campbell by now had the virtual monopoly of Bristol Channel trade and their paddle-steamers *Ravenswood*, *Britannia* and *Glen Gower* were each capable of carrying almost a thousand passengers. To land and re-embark such numbers required additional facilities on the island and the use of three motor launches in the Landing Bay.

The *Gannet*, had resumed its twice-weekly sailing but in 1921 Mr Christie, the then owner, bought the 71 ton Lowestoft drifter *Lerina*. For a while the two boats ran concurrently but on 1 September 1923 the *Gannet* crossed Bideford Bar for the last time with her successor as escort. Built in 1917 the *Lerina* at first used Barnstaple as her mainland base and was fitted with two 16 ft lifeboats on davits to enable her to carry no fewer than eighty passengers. The heavy lifeboats and fittings were found to affect the control of the ship and when they were removed the licence was amended so that ony twelve passengers could be carried.

Civil aviation became fashionable during the 1930s and in April 1934 Mr R.T. Boyd was given permission by Mr Harman to operate an air service to the island. A small area south of Quarter Wall and immediately to the west of the main path was reserved as the airfield. This was provided rent-free but a charge of 1*s* per passenger/flight was levied by Mr Harman. A provisional licence for the airfield was granted by the Air Ministry on 31 May 1934 only three days after Boyd had made the first landing with an Air Ministry inspector using a ten-seater De Havilland Dragon (G–ACCR). The first four passengers crossed on 2 June but the following day the aircraft struck the top of the Brick Field wall and was partially wrecked. Although there were no injuries to the pilot or passengers the Air Ministry cancelled the provisional licence until the wall had been removed, so adding some extra 15 acres to the landing area.

Four days after renewal of the licence on 3 September 1934 Boyd resumed flights using a twin-engined four-seater General Aviation ST3 monospar (G–ACUW) and the following month signed an agreement which granted him exclusive use of the Lundy airfield, made arrangements for the collection of landing fees and agreed freight charges and the use of free passages.

To encourage civil aviation the government offered a subsidy of sixpence (6*d*.) a mile for all commercial flights carrying passengers and freight. As the return trip to Barnstaple from Lundy was 50 miles, the payment for each journey was £1 5*s* (£1.25) enabling fares to be kept down to 15*s* (75p) return – later raised to 15*s* 9*d* (88p)!

From 1 April 1935 the previous irregular flights were replaced by a regular twice-daily mail-carrying service, Boyd added a twin-engined six-seater Short Scion (G–ACCP) to his fleet and from the end of September ran a once-weekly Saturday service throughout the winter. Similar arrangements were carried out in 1936, 1937, and 1938. This Short Scion was badly damaged on Lundy, and probably did not fly again.

To raise more capital Boyd joined Mr Harman to form a limited liability company in 1937. It seems he then acquired two De Havilland twin-engined, twin-seater Moths, one of which was G–AAIM, and also a Short Scion (G–AETT) to replace G–ACCP.

During 1939 the service had to be suspended several times due to a shortage of spares until it finally ceased on 1 September, when all civil flying was forbidden. On the outbreak of the Second World War two days later the Royal Air Force took over Barnstaple Airport, renamed it Chivenor, and greatly enlarged it. They continued to use Boyd's Short Scions until one crashed in February 1940.

P. and A. Campbell's paddle-steamers were taken over by the Admiralty, as they had been in the First World War and, although the *Lerina* continued to serve the island until 1942, having been at first lent, but later sold to the Admiralty, a link was maintained with the island using various commandeered vessels such as the *T.H.E.*, the *Annie Vesta*, the *Pelorus Jack* and a Belgian trawler *De Helige Familje*.

With the end of the war in 1945 and after war duty the *Lerina* resumed the Lundy service under Capt. G. Wilson and others for which a return fare of 25*s*. was charged. Campbells also began to operate a summer service using their new postwar paddle-steamers *Bristol Queen* and *Cardiff Queen* to augment their other vessels which were showing signs of their age and wartime service. The *Lerina* too was becoming increasingly unreliable and had to be laid up at Bideford in 1950 where she was finally broken up.

The island now faced a crisis as the summer steamers were not allowed to carry mail or cargo. The island fisherman volunteered to carry a few passengers to and from Clovelly in his boat, the *Ella Trout* and the landlord of a Bideford inn converted the ex-RNLI lifeboat *The City of Nottingham*, renamed *Margaret Rose*, but this underpowered vessel made only two trips to the island before the owner died and the service collapsed.

Fortunately, Capt. Drabble had started Devon Air Travel using part of the RAF airfield from which he operated his own twin-engined De Havilland Rapide

(G–AKNY) and he was able to provide a regular service to the island. Devon Air Travel was succeeded by Devonair which for the next three years used first a Miles Gemini (G–AKHW) and very soon after a pair of single-engine Austers (G–AJEA and G–AJXC), both of which were owned by Capt. Maurice Looker. These small aircraft could carry only two passengers plus pilot and so from 1953 until 1956 a Miles Aerovan (G–AJIC) was used occasionally until Capt. Looker was able to buy his own ex-Belgian Aerovan (OO–ERY). The service finally ended when the engine of one of the Austers failed while crossing from Lundy. Fortunately, there was no loss of life when the plane sank.

It had become increasingly obvious that the air service which carried the mail and a few passengers, with the rare visits of the Aerovan or a chartered fishing boat from Ilfracombe, could not sufficiently provide for Lundy's transport needs.

Fortunately, Mr Albion Harman was able early in 1956 to buy a 28 ton North Sea trawler, the *Pride of Bridlington* which, renamed, entered service as the *Lundy Gannet* in June 1956. The crew of four provided a weekly winter service and a thrice-weekly summer service for twelve passengers. The vessel plied from Bideford until 1970 when the Landmark Trust, as new owners, transferred its operations to Ilfracombe to avoid the problems caused by having to cross the Bideford Bar at certain states of the tide. They reverted to Bideford in 1984 and have used the port ever since.

Until the Landmark Trust leased Lundy the policy had been to charter large vessels whenever loads of heavy or outsize equipment were needed but, with the extensive building plans of the Trust in mind, the 185 ton Danish ship *Agdleg* was bought for £30,000 in 1971. This ship had been used on the Copenhagen–Greenland route and had accommodation for both passengers and freight. She was renamed *Polar Bear* by the Landmark Trust and from May 1972 ran a service to Lundy in company with the *Lundy Gannet*. This continued until January 1976 when the *Lundy Gannet* was sold for £4,000 leaving the *Polar Bear* as the sole island boat.

Meanwhile the growth in private car ownership, of foreign package holidays, of rising fuel costs and falling receipts finally forced Messrs P. and A. Campbell to abandon large steam-powered paddle-steamers in the 1960s and to use second-hand motor ships. These were the *Westward Ho* (formerly *Vecta*), the *St Trillo* (formerly *St Silio*) and finally from 1969 the *Balmoral*, which ship maintained the Campbells' summer service to Lundy for ten years. During the 1978 season the ailing *Balmoral* was supported by the *Devonia* (formerly *Scillonian*), but the company finally ceased operating at the end of the 1979 season.

For the 1980 season a new enterprise, the White Funnel Steamer Company Ltd, in which the Landmark Trust had a large interest, operated the *Balmoral* but at the end of the season the service was withdrawn.

The Landmark Trust, anxious to make the island accessible to all and to cater for the many visitors staying in the hotel and cottages, entered into an arrangement with the Firth of Clyde Steam Packet Company who undertook to operate their *Prince Ivanhoe* (formerly *Shanklin*) in the Bristol Channel. However, this arrangement was short-lived as the *Prince Ivanhoe* was wrecked on the South Wales coast on 3 August 1981 after only a few weeks of the Lundy service.

Because the *Prince Ivanhoe* had not been able to start its sailings to Lundy until the middle of the 1981 holiday season, the Landmark Trust arranged for an experimental helicopter service to be run by Castle Air Charters of Liskeard to augment the service carried out by the *Polar Bear*, which was still only licensed for twelve passengers.

The helicopter service operated on Sundays and Mondays from Hartland Point carrying six passengers and the pilot to the island in seven minutes. The flights began on 16 April 1981using a Bell Longranger (G–LRII), but difficulties were soon encountered in accommodating six passengers and their luggage and so from 13 July 1981 a Bell Jetranger four-seater (G–BHXU) was used. The day-return fare was £25 though period returns were only £19. Mails continued to be carried exclusively by the *Polar Bear*, as there is no post office at Hartland Point.

The helicopter service proved popular and invaluable after the loss of the *Prince Ivanhoe*. It continued to run on summer weekends and occasionally at other times until October 1985 when new legislation came into force forbidding the flight by single-engined helicopters over water, so making the service impossible to maintain as twin-engined machines would be hopelessly uneconomic.

To augment the weekend helicopter flights and the thrice-weekly visits of the *Polar Bear* an 18 knot, 32 ft dory named *Islander* (BD 29) was bought for £48,000 to carry twelve passengers to and from Clovelly in forty-five minutes. Housed in a special cradle on Lundy, the vessel is launched down the cove slipway when required.

As a private venture, and to replace the services operated by the ill-fated *Prince Ivanhoe*, the MV *Balmoral* returned to the Bristol Channel to accompany the paddle-steamer *Waverley*.

The change in Civil Aviation Authority regulations which had forced the ending of Lundy's helicopter service made the need more urgent for a replacement vessel which would be able to carry more than the twelve passengers to which the *Polar Bear*, and before her the *Lundy Gannet*, was restricted.

After an exhaustive search the 288 ton MS *Oldenburg* was bought from the German State Railways. Built in 1958 the 43 m ship was capable of carrying 267 passengers and 20 tons of freight at 12 knots. With the help of grants from the West Country Tourist Board and the English Tourist Board, the ship was bought by the Lundy Island Company. Following a comprehensive refit she began a regular scheduled service to and from Lundy with her minimum crew of four in May 1986, replacing the *Polar Bear* which was eventually sold for service in the West Indies.

From 1989 the *Oldenburg* became the only passenger-carrying vessel to land at Lundy as problems had arisen with the management of the *Waverley* and *Balmoral*. All passengers were thenceforth scheduled to and from Bideford and, on those occasions when the tide made the use of Bideford difficult, passengers were transported to and from Ilfracombe, so allowing them always to park their cars at Bideford.

MS Oldenburg

The *Oldenburg* is now able to offer a scheduled service during the twelve months of the year carrying staying visitors, day excursionists, mail and cargo in comfortable conditions with facilities which include a shop, refreshment counter and a bar.

Because of the protection afforded by Lundy from westerly gales sailing ships frequently took advantage of the shelter in the Roads on the East Side of the island. The volume of shipping became so great in the nineteenth century that a committee of the House of Commons suggested that it would be desirable to build a harbour of refuge at Lundy. Two years later a royal commission reported that although the site was ideal, the estimated cost of £3 million was prohibitive. The plan under consideration involved the building of 'two piers, one running out from Gull Rock in an easterly direction, leaving an opening of a quarter of a mile; the other pier would run from the former round to Rat Island, leaving an entrance between it and the land. The whole breakwater would then be about a mile and threequarters long, and would enclose an area of about 714 acres'.

Apart from the cost, the advantages of the situation and the ready availability of building materials were offset by the difficulties of navigation due to the frequent fog and tide races, the lack of a suitable beach on which to ground a damaged vessel and the lack of repair facilities. Chanter estimated that 1 million vessels passed Lundy in 1876 and at one time in the 1860s as many as 300 sailing ships sheltered in the Lundy Roads at one time. The volume of shipping increased to such an extent that schemes were reconsidered and the use of convict labour to build a more simple type of harbour was proposed in a report of 1874. This said that 'Lundy Island was offered to the Government in August 1871 by the Proprietor, W.H. Heaven Esq., for the sum of £40,000 having been selected by the Royal Commissioners on Harbours of Refuge in 1859 as the most eligible position for the Bristol Channel'. The Commissioners state in their report: 'That a Harbour of Refuge at Lundy would afford shelter with less risk than any other place. A point of departure from which vessels could get to sea with the first favourable start of wind, large vessels could be towed down from Cardiff, Bristol and Gloucester etc. It is also well situated for the collection of convoys and for a Naval station to watch the Channel. Being subject to no violence from the sea to the eastward, a breakwater would be of the cheapest description, a mere rubble mound, the construction of which requiring little skilled labour, would be well-adapted for the employment of convicts for the safe custody of whom the island would afford every facility.' After a description of the island the report continues:

In 1870 the number of vessels that left the several ports in the Bristol Channel amounted to 39,329 containing 5,634,294 tons of iron and coal, showing that upwards of 78,000 vessels pass and repass Lundy Island in a year amounting to one sixth of the entire shipping of the United Kingdom. . . . There can be no doubt that if the proposed Harbour of Refuge and Convict Station should meet the approval of the present Government and be carried out as recommended it would prove one of the greatest national benefits of the age in rendering most valuable assistance to the Mercantile interests of all nations as also the saving of life and property. The Convict staff and establishment at Portland could be transferred to Lundy Island, as the Harbour of Refuge at Portland is now complete which would prevent additional cost to the country beyond the expense of erecting suitable prisons and barracks.

Discussion of the harbour of refuge continued for some years, occasionally flaring up following a newspaper article or a visit by a local dignitary but, despite the strong recommendations, the proposals came to nothing.

However, steps were taken to inform Lloyds and through them the owners of ships delayed by bad weather in the Lundy Roads. The only existing means of raising contact in such conditions was by lighting a bonfire or by use of a heliograph, and although proposals had been made as early as 1870 for a cable to Lundy, construction did not begin until 1883.

The service opened on 5 April 1884 was operated by two Lloyd's signalmen, William Allday and George Thomas, who opened their office daily from 8 a.m. until

10 p.m. to maintain the link with Hartland Point. The signalmen lived in the twin Signal Station Cottages which were completed in 1885. The previous year a small hut had been built on the Castle Parade to give an uninterrupted view of the channel, and continued to be so used until 1 June 1909 when Admiralty coastguards took over Lloyd's duties, and built themselves the station on Tibbett's Hill where the site had been leased at £104 per annum.

The value of the shelter given by the crumbling shale saddle to shipping sheltering in the bay was recognized by the merchants of Bristol who are reported to have offered £8,000 to reinforce it.

Somewhat late in the day the Mayor and Corporation and the Harbour Commissioners of Swansea visited Lundy on 15 June 1888 to view the site of the projected harbour of refuge. No doubt fortified by the presence of the Swansea Police and their band and 'a sumptuous repast at which about fifty sat down' the worthies concluded that Lundy 'offers the most desirable position in the Channel'.[6]

The cable link with Lundy was a private venture and after it had broken several times on the rocky seabed at Shipload Bay, Hartland it was finally abandoned in 1887. For six years there was no telegraphic link, until in 1893 the GPO installed a new cable from Croyde Coastguard Station which ended on Lundy in the hut specially built against the north wall of the castle keep. The first message sent by Mr Heaven read: 'The Kingdom of Heaven rejoiceth', but when the cable broke in June 1896 on the sandy seabed 4 miles out from Croyde the engineers expressed surprise as they had expected the rocky seabed nearer Lundy to be the cause of breakages.

The cable parted several times subsequently, on occasion so close inshore to Lundy that it was suspected that it had been deliberately cut after fouling the anchors of ships moored in the Roads. Repairs were usually made immediately but when the cable broke during the war in 1917 two years were to pass before repairs could be undertaken,[7] and when in 1928 it broke again within a few months of repair, it was finally abandoned.

Early experiments in wireless telephony had been made in 1900 and again in 1911 and 1912 but these were not followed through for many years. However, when the Lundy cable was finally abandoned the Marine Department of the Board of Trade which was responsible for the safety of shipping, came to an agreement with Mr Harman who undertook to be responsible for watching the coasts of Lundy. Station No. 6078 opened on 3 May 1930 and operated from the Old Light using a 100-watt Marconi XMB–1A transmitter and XMC2 receiver in contact with Hartland Point Coastguard Station where similar machines had been installed. It was agreed that private messages as well as shipping information could be transmitted and that the Lundy sets could be operated by an uncertificated operator, a duty which Mr Gade performed from the closing of the Admiralty coastguard station on Tibbett's Hill in August 1928 until January 1974.

The original transmitter was replaced in 1945 by a naval TV5 set which operated twice daily on 183 metres. In the spring of 1971 these arrangements were supplemented by a UHF transmitter/receiver installed in the island office which gave direct contact with Barnstaple, and from November 1974 a direct link was established with the mainland telephone service using a transmitter working on 157.55 MHz from Lundy and 162.15 MHz from the mainland on Channel 31. The telephone number of Lundy has altered over the years and is now 0237 431831 with a Fax number 0237 431832.

The diaries of the Heaven family for 1894 show that an overhead telephone line connected Millcombe House with the cable hut at the castle but no mention is made of other branches. In 1910 a telephone line was built to link the North and South Lighthouses with the coastguard station on Tibbett's Hill. Later the Old Light and the Old Hotel were connected to this line but in 1966 the Old Light telephone was transferred to nearby Stoneycroft. The wiring was modified in 1971 but finally in 1976 all but the ten southernmost poles were removed as the overhead line was replaced from the North Light to a point just below the Battlements by a buried ten-core cable. South Light was then able to control North Light as an unmanned 'slave' station. The Old Hotel, Old Light and Stoneycroft all lost their telephones though an underground line linked Millcombe to the office.

In 1991 the telephone system was completely revised. A radio-telephone aerial dish was installed by Barton Cottages and at the same time a new internal system linked every staff residence with the office. This system links with the hand-held appliances used on the beach and with the bridge of the *Oldenburg*.

The radio-telephone aerial dish, installed in 1991

Chapter Seventeen

SHIPWRECKS

It is only to be expected that an island in Lundy's position should have a history of shipwreck but, quite apart from the problems of tide, wind, darkness and fog, this island has other hazards. Halftide Rock at the south-west and the Hen and Chickens reef at the north-west, as well as the Stanley Bank and East Bank, pose problems enough, but in 1965 after two coasters had reported scraping their hulls in a trough during storms off the West Side, Admiralty surveyors discovered three pinnacles of undersea rock and to avoid further trouble blasted away the tallest of the three.

Many ships are listed as having sunk near or around Lundy but only those that have struck the island are listed below. Stone cannon balls dated from 1575–1600 have been recovered recently from the seabed around Lundy by divers, but the earliest named wreck is that of the *Marie*, a collier that was lost on 19 September 1757. On 12 July 1792 the briganteen *Jane* 'put ashore' on Lundy to save her crew and some of her cargo of coal was saved. In December 1796 the brig *Wye*, less than a year old and plying from her home port of Chepstow to Plymouth, was lost on Lundy and 'every soul perished'.[1]

The *Jenny*, which had had an adventurous history of trading for the Honourable East India Company and in the Pacific, was wrecked on the West Side on 20 February 1797 at a point since known as Jenny's Cove. The 78 ton three-masted schooner which mounted 'eight old and very bad two-pounders for which we had scarce any shot, two swivels, some wall pieces and twelve muskets'[2] with its usual crew of thirty, was homeward bound to Bristol from Africa with a cargo of ivory and gold dust when she struck, broke up, and 'all hands, including four or five passengers, being lost, with the exception of the chief officer who was sent back to Lundy to see if any salvage could be affected'. Apparently much of the ivory was salvaged but the leather bags containing the gold dust were soon washed away.

In January 1800 the *Myrtle Tree*, bound from the Baltic to Dublin, was lost on the island and in 1811 the *Estrella de Mar*, a thirteen-year-old 104 ton schooner of St Ubes, Portugal, en route to Bristol, was wrecked without loss of life near the Battery.

On 17 November 1816 the 40 ton sloop *Rover* bound from Newport to London with a cargo of coal was wrecked on the Knoll Pins. Four years later on the night of 20/1 January 1820 the schooner *Lamb* went ashore in the cove immediately north of the Battery – a site known for some years afterwards at Lamb Cove. She was lost with all hands, though three bodies and an oar marked 'Lamb' were later washed ashore.[3]

The smack *Fame*, bound for Cork, was wrecked on 7 February 1822, but the crew were saved.

The following year the agent on the island reported to the owner: 'There was a great misfortune happened hear [*sic*] on the 30th October [1823]. An Irish brig called the *Marriston* was wrecked here and 25 persons drowned, besides 250 pigs. The Captain and three men saved their lives on a part of the mast but one of the men died after he came ashore and we buried him and another man that was picked up on the island. We could save none of the wreck; she went to pieces.'

Two wrecks occurred in 1825 – the first, the *Commerce*, a Jersey brig of 154 tons bound for Swansea in ballast to load coal, struck the Shutter on 14 April 1825 and broke up. Fortunately all the crew were saved, but later that year an unknown ship was wrecked and 'several shipwrecked mariners were interred' in the burial ground.[4]

On 21 March 1829 the 372 ton barquentine *Francis Anne* sank after striking a sunken rock 'south by west about three cables length from the east end of Rat Island'.[5]

Another British collier, the *Rapid*, bound from Llanelly to London, was wrecked on the east coast on 21 August 1835, but the more fortunate barque *Abbotsford* of 407 tons bound from Bristol to Boston which went ashore in April 1836 was later refloated and taken to Ilfracombe.

A wreck which occurred in 1838 was mentioned in evidence given to a royal commission[6] by William Yeo of Bideford who told of being anchored on the East Side of Lundy when the wind suddenly changed direction to the east. 'We managed to get our anchors, but a ship belonging to Shields which lay alongside of us could not. She went ashore and went to pieces.'

On 19 March 1842 the 76 ton smack *Mariner* of Dartmouth was lost in Lundy Roads but no details are known.

The 200 ton brig *Crescent* (Capt. James Pain) of Exeter sprang a leak a short distance from Lundy Roads on 25 June 1842. The master and crew abandoned her, after which she went down with her cargo of coal from Swansea. 'The crew reached Lundy where they took shelter in the hole of a rock for two nights and a day, and we regret to say that although under such perilous circumstances and fatigue, the people of the island neither offered or rendered the sufferers the least assistance, or served them with any provisions during the whole time they were on the island. The Trinity Steamer *Argus* took them off and landed them at Appledore, the captain hailing them with the greatest kindness and humanity.'[7]

On 2 February 1848 the fifty-year-old 104 ton St Ives brigantine *Ann* (Capt. Richards) struck the West Side and only a boy passenger was saved. Ten days later, on the 12th, all the crew escaped when the 379 ton Norwegian barque *Sylphiden*, carrying coal from Newport to the West Indies, went ashore on the West Side in fog. When the US ship *Archelaus* of 590 tons sank in the Roads on 7 November 1849 the three pilots, based at Pill, Bristol, who rescued the crew of twenty-two were each later awarded £5.

From 1850 until the First World War an Annual Register of Wrecks[8] gave full details of most of the wrecks around the coasts of Britain. The first Lundy record in the register occurs on the second day, 2 January 1850, when an unknown barque sank in the Roads with the loss of four lives. On 18 January 1850 the 195 ton brig *Thomas Crisp* was wrecked on Lundy during a gale and one life was lost. A month later, on 18 February 1850, the wreck of an unknown trawler was found 'on the west point'. Although the 348 ton barque *Glenlyon* went aground on Lundy on 29 May 1850 she was later towed off to Ilfracombe.

In a storm on 9 January 1851 a French lugger was wrecked with the loss of her crew of four, but there was one survivor from an unnamed schooner with a crew of five which was wrecked in the same storm. A year later on 13 January 1852 the 58 ton schooner *Wizard* (Capt. Guille) bound from Bristol to St Michael's was wrecked on the cove. Her crew of six escaped and the wreck was 'sold for £40 on the beach'.

The *Ariel* is reported to have been wrecked near the Landing Beach in 1853 but is not mentioned in the wreck register. This register gives no more Lundy wrecks until 14 May 1855 when the sailing vessel *Joseph F. Votsam* was stranded at night on the Hen and Chickens with sixty-two people on board. An anonymous islander writing some fifty years later in the *Western Mail* recalls: 'I remember another morning when we were roused from our sleep by a lot of boats, full of people, in a state of great privation, being rowed ashore. There were men, women and children. It turned out that they had been taken off an emigrant ship which had struck on the north reef of the island, which is known as the Hen and Chickens. The vessel came from Cardiff and nearly all the people were Welsh.'

The following day 15 May 1855 the 408 ton British barque *Avon* (Capt. Moor) laden with copper ore from Cuba sank on the north-west side.

There is evidence of two further wrecks about this time – one of which may have been the *Wesleyana*, which struck the North East Point in 1856. A report of that year mentions a party of divers 'exerting their skill aided by the appliances of science but hitherto without any decided success in raising the precious things from the sunken vessels around the island. The *Loire* steamer sunk some time ago as she was on her voyage from Cardiff to Rouen, laden with coals, still lies snugly in custody of Davy Jones . . . her whereabouts is now difficult to find; the masts which served as a buoy, have been washed away by the action of the sea.'[9] Some seven weeks later the same paper reported that two tons of copper ore had been recovered of the 560 tons carried by the *Avon*.[10]

The next entry in the wreck register is for 13 March 1858 when the *Charles*, a 240 ton schooner, was wrecked in a Force 8 gale with the loss of five lives. On 15 April 1858 the 41 ton smack *Trident* carrying coal from Cardiff to Plymouth was wrecked in a Force 9 easterly with the loss of the mate.

The great gale of 24/5 October 1859 wrecked no fewer than seven vessels on

Lundy. These included a barque, a schooner and a brig – no lives were saved and a resident reported that 'the only bodies we recovered were those of four foreigners, and their bodies were buried in the churchyard'.

Fog was the cause of the wreck on the West Side near the Old Light of the 53 ton brig *Valentine* (Capt. Williams) on 23 May 1861 but fortunately all the crew were saved.[11]

The Glasgow steamer *Iona II* of 246 tons was also the victim of fog on 2 January 1864. She had been built by James and George Thomson of Glasgow the previous year and was engaged on blockade-running during the American Civil War. A great deal of confusion was deliberately generated because of pressure by the American Federal states on the British government to stop the use of vessels by the Confederate states. The last journey of the *Iona II* is surrounded by false reports and dates, but news leaked out after the end of the war that 'during the late war between the northern and southern states of America a large steamer, a blockade runner, laden with a valuable cargo, ran into Lundy Island in a thick fog and soon went to pieces'.[12] She was 245 ft long, 25 ft wide, had a draught of just over 9 ft and was very fast. She was possibly sailing without lights at the time.

More prosaically the SS *Hector* also struck the island in fog that year, on 28 March, but she was eventually refloated and taken to Cardiff for repairs.

The only wreck recorded in 1865 was that of the sailing vessel *Eclipse* which was stranded on 5 April.

A vivid account of the wreck of the *Hannah More* on Rat Island on 10 January 1866, when nineteen of her crew of twenty-five were lost, is given in a local paper of the period.[13] The 1,129 ton ship had arrived in Lundy Roads two days previously with a cargo of guano.

On the Wednesday [10th] night a great gale began to blow and the wind chopped to every quarter in hurricane force. The *Hannah More* attempted to set her canvas to beat off the shore, but her sails were blown to fragments. She began to drag and one cable parted. The ship swung broadside to the seas, and her decks were swept of everything, including bulwarks and boats, and her topmasts went overboard. In the following gleam of morning, those on shore saw the crew clinging to the lower rigging. A rescue was organised by a young surgeon on a visit to the island. Two Bideford men, Thomas Saunders and Samuel Jarman went out in Mr Heaven's small punt and made two attempts to take out a line . . . a giant wave lifted the ship onto Rat Island on her side and in twenty minutes she had disintegrated. All but six of the crew were washed off, but these six remained on a portion of the wreck from daylight until 4 p.m. After five attempts to reach them in the small punt they were at length brought back to the beach. The remainder were seen clinging to spars and were carried by the eddy round Rat Island to the westward, where they drifted for hours to and fro in the currents before many of them were dashed against the rocks.

On 27 October of the following year, 1867, the Genoese wooden barque *Columba* was wrecked on the Landing Beach and became a total loss. The 351 ton vessel, built in 1853, was beached by the captain who reported that he had a leak to stop. He wanted to shift some cargo ashore and work on her at low tide. The crew came ashore for supplies leaving only one man, Agostino, in charge. He smelt burning and found oil upset in several places and for this one of the sailors was suspected. Fortunately drizzling rain and flowing tides reduced the smouldering timbers, but it was subsequently learned that the vessel had been heavily insured.

The crew were busy for the following week removing everything that they could salvage from the wreck, storing goods in the cave and Fish Palace on the beach and hauling timber which was stored at the side of the Beach Road almost as far as Millcombe gates!

The only wrecks recorded for 1868 are those of the 44 ton Barnstaple smack *Caroline* which was carrying granite from Lundy to Fremington. She became stranded on the beach and by 19 February had become a total loss. In August the barque *Admiral* of Jersey was 'dashed to pieces on Lundy and all hands perished except one man who was picked up by an Ilfracombe Pilot'.

On 20 March 1869 the *Albion*, Bristol pilot cutter No. 9, dragged her anchor in the Roads and was wrecked ashore. The crew were rescued by fishermen rowing through the breakers. In thick fog a few weeks later on the evening of 6 April the 156 ton brigantine *Belinda* with a cargo of 220 tons of copper struck the cliff east of the south-west point and was wrecked. The following month a fishing boat raised 15 tons of copper ore in bags while fishing near the scene. At the end of that year, on 30 December 1869, the 32 ton smack *Eliza* was lost with all her crew off Lundy.

The one wreck recorded in 1870 was that of the 219 ton brig *Mary* of the Scilly Isles and outward bound from Swansea to Bordeaux with a cargo of coal. She struck Rat Island on 17 December, fortunately without loss of life. The Trinity House staff were commissioned to act as Receivers of Wreck and a few months later sold the *Mary*'s mainmast to Mr Heaven for 10*s* (50p).

On 14 February 1871 the 958 ton barque *Brenda* bound from Newport to New Orleans with a cargo of 'railway iron' grounded just north of Brazen Ward. Subsequently, after removal of all her cargo, she was pulled off on 1 July.

An iron brig, at anchor in the bay on 7 May 1872, was struck by the 152 ton wooden brigantine *Gertrude* which promptly sank, though all the crew escaped. Later that year on 5 September the St Ives sailing vessel *New House* was wrecked though no details are known.

The one wreck recorded in 1873 was that of skiff No. 34, from Pill, which sank on 23 October without loss of life. Another skiff, No. 19, sank the following year on 7 June at the North East Point while on 30 September 1874 the 30 ton smack *Fanny* (Capt. Luard) which had come for cattle went aground on the beach and soon broke up when the wind suddenly backed from SW to NE.

The one-year-old 100 ton French schooner *Jean et Robert*, carrying coal from Newport, was anchored in the Roads when the wind rose to a gale. She slipped her

A wreck at Brazen Ward (unknown)

anchor but could not work out of the Roads and so went ashore on the beach on 21 January 1876. By 2 p.m. she was reduced to 'firewood' and although the captain, apprentice and cabin-boy were drowned, the remaining crew of four were saved and some two tons of the scattered cargo was secured. In thick fog on 6 February 1877 the 811 ton iron steamer *Ethel*, laden with iron ore, was wrecked on Black Rock. Of the crew of twenty the only survivor was John Lawrence, the mate, who landed on Lametry Beach, climbed the cliff and went to Millcombe House.

Fog was again the cause this time for the grounding of the 547 ton Italian barque *Paola Ravello* near the quarries on 1 September 1882, but when pulled off by tugs later that day she was found to be 'so damaged that she was run onto [the landing] beach where some 70 tons of her cargo of steam coal was discharged. She was bought by Fishwick of Appledore, refloated and taken to Barnstaple where, after repairs, she was renamed *Claudine* of Barnstaple.' At the time of her grounding there was a suspicion among the islanders that a plot was afoot similar to that centring round the *Columba* fifteen years earlier, as the captains of both vessels came from Genoa and knew each other. This was strenuously denied by the *Paola Ravello*'s captain.

Two vessels went ashore in dense fog on the morning of 13 December 1882. One was the barque *Burnswark* of 253 tons which struck near Quarter Wall while steering north-westwards in an attempt to clear the island. The crew of thirteen led by Capt. Luke was rescued by pilot cutter No. 22. The cargo of spirits, porter and tobacco was undamaged and the vessel was later towed off to Ilfracombe. The second vessel, the 388 ton wooden three-masted brigantine *Heroine* (Capt. Kirby) struck Seal Rock and 'all the crew [of ten men] came ashore in their own boats, and scaled the cliffs at the north end of the island'. The subsequent Board of Trade inquiry questioned whether a light should be shown at the south end of the island, and while the captain alleged that this would have averted the shipwreck, he was nevertheless found guilty of negligence and his certificate was suspended for three months.

The only mention in the Heaven diaries of a wreck in 1883 is that on 23 September when the *Little Ruth* caught fire and was driven on to the beach. The fire must soon have been brought under control as she was towed off two days later. The following year in thick fog on 27 June 1884 the SS *Wimbledon* and the SS *Baines Hawkins* both out of Cardiff laden with coal, struck the East Side and were stranded. Thick fog on 12 February 1885 also caused the loss of the 1,813 ton steamer *Peer of the Realm* (Capt. Knowles), which struck near Knight Templar Rock. No lives were lost and although the crew were reported to have been 'troublesome', attempts made to refloat her had to be abandoned.

The *Inversnaid*, an iron ship of 1,549 tons, bound with coal from Cardiff for Singapore, went down with her crew of thirty off Lundy in a Force 10 northerly on 16 October 1886, after narrowly missing being wrecked on the Hen and Chickens.

In January 1888 the 2,374 ton steamship *Elsie* struck Brazen Ward, again in dense fog, provoking the tenant farmer, Mr Wright, to complain that 'we have no means of saving life' – a plea which must have been noted by the Board of Trade who in 1893 provided a complete life-saving apparatus. The *Elsie* was later towed off to Cardiff, whence she resumed her voyage.

A 52-year-old 24 ton pilot cutter, the *New Prosperous*, was wrecked just north of the landing place on 14 February 1888 and later that year, on 9 May, three vessels struck in the morning fog. One was the 12 ton wooden steamtug *Electric*, which broke up on Pilot's Quay after the crew of five had escaped. The 812 ton screw-steamer *Radnor* was beached on the East Side close to where an unidentified French steamer also went aground, but which later got off undamaged.

In 1889 the *South Australian* when down off the North West Point and on 16 December the 63 ton wooden schooner *Eliza Jones* was lost on the Rattles with her crew of three.

The entire crew of the *Ashdale*, which was wrecked on 10 September 1890, landed safely, but newspaper reports were critical of their treatment by Mr Wright.

A notable feat of life-saving followed the wreck of the *Tunisie* of Bordeaux on 19 February 1892. The vessel struck near the Sugar Loaf and twenty-one Frenchmen were rescued by John McCarthy, the lighthouse keeper, who got a line to the ship using an explosive fog-signal rocket and an improvised breeches buoy made from an old coal bag. The minutes of the Royal National Lifeboat Institution record 'That the thanks of the Institution inscribed on Vellum and the sum of 15/- be presented to Mr J. McCarthy, Principal Lighthouse Keeper at Lundy Island and 15/- each to the two assistant light-keepers and eight other men for saving by means of lines the crew of 21 men from the S.S. *Tunisie* of Bordeaux which stranded under a high cliff on the east side of the island in a strong easterly gale, a snow storm and a very heavy sea on the 19th February 1892'. At a simple ceremony on Lundy in August 1892 the eleven rescuers were each presented with three sovereigns by the Revd Mr Heaven on behalf of the Board of Trade and George Thomas also received a medal inscribed with the words 'Awarded by the Board of Trade for gallantry in saving life at sea', and on the reverse with the monogram and head of Queen Victoria. The rim of the medal read 'George Thomas, wreck of the *Tunisie* on 19th February 1892'. The ship was not badly damaged and was towed off on 23 September.

Meanwhile on 21 May 1892 the fully laden British collier, the SS *Ackworth*, was stranded on Lundy in fog. The crew were taken off but the vessel sank the following day.

The SS *Charles W. Anderson* ran ashore on the beach on 13 August 1893 but was able to pull off later, though on 1 December that year the 210 ton wooden brigantine *Ismyr*, laden with coal, dragged her anchor in a choppy wind and was wrecked on the point of Rat Island with the loss of two members of her crew of eight.

Meanwhile as a result of the attention drawn to the wreck of the *Tunisie* a regulation rocket apparatus was fixed on the island and in 1893 Mr Wood was appointed to the Lloyd's signal station.

The 1,580 ton Dutch steamer *Marie* laden with coal struck the East Side in fog at 5.30 a.m. on the morning of 19 September 1895 in the same spot which the *Tunisie* had struck. Her crew of twenty-five were thought by the islanders to have 'been drunk' as it was flat calm and although the crew said that they had heard the fog-rockets and seen the flashes 'they thought they were thunder and lightning'. The vessel was later refloated.

On 11 November an unnamed vessel being towed by a tug broke its hawser off the North End. The two vessels collided and the tow capsized – 'we could not find it or anyone'.

Two small wrecks were reported in 1896. The first, that of the 12 ton wooden pilot cutter *Dyfed*, happened during a Force 10 north-easterly on 22 January while in June the schooner *Kate*, owned by Messrs Britton & Pickett of Ilfracombe and used by them to carry building materials for St Helena's church, was lost on the East Side. She was soon salvaged and continued in use.

There are five incidents recorded for 1897. The first happened in dense fog on

20 March when the 5,000 ton SS *Cam* ran ashore under Tibbett's Point. Fortunately the engines were reversed just before impact so the damage was slight, the ship being able to refloat on the high tide and to be taken to Cardiff the following day. On this very day the 2,188 ton steel steamship *Salado* with a crew of twenty-two, three passengers and a cargo of coal struck the Mouse Hole and Trap in fog in a Force 2 wind. The crew were housed in Lloyd's signal station cottages while four of them rowed to Ilfracombe to report the wreck. No lives had been lost but the ship broke up in November 1901. A few weeks later on 1 April 1897 the 51 ton wooden ketch *Millicent*, with a cargo of coal, anchored in the Roads. She sprang a leak and quickly broke up. On 19 May the ketch *Infanta*, which had come from Appledore to work on shipwrecks at Lundy, was herself wrecked at the North End. Finally, on 1 November the 45 ton steel steamship *Ballydoon*, which had sprung a leak the previous day when she struck a submerged wreck, herself sank on the West Side in an easterly Force 6 gale.

On 6 April 1898 the 2,830 ton steel screw schooner *Darial* struck in thick fog. She was refloated on the next tide but claimed that the new North Light fog signal had not been working when she struck. The 146 ton wooden wreck-barge *Rover*, which had been moored to the wrecked *Salado*, sank on 31 August 1898 during a Force 7 north-easterly when nobody was aboard. Later in the same year a similar wind on 28 November caused the 147 ton iron steamtug *Earl of Jersey* to strike a half-submerged rock at the Rattles and to founder gently, giving the crew of six ample time to escape.

Three ships struck in 1899. The first, on 31 March, was an unnamed Italian steamer under the Quarter Wall cottages. The second was the steel SS *Kaistow* of London which struck the Sugar Loaf in fog but was soon towed off on 22 May. On 6 July the 61 ton ketch *Star of St. Agnes* was wrecked on the West Side, but her crew of three 'were cared for'.

The 2,431 ton steamship *Bath City*, only five months old, was returning to Bristol from New York laden with grain and tramway equipment when at 11.15 p.m. on 14 February 1900 in bad weather and thick fog she struck the Needle Rock. The captain backed her off but she sank twenty minutes later. The crew escaped in two lifeboats and were taken to Swansea, where a roll call discovered that one crew member had been lost. Later that year, on 24 April, wreckage was discovered of the *Ruby* of Lerwick, while on 7 May the small ketch *Fiona*, laden with coal from Cardiff, was wrecked on the East Side below Quarter Wall, though all the crew escaped.

That the list of wrecks is not complete is shown by the report of the 1859 royal commission which was charged with investigating the possibility of building a harbour of refuge in the Bristol Channel. They noted that 'out of 173 wrecks in the Bristol Channel in 1856–7, 97 received their damage and 44 lives were lost east of Lundy while 76 vessels were lost or damaged and 58 lives sacrificed west of Lundy, thus showing that the island to be nearly in the centre of the dangerous parts'.

At a meeting of Bideford Council in 1904 it was said that 'over 137 lives, roughly, had been lost in the Bristol Channel area in twelve months, but in October 1886 over 300 lives were lost "inside Lundy" and from 18–20 steamers foundered'.

HMS Montagu *(unknown)*

Perhaps the most unfortunate and certainly the most famous of the wrecks that have occurred on Lundy was that of HMS *Montagu*, a first-class battleship of 14,000 tons displacement which had cost approximately £1 million to build. The *Montagu* was launched at Devonport in 1901 and completed two years later. Her speed was 19 knots and she was armed with 16 guns and had a complement of 750 men. At 2.10 a.m. on 30 May 1906 in thick fog she struck a point to the north of Great Shutter Rock, fortunately without loss of life or injury to any of the crew. She was serving with the Channel Fleet and was testing new radio equipment.

The subsequent official report of the wreck states that

it was the opinion of the Officer Commanding that they had gone ashore at or near Hartland Point, and an Officer and a small party of ratings was sent to investigate. Thinking they were south of Hartland Point they rowed northwards and landed below North Light, climbed up the very dangerous rock face and after much struggle reached the top. They then struck the path leading down to the North Light where they greatly astonished the keeper on duty by peering through the windows. So convinced was the Officer that he had landed at Hartland that 'words passed' ending when the Keeper assured him that he did really know which lighthouse he was in charge of!

This conversation weighed heavily against the commanding officer and his navigating officer at the court martial as proof of how far out they were in their reckoning. Both Capt. T.B.S. Adair and Lt. Dathan were severely reprimanded and dismissed their ship, and Lt. Dathan also lost two years' seniority. Capt. Adair retired as Rear Admiral a few months later and joined the shipbuilding firm of Beardmore & Company of Glasgow with whom he remained for twenty years.

The *Montagu* listed heavily to starboard, lost both propellers, the wireless telegraphy apparatus was shaken out of the rigging and she was holed so that several compartments, including the engine rooms, boiler rooms and stokeholds were flooded. The battleships *Duncan*, *Albermarle*, *Cornwallis* and *Exmouth* (flagship of Admiral Sir A.K. Wilson), the cruiser *Aeolus*, and several tugs were ordered to go immediately to the scene of the accident; the Liverpool Salvage Association dispatched 'two of their finest salvage steamers afloat, the *Ranger* and the *Linnet* . . . with eight powerful steam pumps and a full equipment of salvage appliances and a large staff of divers under the command of Capt. F.W. Young'. There were rumours that a floating dock was to be brought from Bermuda to receive the *Montagu* when refloated.

On 1 June 'the Commander in Chief with *Aeolus*, *Empress* and *Industry* with two lighters in tow' arrived and at once began to remove as much as possible from the *Montagu* in an attempt to lighten her, prior to refloating. The following day, one of the lighters which was carrying four 6 in guns and torpedo nets from the *Montagu* sank at the Rattles, but it was hoped that the vessel would 'ebb dry on the spring tides about the middle of the month'. The following day yet another battleship, the *Mars*, was ordered to Lundy to help.

By the time the SS *Ranger* arrived on 26 August it had become clear that the *Montagu* was a total wreck. The *Ranger* removed the fore 12 in guns early in September and completed the removal of the aft guns by the end of the month, during which time HMS *Doris* was 'in attendance'. Seaborne work ended in October and the following months were spent in rivalry between the Admiralty salvage and civilian salvage.

The wreck was sold to a consortium in 1907 for £4,250 – less than half of 1 per cent of the cost to the taxpayer of this modern ship only five years previously. A 500 yd aerial footway was strung between the ship's charthouse and the cliff head from where a path cut into the cliff allowed safe access for the salvors who were living on the island. The scrap was ferried to Ilfracombe and operations continued at intervals until as late as 1922. Loyd, writing in 1925, said that the barbettes were still visible at low water, but today no trace remains above water though the cliff path with its steps cut down to the site of the aerial footway is still called Montagu Steps.

The 815 ton *Auricula* ran aground near the *Montagu* on 1 May 1908 but was later refloated. During a severe gale in November 1909 the *Thistlemore*, on passage from

A 'Kaaksburg' propellor and 12 in shell from HMS Montagu

Cardiff to Cape Town, was sheltering in the Roads when her boilers blew up killing all the crew except for nine. The fate is not recorded of the sailing vessel *Augoustis* which ran aground on 30 November 1912 in Halfway Bay. In 1913 the SS *Clutha River* went aground on the island but was later refloated and towed to Cardiff where she was beached on the mud flats for inspection and repair.

The first recorded wreck of the First World War occurred when the 151 ton three-masted schooner *Arthur Edward* struck just north of Jenny's Cove on 1 January 1917. One man, an Australian, was drowned but the mainmast broke and fortunately fell against the cliff so allowing three men to clamber along it to safety before the wreck was washed away. On 20 August the 532 ton Norwegian steamer *Knatten* caught fire off the west coast. The crew managed to escape in boats but the steamer drifted with the tide on to the Hen and Chickens where she broke up. A gale later that year on 19 September caused the Glasgow schooner *Mary Orr* to drag her anchors while sheltering in the Roads. She was abandoned and her crew of four were taken to Ilfracombe by the Ilfracombe lifeboat. Finally, on 30 November 1917 two steam trawlers, the *Courage* and the *Gazelle*, were both stranded on Lundy.

The war had ended when on 5 December 1918 the 2,214 ton SS *Enfield* was stranded at the quarries. The crew of thirty-five escaped injury and the following April the ship was refloated.

In 1927 the *Annie-Kate*, a Padstow herring boat owned and used by two fishermen who lived and worked from the island during the season, tore its moorings while tied in the cove and with the rising tide was thrown on to the shoreside boulders and there damaged beyond repair.

Two years later, on 25 March 1929, the 1,556 ton Greek steamer *Maria Kyriakides* ran aground in almost the same spot as the *Enfield* at the quarries. Her crew were saved and after seventeen months the ship was refloated and taken to Ilfracombe, where after repairs it was relaunched as the *Newlands*.

Mr M.C. Harman reached an agreement with the Board of Trade on 25 November 1929 that he would report movements of shipping around the island and maintain the rocket life-saving apparatus in an efficient condition. He also undertook to carry out four drills a year and to pay the volunteers for any drills or services to wrecks that it might perform. Within two years the team, led by Mr Gade, was called upon to rescue the crew of twenty-four from the Greek SS *Taxiarchis* which had been driven ashore on 29 March 1931 at the quarries. Again this wreck was refloated and after two years was towed to the mainland for scrap.

On 20 October 1933 the cutter *Mayflower* had requested a tow to Lundy but the skipper apparently cast off the tow before the *Mayflower* had reached the safety of Lundy's Landing Bay. The boat was sighted in the tidal ebb and flow around Surf Point. The Appledore lifeboat was called but found nobody on board: the owner, an eccentric and apparently penniless character named Bolitho had vanished without trace. The abandoned *Mayflower* was towed into the bay where it was anchored. During the night the wind increased and in the morning the boat was discovered, reduced to matchwood, on the beach.

Outward bound from Cardiff to Genoa with a cargo of coal, the 5,287 ton Italian steamship *Carmine Filomena* (Capt. Attilio) struck Rat Island in morning fog on 2 July 1937. The crew landed safely but the ship soon broke into two and became a total loss. Only eleven days later the SS *Nellie*, a Belgian ship of 640 tons and then only one month old, turned turtle after striking the Hen and Chickens, where she sank. The crew were all rescued by the SS *Ranger*.

The SS *Greyfriars* (Capt. Husband) of 1,142 tons, on passage from Plymouth to Swansea, reported on arrival that she had been ashore on Lundy on 11 February 1939 but subsequent drydock inspection showed that she had suffered negligible damage.

Just before the outbreak of the Second World War Dr J. Sewart, his wife and four children were rescued when their 12 ton motor yacht *Freckles*, which had been converted from a former RNLI lifeboat, was swept on to the wreck of the *Carmine Filomena*, where she broke up and sank on 13 August 1939.

Five incidents occurred around Lundy during the Second World War. The first was on 27 January 1940 when the SS *Halton*, a 460 ton vessel registered in Liverpool with a cargo of coal outward bound from Cardiff, ran aground on the beach after being holed at the Knoll Pins. She was repaired and later towed off.

On 23 March 1941 the trawler *Kestrel* was beached after an attack by a German warplane during which the mate was killed. A salvage crew managed to weld up the bullets holes in the hull and the trawler was able to reach Ilfracombe. Very soon afterwards a similar attack forced the Norwegian ship *Knoll* to beach and make temporary repairs.

The 335 ton Dutch ship *Atlas*, sailing in ballast from Hayle in Cornwall to a port in the Bristol Channel, had been requested to join the first available convoy, but the master, making his first trip in her, decided to set off alone. At 2 a.m. on the morning of 9 October 1942 in poor visibility, during a Force 6 westerly gale, the vessel struck just north of the Great Shutter Rock. There was only one survivor from the ship which quickly broke up and sank.

The final wartime victim was the SS *Alcoa Master* of New York, which grounded on Rat Island on 17 February 1945 but was refloated with the tide.

In the early hours of 18 July 1948 in calm weather but in thick fog the Dutch MV *Amstelstroom* of 395 tons stranded on the West Side just north of the Battery. The impact was so gentle that the crew of eleven were able to walk over the bow which was touching the cliffs and clamber up to safety.

Mr Summersby, the then resident fisherman, lost his boat the *Ella Trout* in 1950 when it sank at its moorings and in heavy weather on 9 September 1952 two launches belonging to Messrs P. and A. Campbell, the *Cambria* and *Devonia* broke adrift and were lost.

During the winter of 1954/5 a tug that was towing a condemned LCT (Landing Craft Tank) was in trouble to the north-west of the island. The tow parted and the LCT, with no men aboard, struck immediately north of Battery Point and within a month had broken up and disappeared.

The yacht *Elan* of Minehead lost its moorings in bad weather on 15 September 1968 and smashed to pieces on the Sentinels. Fortunately the owner and mate had left the yacht earlier and were able to spend the night in the cave on the slipway. The following day the Campbell launch *Waverley* sank.

The yacht *Sarcas* of Newport was struck by an easterly gale while moored in the Landing Bay, causing it to drag its anchor and to be dashed on to the beach, resulting in irreparable damage.

On the morning of 6 November 1980 at 2.30 a.m. and after three days of easterly gales, two German ships were heard in agitated conversation on a distress radio frequency. After a few minutes the *Padberg* broadcast a Mayday distress signal that the *Kaaksburg*, a 468 ton coaster, was ashore on the East Side of Lundy after her engines had failed. A Dutch trawler, the RNLI lifeboat 70–001 and a Sea King helicopter at once made for the island. Meanwhile the *Kaaksburg* radioed that she had a crew of seven, was in ballast and was hard aground with her engine room flooded. The Lundy Coastguard Rescue Company reached the scene at the north end of the quarries, to be joined by the RAF rescue helicopter which reported no sign of life on the vessel, but faint lights above it on the cliffs. The coastguards and helicopter winchman climbed down to meet the crew, who were in nightclothes, and were able to help them reach the summit from where they were flown to RAF Chivenor. The vessel soon became a total loss, broke her back, and during the winter of 1981/2 the aft portion slipped back into deep water and sank. The bow had been driven hard into the cliff-face, where it has since slowly disintegrated.

As recently as 1983 the MV *Inshaalah* broke her moorings in rough weather on 6 June and was driven ashore, where she became a total loss.

Undoubtedly radar has already reduced, and satellite technology will still further reduce, such hazards as Lundy presents to shipping but the walls of the Marisco Tavern will continue to carry, as reminders of the past, the relics from wrecks. There are life belts from the *Carmine Filomena, Cambria, Maria Kyriakides, Atlas, Devonia, Taxiarchis, Elan, Waverley, Amstelstroom* and *Halton*. There is a piece of timber from the *Ella Trout*, the flag from the *Freckles*, and lanterns from the *Nellie, Kestrel* and *Mayflower*. There is also part of a rescue rocket with a brass plaque inscribed:

This rocket was fired by F.W. Gade at the rescue of 24 lives from the Greek ship *Taxiarchis* which ran ashore on Lundy 28th March 1931. Rocket Crew: F.W. Gade; S. Stookes; J. Crews; C. Smaldon; J. Bament. Assisted by Mrs F.W. Gade and Mrs Morryot.

Chapter Eighteen

LIGHTHOUSES

The need to warn shipping of Lundy's presence became more urgent towards the close of the eighteenth century because of the rapid rise in the volume of shipping drawn to the busy and expanding port of Bristol.

Navigation then lacked the many refinements known today and the position of the island across the channel, with its dangerous rocks and tidal races, constituted a serious hazard to sailing vessels. Trinity House Minute Book for 7 September 1751 records a letter from Thomas Benson 'praying the Corporation to give their opinion on the erection of a lighthouse on the said Island of Lundy'. The clerk was ordered to reply to Benson explaining the correct procedures to be adopted.

Four months later the minute book records another letter from Benson and also three petitions – one from Bristol, one from Bideford and one from Clovelly 'setting forth that the erection of a light on the Island of Lundy will not be so useful as on Hartland Point . . . '. However, by 1786 the merchants of Bristol had changed their minds and now considered the danger to be so great that they offered to build a lighthouse and maintain it at their own expense if the then owner, Mr Cleveland, was agreeable.

Whether the 'plan . . . suggested by Capt Rogers of Hayle in Cornwall for erecting a Lighthouse on the island of Lundy; which in appearance and effect will be totally different from every light in England'[1] was in the mind of Mr Cleveland when his party decided that the highest point and therefore the most suitable for the lighthouse was on Beacon Hill is not clear. However, on the afternoon of 7 July 1787 'they laid the foundations for illuminating the island and the surrounding element'.[2]

Lundy proved the perfect rendezvous for pilots awaiting incoming ships and a suitable setting-down point for ships heading for the open sea. The earliest reference to pilotage dates from 3 October 1782, when Mr William Walters was taken aboard one of His Majesty's ships at Lundy to pilot her 'safely up to Flat Holmes'. Pilot's Quay on the West Side would seem to date from this time, used when landings on the beach were not possible. On early nineteenth-century maps the site is marked as 'Pile's Quay' and as one of the recorded pilots is so named, it seems likely that he pioneered its use.

By 1807 the need for pilotage had so increased that Parliament passed the Bristol Wharfage Act which decreed that 'from the first day of October next after the passing of this Act all vessels sailing, navigating or passing up down or upon the Bristol Channel to the eastward of Lundy Island (except coasting vessels and Irish traders) shall be conducted, piloted and navigated by Pilots'. The procedure adopted was for a pilot to join ship on leaving port and later to join a homeward bound ship. Fog and wind sometimes made this impracticable and at least one pilot was obliged to continue with his charge to New York.[3]

In their heyday pilots would walk to Beacon Hill with their telescopes to catch sight of an expected vessel bound for the channel ports, and then when sighted would rush down to up-anchor and hoist sail to waylay her for pilotage. This often meant a race between other pilot boats to reach their quarry first, especially if another boat was cruising off or under the lee of the island.

This happy period when pilots waited on Lundy was to last only just over fifty years as the Bristol Channel Pilotage Act of 1861 allowed vessels bound to and from Cardiff, Newport or Gloucester to proceed in the Bristol Channel without pilots. The need for pilotage was further curtailed in 1891 when the area of compulsory pilotage was reduced to the limits of the port of Bristol and was served by pilots based there.

In 1928 the Treasury confirmed that Barnstaple should continue as a port, and defined its limits: 'Lundy Island in the Bristol Channel and the sea surrounding it to a distance of three miles from low water mark, shall form the Port of Barnstaple. This Warrant annuls all former limits of the Port of Barnstaple as from April 18th [1928].'[4]

Once Trinity House had made the decision to build a lighthouse a survey was made in 1817 marking the bearings to mainland features from the two short-listed possible sites – one on Beacon Hill and the other some 500 yd northwards on a 'High Hill, six feet [lower than] Chapel Grounds.' (Engineers Office. Drawing No. 1317.)

The Trinity House Engineers Office Drawing No. 1318 taken in February 1819 concentrates on bearings from Beacon Hill and shows that the more northerly site had been rejected. At a meeting of the Trinity House Board on 29 April 1819 the deputy master reported that an 'agreement had been entered into with Sir Aubrey de Vere Hunt for two acres of the land, at a rate of 15 guineas per annum, on lease for 999 years and to pay the Proprietor . . . for the right of quarrying all such stone as may be requisite . . . for the sum of £500'. On agreement to this, Capts. Lewin and Gooch were sent 'to select a proper scite [sic] for the Light-House'. On 27 May 1819 they recommended 'Chapel-Hill as the fittest situation . . . the height of the tower to be 80 feet'.

All was agreed and the lease signed on 1 July. Construction began at once obliterating completely any remains of an earlier fire beacon, from which the hill took its name, that had served either as a maritime warning or as part of a national anti-invasion alarm.

The buildings were designed by Daniel Asher Alexander and built by Joseph Nelson within one year. The 96 ft high tower was of advanced design incorporating cavity-construction 3 ft 6 in thick at the base rising to 2 ft thick at the lantern with a

The Old Light, 1889 (unknown)

consistent cavity of 3 in. There were 147 steps leading to the lantern which was decorated with wrought-iron balusters. The cost of quarrying the granite was £10,276 19s 11d; the tower cost £9,781 17s 11d and the adjacent buildings £395 2s – the total complex costing in all £36,000.[5]

Mr Nelson returned for three months in 1826 with a team of eighteen men to build 'two or three small buildings' in the lighthouse yard.

When the light was first brought into use on 21 February 1820 the upper light, rotated by clockwork, showed a flash every two minutes and was visible for some 32 miles. Originally fitted with reflecting mirrors to form a catoptric system, the light was replaced on 1 November 1840 at a cost of £1,902 18s 4d by a dioptric system using '24 zones of prisms'. The lower light consisted originally of a row of nine red lamps hung 30 ft below, under the stone canopy that can still be seen on the west face of the tower. These lights were visible over 90 degrees from NNW to WSW and the angle of the canopy was so arranged that the light was visible to ships only when they were 4 miles or less from the island, so serving as a warning that they would have to alter course if they wished to clear the island. If course were not altered the light disappeared completely on being interrupted by the cliff's summit and when this happened the danger was imminent.

Unfortunately, experience showed that at certain distances the red light merged with the upper light, thus rendering it ineffective as a warning. In an attempt to counter this, a room some 3.5 m by 2 m was built in 1829 at the foot of the tower and was in use from 1835 until 1842. Behind a glass window were 'placed nine hemispherical reflectors made of copper, polished and silvered within their concavity. They are set in two rows, four above five, arranged in the arc of a large circle. A lamp is placed in the focal centre of each, the smoke which is led off by a tube, passing through each reflector to a common chimney behind.'[6] Although this had a range of 25 miles it proved difficult to see the lower coloured light at any distance, but the greatest disadvantage, as Mr Heaven wrote in April 1858, was that 'The Light is not of the slightest use to vessels when most in want of it, in thick and blowing weather, but also in many dark nights, because when the island itself is free from it, the Lighthouse stands so high that it is capped by fog.' He suggested 'low lighthouses on north and south extremities of the island, one with bell and the other with gong or cannon'. The Elder Brethren were still considering the additional marking of the island but proposed 'to place a gun on the west side of the island'.

A site was agreed, two 18-pounder guns were brought to Lundy and on the West Side cliffs, at a spot since known as the Battery, the two guns were mounted in a gun house and the building of a powder room, plus a pair of cottages to house the

Signal Rock at the Battery, c. *1890 (unknown)*

gunners and their families, completed the emplacement. During fog one gun was fired every ten minutes, and on one occasion the firing lasted for seventy-two hours without interruption. The principal lightkeeper was paid £65 per annum and his deputy £46 10s, each with a suit of clothes annually and coal, oil and furniture for the dwelling. The Battery gunners were paid £45 per annum and £39 per annum plus similar perquisites, but the three-roomed cottages were really inadequate for the two gunners and their families. Gunner Blackmore, 'an inveterate poacher', had seven children who were obliged to run up the sideland and hide when the visiting Trinity House yacht was sighted, only being allowed to return home when the Brethren had started for the beach!

Trinity House ordered that the buildings on Beacon Hill be enclosed and in 1865 the wall surrounding their property was built. For an uncertain reason the Battery guns were not used after 1 August 1878 when cotton powder rockets were substituted. In 1881 the Elder Brethren considered moving the lower lights from the lighthouse to the Battery and actually experimented with bells, hooters and communication whistles, but when these all proved unsatisfactory laid plans in 1886 to place a rocket station at the South End and a siren at the North. These schemes were delayed for financial reasons until, in 1896, Mr Heaven's scheme for the building of two new lighthouses, one at either end of Lundy, was begun.

The lighthouses were completed in the following year when machinery from the Old Light was dismantled and taken by cart to a wooden platform built at Benson's Cave, just below the castle, from where it was carried by aerial cableway to the South Light. The substantial bungalow in the Old Light compound which had been the residence of the principal keeper (Mr J. McCarthy until 1889, and J. Trehair from 1893) was also dismantled by the contractors, who were housed in temporary wooden huts just to the east of the present-day South Light wall.

With the surrender of its right of way across the island, Trinity House abandoned the Battery while leaving the cannon in place. The buildings have not been used since and are now in ruins. The Old Light was similarly abandoned but it was soon used as holiday accommodation and when Martin Coles Harman founded the Lundy Field Society in 1946 he allowed the Old Light and the adjoining buildings to be used as a headquarters and as accommodation for visiting members. Until 1952 the building also housed the radio transmitter, whose aerial was suspended from the tower. The tower and lantern were restored and reglazed and extensive work on all the buildings was completed by the Landmark Trust in 1982, since when the keepers' quarters have become two holiday flats.

The lantern at South Light is mounted in a 16 m tower, built at 53 m above mean high water in the south-east corner of the island on the Lametor promontory. The original paraffin burner had a candlepower of 40,000 with a maximum of 60,000 and every minute showed a flash which was visible for over 19 miles. In 1925 the mechanism was modified to flash every thirty seconds. The entire apparatus was replaced in 1962 by a 1,000 watt electric lamp powered by duplicate 1,500 watt generators producing a flash for a third of a second every five seconds and visible for 24 miles. In thick weather when the Knoll Pins were not visible from the lighthouse a signal charge of 4 oz of Tonite (a form of gunpowder) was detonated every three minutes, for which the keepers received a bonus of 6*d* an hour. Originally supplies were raised to the lighthouse by a winch and fixed cable worked by a steam-driven donkey engine, but improvements in 1960 substituted a diesel motor and the explosive fog-signal was replaced by a compressed-air horn blowing at twenty-five second intervals. The buildings were rewired at 240 volts and from 1970 the keepers were entrusted to make observations as Meteorological Office No. 702. The winch house and cables at both lighthouses have been removed as all Trinity House supplies are now brought ashore by helicopter.

The North Light stood in a tower 17 m high and 50 m above mean high water at the North West Point. It cost £45,000 to build and gives a flash of 81,000 candlepower every twenty seconds. Two powerful compressed-air horns were originally installed and together with the disturbance caused during the building work are thought finally to have driven nesting gannets from the island. The radio beacon, added in 1927, transmitted the morse letters NL automatically every five minutes.

In 1976 a cable was laid, underground for most of its length, between South Light and North Light to enable the latter to be operated as a slave station by the South Light keepers. The North Light keepers' quarters were abandoned, the overhead landline and telegraph poles were removed, the original North Light

The North Light

lantern was replaced and the original air-driven foghorns were replaced by electronic loudspeakers. The new speakers which sounded the morse letter N every thirty seconds during fog were in use until 1987 when the North Light went silent.

Meanwhile in 1985 earthworks were begun to install a new modular lighthouse at North End but this was abandoned after a few weeks' work as agreement could not be reached. Similarly plans to build a helicopter landing pad on the roof of the quarters were never implemented.

Early in 1991 the lantern in the North Light tower was abandoned to be replaced by a compact but equally powerful light, powered partly by a bank of solar cells installed on the roof of the disused foghorn house, which building has now been physically separated from the original staff quarters and light tower. Control of this new light is effected by radio from Nash Lighthouse across the channel, so rendering obsolete the underground cable which formerly controlled Lundy North from Lundy South. However, with modern satellite communication now carried on the smallest of vessels, the entire future of the lighthouse service is under discussion.

The duties of the four keepers at South Light are divided into periods of four hours' watch followed by eight hours off duty during a twelve hour period. Lundy is classified as a rock station but is probably the most attractive of all such postings as keepers are able to move about the island and visit the stores and tavern.

Chapter Nineteen

GEOLOGY

The first complete geological study of Lundy was made by Dr A.T.J. Dollar, who described Lundy's granite mass as 'the denuded core of far more lofty mountains piled up during the Armorican folding . . . half liquid magma pushes up into the cavities at the base of the mountainous folds of rock and solidifies. Then, as millions of years go by with their millions of seasons of rain and frost . . . denude . . . the . . . masses . . . until a time may be reached when the granite core, the solidified magma so much harder than the overlying rocks is all that remains.'[1]

'Up to the early 1960s the Lundy complex was assumed to be of Hercynian (Carboniferous) age, a view reinforced by the similarity of the granites of South West England. However, age dating of the granite in 1962 (Dodson & Long) indicated that the granite and dykes were of Tertiary age.' The granite was dated in 1990 at 59 million years (by Thorpe et al. 1990) and as a result of the analysis of samples of dyke rocks collected in 1988, Thorpe and Tindle suggest that Lundy may have been the site of a Tertiary volcano. Such a volcano is conjectured to have been about 20 km in diameter and these findings are supported by recent (1991) geomagnetic investigation.[2]

This Tertiary igneous area extends to the Faroes, Iceland, Greenland, Jan Mayen and Spitzbergen, and although volcanic activity in Britain lasted for only a brief period, it is still prevalent further north, as in Iceland.

The south-east corner of Lundy is all that now remains of the original overlying slates formed 170 million years ago. This now joins the granite in a distinct line from the Sugar Loaf to the Rattles. The slate is similar to the Morte slates of North Devon and may be called Upper Devonian.

The island plateau, which forms an almost level marine plane similar to many in southern England at the 400 ft contour, is bounded on all sides by steeply inclined sidelands, at the base of which are vertical cliffs.

Of the several intrusive dykes of igneous rocks, one which rises vertically near the Landing Beach presents a large face which prevents the further erosion of the shale between the castle and the South Light. This unique microgranite has been named Lundyite.

Dollar classified the Eocene granite into three types: G1, which is an even-grained white orthoclase variety; G2, a variety with phenocrysts of orthoclase and quartz set in a microgranite groundmass; and G3 and G3a which are microgranites.

Virtually all the streams have developed along the joint-planes in the granite or along the dip and strike of the slates, and their erosive action has been minimal. These stream valleys fall into two systems – that in the northern part of the island is known collectively as Gannets' Combe and drains eastwards. The volume of water in the main Gannets' Combe stream is no greater than that in the Punchbowl stream which is the largest stream on the West Side of the island and whose valley is considerably smaller than Gannets' Combe. The presence of gravels and roche moutonées near the North End led Mitchell[3] to believe that an ice sheet had passed over this area which, on retreating, had allowed the outflow to deposit gravels and to carve Gannets' Combe. Mitchell believed that the rest of the island stood up as a nunatak above the ice surface. Recently it has been argued that the gravels noted by Mitchell are in fact the remnants of imported gravel used by GPO engineers when they cemented in the telephone poles in 1910. Taylor[4] believes that Millcombe and St John's Valley at the southern end of the island and which drain most of the island south of the lighthouse wall, began as U-shaped valleys, but as such do not extend right down to sea-level. St John's Valley is in a hanging position in relation to Millcombe at the confluence of the two valleys, and Millcombe ends at 55 m (180 ft) above sea-level. Below this the valley is 'very youthful' until it drops over the cliff-edge in a small waterfall.

Many of the tors and granite ridges around the coastal strip have been eroded into regular shapes so that they look like steps and many of them are at levels that correspond with late Pliocene and early Pleistocene sea-levels. On the adjoining North Devon coast these levels are known as the Georgeham 131 m (430 ft) and Instow 85 m (280 ft) levels. It is conceivable that much of the island's plateau surface above the 120 m (400 ft) contour can be correlated to the Georgeham level and the Logan Stone at Halfway Wall corresponds to this height. The Instow level relates to many island features. The raised cliffs at Jenny's Cove all have their base at 85 m and The Cheeses, which extend down to sea-level, have a step at 85 m. On the East Side there are raised beach remnants and Hangman's Hill is most interesting. Here the small eminence is separated from the main part of the main sideland slope by a col at 85 m. This col is on the line of the dolerite dyke which separates the granite from the slate and is also in a direct line with the upper section of the Millcombe stream.

With the change from Georgeham to Instow levels, streams would have established themselves in order to drain the enlarged island. With no great catchment area the small streams would barely have cut furrows in the island's surface and their line must be much the same as the higher stream levels today. They have naturally developed along the joint systems in the granite and down the dip slope of the slates. The predecessors of the Millcombe and St John's Valley streams presumably flowed, as do all other stream valleys, straight down the dip slope of the slate into the sea. But a little stream-capturing took place and St John's

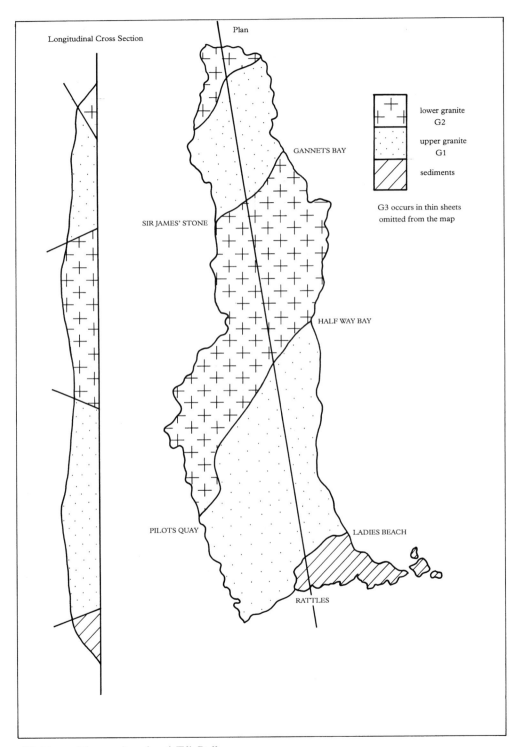

Longitudinal Cross Section

Plan

GANNETS BAY

SIR JAMES' STONE

HALF WAY BAY

PILOTS QUAY

LADIES BEACH

RATTLES

lower granite
G2

upper granite
G1

sediments

G3 occurs in thin sheets
omitted from the map

Divisions of the granite, after A.T.J. Dollar

stream could have developed a tributary along the strike of the slate at a point near the present Millcombe House gates. As this developed northwards it would have captured the upper waters of the Millcombe stream, so that the abandoned course through the col by Hangman's Hill would be left high and dry. At this stage the valley systems would still have been V-shaped and not U-shaped as today.

While the 85 m level shows up on the coast and in the col, it does not show up in the southern stream valleys and Taylor believes this shows that some other force had been in action.

Mitchell believes that the ice which reached the Isles of Scilly also passed Lundy but only reached the 106 m (350 ft) contour. He suggests that the part of the island above this height stood up as a nunatak, even though it would have been a low one. He bases this on features at the North End of the island without considering those at the south. Northern features are roches moutonées, erratics, and Gannets' Combe Valley system, which Mitchell believes was cut by melt-water. The type of erratics suggests that the ice came from the Irish Sea area to the north-west of Lundy. Some of the ice would pass over the lower parts of the island, but some would be deflected south by the island mass until it was possibly thick enough to traverse the southern end of the island. The area to the south of Beacon Hill, where the ice could have passed over to the east, is almost flat just below the 122 m (400 ft) contour. In part it is hummocky ground and one area to the west of the church has been the site of sand excavation. This area is drained by the Millcombe and St John's Valley streams and it would have been quite straightforward for the ice to pass down these valleys and widen and overdeepen them. As any ice passing over this area would have reached Millcombe before St John's Valley, the latter would have been excavated to a lesser extent and this would explain its hanging character.

K.S. Gardner[5] had earlier suggested that Lundy formed a Mesolithic peninsula at the southern edge of the River Severn based on seismic surveys which show a flooded river valley system at −150 ft. Gardner suggests that the post-glacial sea-level at −150 ft existed in the Bristol Channel until early Mesolithic times and that Lundy last became an island about 7000 BC.

Of the many minerals present on Lundy two have been investigated in the hope that they might be commercially workable. Copper ore is found at the junction of the granite and slate just east of Benjamin's Chair and three adits were driven there in the nineteenth century as were three adits similarly driven at Long Roost.[6] During the Second World War an inspector visited Lundy to see if the molybdenum ore, of which there was then a shortage, could be worked. All these commercial investigations came to nothing.

Other minerals recorded are:

Beryl	in small white-yellow columnar crystals
Felspar	in white tubular crystals
Fluor	crystalline and massive
Garnet	

Mica	in plates and hexagonal crystals
Rock crystal	transparent, frequently dark brown or black
Schorl	
Thorian uraninite	(Thorpe 1990) ((U2Th)02)
Xenotime	(Thorpe 1990)
Ytterbium phosphate	(YP04)
China clay	formed from disintegrating felspar, present in small quantities but too impregnated with iron to be useful

In the slate are veins and strings of Gossan containing:

Blende	sulphuret of zinc in traces
Towanite	copper pyrites
Magnetite	magnetic iron ore, found in a vein below Benjamin's Chair
Quartz	amorphous and crystalline found in veins crossing the slate in every direction. This is the most abundant non-metallic mineral
Limestone	a seam appears on the Landing Beach and passes south-eastwards through Hell's Gates. This fault of a soluble mineral probably accounts for the separation of Rat Island from the main island.

Chapter Twenty

THE GRANITE QUARRIES

Willi
illiam Hudson Heaven bought Lundy in 1834 with money acquired in recompense for his estates in Jamaica following the emancipation of the slaves. He soon discovered that it was more expensive to maintain a pleasant family seat on an offshore island than on the mainland and he quickly sought ways to augment his income.

The commercial possibilities of Lundy are few. Tourism and holidays, as we know them, were non-existent before the coming of the railways and the island had little accommodation to offer would-be sportsmen. The island's one asset was its granite and with the Industrial Revolution gaining pace there was a big demand for stone, not only for such public works as city kerbstones and gateposts and lintels for factories, but also for the ecclesiastical demands of the Gothic Revival church builders and the monumental masons of the municipal cemeteries.

William Heaven, already mortgaged and in debt to his relations, leased the island on 31 August 1862 for fourteen years to a Mr W.C. McKenna on the following terms:

> Lease of the island, with the exemption of the reserved portion (see map) with the right to quarry, work and remove granite. Right of access and right to build as necessary and to construct tramways etc.
>
> Annual Rent £500.
>
> Shooting, fishing, right to collect eggs and mushrooms excluded from rights accorded to tenant.
>
> Term of 14 years at a yearly rent of £500 plus £200 per annum rent of granite and royalties of 6d per ton on pitching stone and 3d per ton on rubble waste; these royalties part of the £200. [That is, the £200 was payable whether the granite was sold or not, and more was payable if the royalties due exceeded £200.]
>
> The stone to be weighed and the weighing to be notified to the lessors who are entitled to be present.
>
> The lessee to be responsible for repairs to the Farm, existing buildings, and buildings he erected, with the exception of roofs and outer walls of buildings already existing.

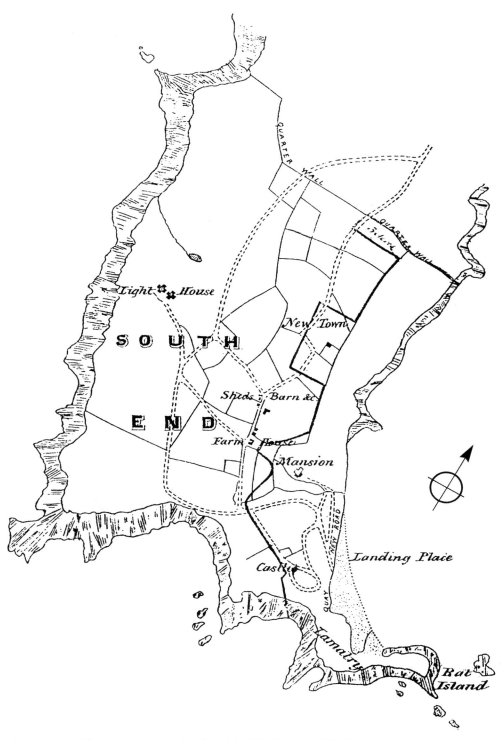

A photocopy of the map accompanying the original deed between Mr McKenna and Mr Heaven

The Lessee to spend at least £100 per year in the first seven years in draining and fencing the agricultural land and there are specifications of a general nature about the cultivation of the farm.

The lessee to provide transport for the lessors, their servants and visitors, stores, provisions, luggage and effects, both by boat and by haulage on the island. Also to land and haul coal, culm and fuel at stated rates of charges. The lessee undertakes to dismiss any staff to whom objection is made by the lessors.

The lessee to supply farm produce at fair average market price.

The lease is terminable after 7 years, renewable after 14 years.[1]

From the map accompanying the original deed (see opposite), the demarcation line drawn by Mr Heaven explains many of the subsequent walls and boundaries. The enclosure of what was to become the Tillage Field forced the main East Side path on to its present, straighter, course, the curved wall separating St Helen's Field from Millcombe Valley runs almost parallel to an earlier wall, traces of both of which are still visible and the curved partition skirting the common as far as the crossroads at the head of St John's Valley was to be replaced by the battlemented wall in 1872.

On 10 July 1863 W.C. McKenna transferred this lease of the island to his brother J.N. (later Sir Joseph) McKenna, a director of the National Bank who was about to float the Lundy Granite Company Ltd with a capital of £25,000.

The Lundy Granite Company agreed to pay W.C. McKenna 1s a ton for granite block with a guarantee of at least 4,000 tons annually, 6d a ton for the rubble, with a rent of £500 a year for the farm.

The company prospectus was issued on 18 July 1863 and work began immediately. Trial pits were dug in many places and these were characterized by clean vertical cuts where the prospects of finding good stone must have seemed justified. Two of the largest are the High Pond Quarry on Acklands Moor (1324.4476) and the Rocket Pole Pool (1347.4366), both of which have now filled with water. There are further trials around the Rocket Pole Pool – two to the north, two to the south, and a large depression to the east. Other trials, which were probably abandoned at an early stage, are the two ponds just to the east of the main path on the north side of Quarter Wall, which again have now filled with water. There are further pits west of St Helena's church and others east of Pondsbury.

Evidence of the Granite Company's attempts to farm the island can be found on many of the large stones or outcrops occurring in the island's fields. Attempts have been made to split these to make removal easier and lines of drilled holes, each of exactly ¾ in, 1 in, or 1¼ in diameter, can be found where attempts have been abandoned. The company tendered 'for a large contract for supplying granite to the Thames Embankment and sent up a specially picked stone as a sample'.[2] *The Times* of 28 October 1863 reported that the company had 'received a contract to supply stone for the first section of the Thames Embankment'. On this optimistic news the company capital was soon raised to £100,000 in £5 shares of which 15,480 were

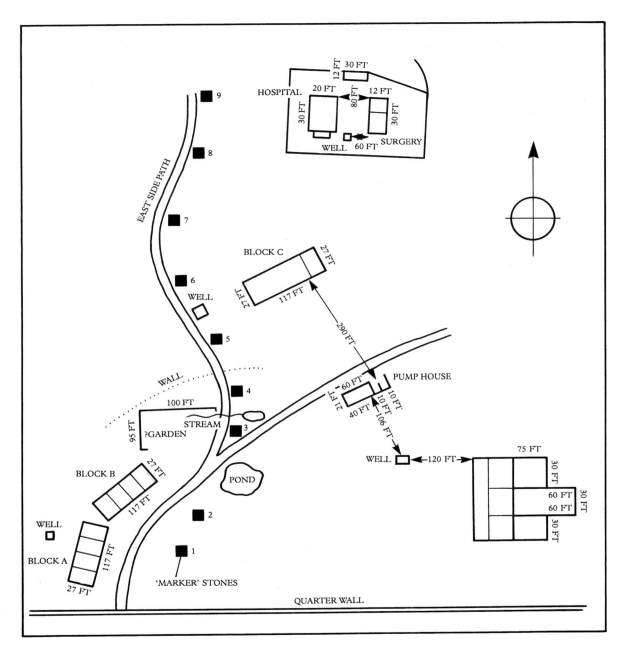

The Quarter Wall Village, Lundy, 1863–8

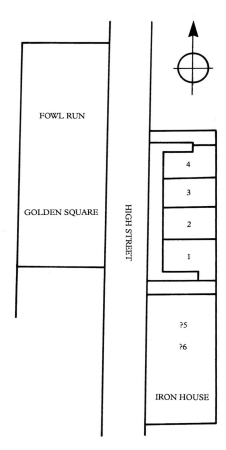

The Lundy Granite Company's buildings on High Street. Apart from the dwellings in the Fowl Run, it is known from census returns that there were six other dwellings and the 'Iron House'. These almost certainly include the four Barton Cottages. It is known that the 'Iron House' stood on the present-day site of the sheep dip, as probably did the other two dwellings

taken up, providing over £77,000 of working capital. Even Mr Heaven was honoured and appears to have been awarded a medal inscribed: '1862 LONDINII. HONORIS CAUSA' with 'Wm H Heaven Class III' around the rim.[3]

Apparently the first consignment of stone did not live up to the quality of the sample, the contract was cancelled and Lundy granite was not used for the Thames Embankment.[4] A rumour that it was to be used for the building of Charing Cross Station Hotel seems most unlikely.

They engaged fifty stone-cutters from Scotland on a three years' agreement at 5s a day and housed them in temporary buildings. 'Where the Fowlrun now is were three or four dormatories . . . wooden buildings covered with felt, tarred black, and in derision called "Golden Square", and the "Iron Hall", built on the site of the present sheepdip and probably used as a refectory, was taken away by the insolvent Granite Company'.[5]

Once permanent building was possible, the company quickly built two blocks, one of four, the other of five houses to the north of Quarter Wall and a further block

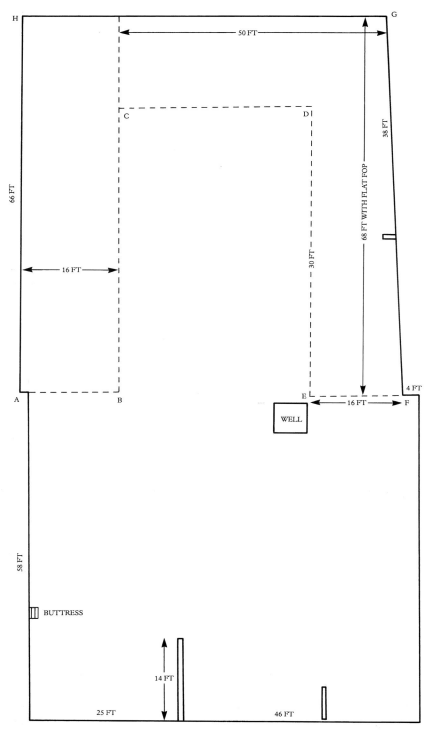

The Fowl Run, 1989. This enclosure, now known as the Fowl Run, would appear to be the site of 'Golden Square', constructed by the Granite Company and containing six dwellings. The area ABCDEFGHA shows evidence of dwellings of 25 ft frontage and 16 ft depth. Scale: 1 cm = 7 ft (approx)

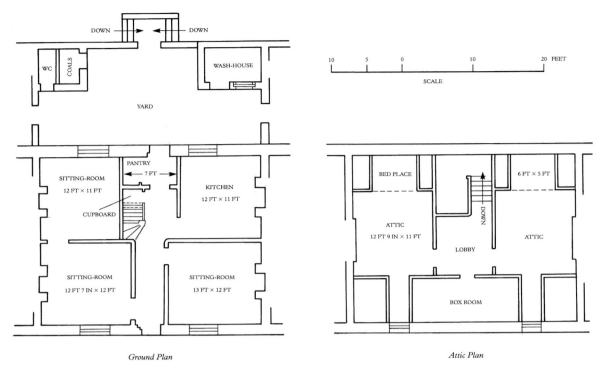

DOWN

DOWN

WC

COALS

WASH-HOUSE

YARD

10   5   0   10   20 FEET

SCALE

PANTRY

← 7 FT →

SITTING-ROOM

12 FT × 11 FT

KITCHEN

12 FT × 11 FT

CUPBOARD

SITTING-ROOM

12 FT 7 IN × 12 FT

SITTING-ROOM

13 FT × 12 FT

BED PLACE

6 FT × 5 FT

ATTIC

12 FT 9 IN × 11 FT

DOWN

ATTIC

LOBBY

BOX ROOM

Ground Plan

Attic Plan

Plan of the quarry officer's house, 1905

of three houses nearer the cliff-edge – the south one to house Dr Linacre (and later Dr Snow) the company surgeon, the middle one for Mr Ryle, the company engineer and the north one for Mr Gray, the foreman of works. In the High Street the Fowl Run wall incorporates two walls of a building dating from this time. The Granite Company also built the storekeeper's cottage adjacent to the building which housed the stores and the bakery, over which the baker lived. They built too the Linhay, the old brewhouse, and the barn as well as the Barton Cottages, and the third workers' block ('B' on map) was started to replace the wooden buildings. The hospital is a little to the north, and to its east was the surgery, of which only the foundations remain.

Once the eastern siding had been chosen and accommodation provided, the island must have presented a busy scene and, despite the loss of all first-hand records (sold as wastepaper for 30s (£1 10s) on the eventual collapse of the company), the method of working the quarries is quite clear.

The oldest quarry is the southernmost (Quarry 'A') at 360 ft above sea-level. Stone from here was dressed at the quarry mouth and the waste removed by tramway tub to a tip towards the south. At this early stage various 'overseers of the granite company' ate and probably lodged in the farmhouse (1864) and their

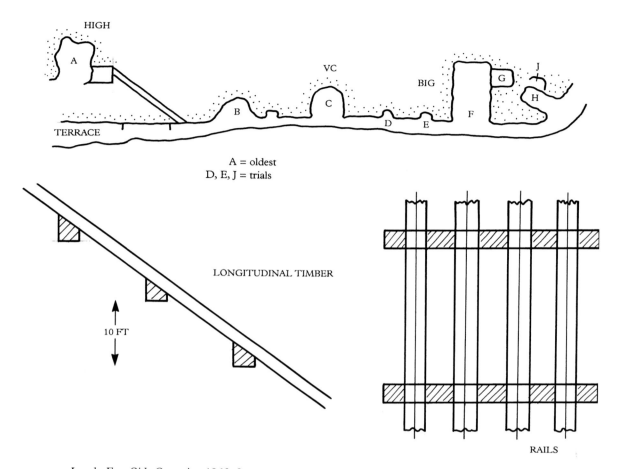

A = oldest
D, E, J = trials

Lundy East Side Quarries, 1863–8

intention to manage the farm seriously is borne out by the large number of drill holes made on exposed large stones all over the island by quarrymen anxious to remove them from fields.

Quarry 'A' was, however, soon abandoned when the main series of quarries was begun. To this end a large terrace was built at 275 ft above sea-level, big enough to house the stables needed for the horses used on the tramway and for sidings, where wagons or tubs were stored while skilled masons dressed the stone.

The first of the lower quarries (Quarry 'B') was at 278 ft above sea-level and the small excavation into the cliff-face, just to the north of this, probably served as a lavatory. The next quarry (Quarry 'C') is at 283 ft and is known as V.C. Quarry. Beyond this is a small trial quarry ('D') and an even smaller trial quarry ('E'). The largest quarry (Quarry 'F') at 319 ft provided the finest stone and, being so large, had two spoil tips.

Just before the rising path reaches the plateau there are trial digs (known as

Quarry 'G') on the plateau near the north-west end of Quarry 'F' and a small north-facing trial dig (Quarry 'H') at 345 ft above sea-level.

The tramway continued on this steadily rising gradient to reach the plateau at the 364 ft level, where a terminus enabled horses to be changed or acted as a loading site for heavy materials that had been carried across the island.

The tubs used in each quarry carried spoil to be tipped over the edge. By using a turntable at each quarry mouth, laden tubs of useful stone could be moved on to the main downward-inclined tramway, moving towards the terrace by gravity or restrained by an attached horse walking behind. The sleeper grooves of this tramway are still easily traced at roughly 3 ft intervals with each sleeper about 51 in long supporting the 18 in gauge track. The space between each sleeper has been made up to provide a smooth path for the horses needed to haul the empty tubs back to the quarries.

On the terrace the tubs were marshalled into sidings and the stone prepared and dressed prior to shipment, waste from which remains in two small tips of chippings on the seaward side of the terrace edge.

Stone was lowered from Quarry 'A' to the southern end of the terrace down an incline which ran from the north edge of the timecheck platform at a gradient of 1 in $2^1/_2$. On the well-built timecheck platform stood a brake drum with a wheel around which a cable ran to the trucks being used to lower stone from the high tramway to the terrace. Progress down the incline was controlled by the brake drum and counter-balanced either by a weight or by an empty truck.

From the south end of the terrace a longer and steeper incline ran in a slightly different direction down to Quarry Beach and carried the finished stone from all the quarries. This lower incline had a gradient of 1 in $1^1/_2$ and the controlling cables ran up to a point in the sidings about 360 ft above sea-level. At the beach the stone was carried on a horizontal tramway to the jetty to be loaded into waiting ships.

Still to be seen on the beach is a line of keyed blocks which trace the outline of a granite quay from which a wooden jetty, now lost, would run at right-angles out to sea. This arrangement could not have been ideal as the Lundy Island Floating Breakwater Company Ltd was registered on 23 December 1863; 'the Objects for which the company is established are the construction of a floating breakwater within the roadstead on the eastward side of Lundy Island. . . . Also to provide for the maintenance of the structure and the purchase of a steam tug vessel.' The company had a capital of £2,000 as 400 shares of £5 each.

Meanwhile, the Lundy Granite Company had bought a new, small 56 ton 35 hp iron screw-steamer, built at Rutherglen and registered at London. This vessel, named *Vanderbyl* after one of the directors, carried most of the company's exports although some stone was carried in sailing ships – ships which were to have benefited from the services of the 'steam tug vessel' proposed by the Lundy Island Floating Breakwater Company Ltd. However, nothing appears to have been achieved as Capt. Christopher Claxton, who was named as the original subscriber, disappeared and in the absence of any returns, or directors, the company was dissolved in 1882.

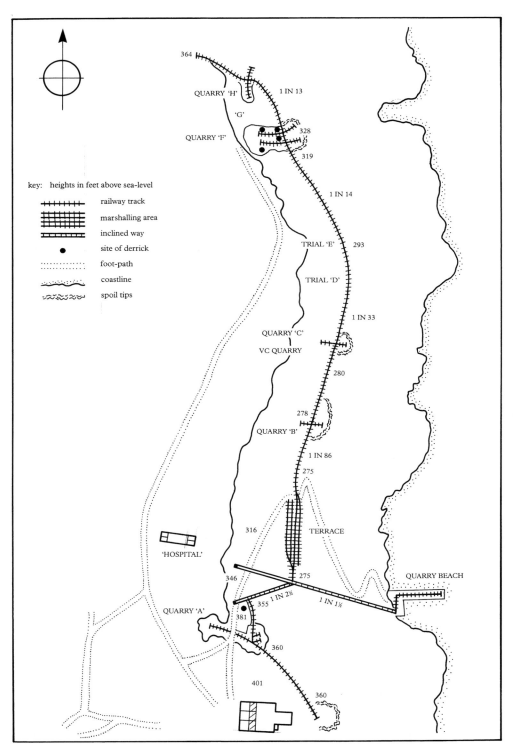

Lundy Quarry Railways, 1863–8

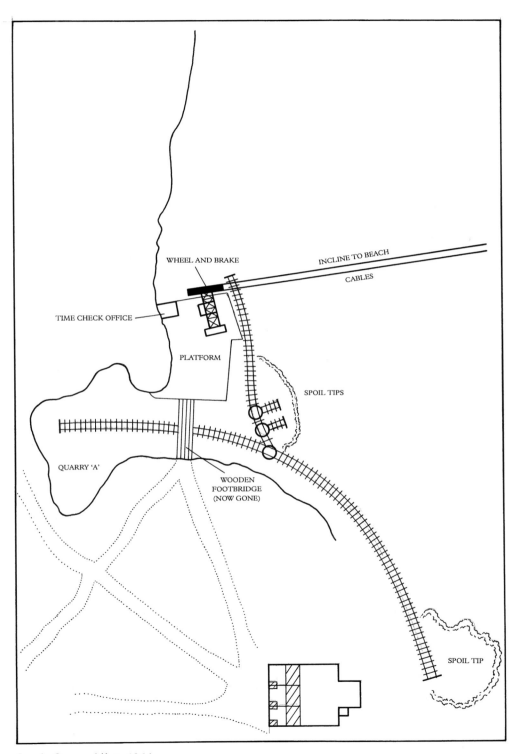

WHEEL AND BRAKE

INCLINE TO BEACH

CABLES

TIME CHECK OFFICE

PLATFORM

SPOIL TIPS

QUARRY 'A'

WOODEN
FOOTBRIDGE
(NOW GONE)

SPOIL TIP

Lundy Quarry 'A', c. 1864

By the summer of 1864 the *Vanderbyl* was regularly visiting Barnstaple to load cattle and other supplies for the Lundy Granite Company and although she carried granite at times as far as Tenby her regular mainland destination was Fremington Quay, where Mr John McKenna (the 1862 lessee of the island) was 'proprietor of the Granite Works'[6] and where the recently built railway link to the quay provided nationwide connections.

Capt. William Dark, who was later to captain the island supply skiff *Gannet*, served under Capt. Press on the *Vanderbyl* which was reported in January 1867 to have 'left Appledore Pool at 10 am on Tuesday morning for Lundy, took in a full cargo of granite, with which she returned to Appledore by the evening tide'.[7] Shipment was not always so easy. The company is reputed to have lost 'a barge' laden with granite which was driven on to the Landing Beach in a storm and square sea-rounded granite blocks were still to be seen on that beach a century later. Later in the decade, possibly on charter, the *Ogmore* of Swansea, a 101 ton 25 hp steamer, was used to carry granite and continued to visit the island after the collapse of the Lundy Granite Company to transport scrap metal and other salvaged materials for disposal on the mainland.

Things did not go well for the Lundy Granite Company. From the start there was friction between the Heaven family and the hard-working, rough-living labourers. As early as March 1864 George Cauridge, the company clerk, hanged himself in his

The ruins of a probable quarry company cable house

island cottage and his body was taken to Ilfracombe for an inquest. The 'company, if unsuccessful as stone merchants, were worse as farmers, and let the island deteriorate greatly . . . the three hundred quarrymen and labourers – it is said that there were a hundred English, a hundred Scots, and a hundred Irish – confined in a small island found their leisure time heavy on their hands. At any rate they got into all sorts of mischief – poaching, trespassing, trampling down the crops. . . .'[8] There were allegations of damage to walls and cultivation, drunkenness, and evidence that the workforce contained undesirables who had mainland debts. Even the company surgeon, Dr Linacre 'who had come to Lundy to overcome a craving for drink – unsuccessfully'[9] had to be replaced by Dr Snow.

The Bideford County Court judge in 1864 described Lundy as 'a refuge for the destitute' and labelled some of its inhabitants as 'the fag ends of society'. In spite of protest meetings held in the island canteen (now the tavern) where the islanders' 'bottled wrath' was allowed expression, the granite company brought the county court bailiff aboard the *Vanderbyl* in June 1866 on a visit. He was well received and later spoke well of conditions on the island, having been most impressed by the company's hospital. However, the Heaven family papers frequently mention the poor state of the farm and comment on the years of hard work that would be needed to repair the neglect.

The physical problems of transporting the stone ashore when easterly winds made it impossible for ships to come alongside the jetty for weeks at a time, with the consequent lost contracts; the halted work, the idle labourers with more time for mischief, all took their toll but above all there was the growing suspicion that the company was acting fraudulently.

In an interview in the *Western Mail* of 9 August 1906 the Revd H.G. Heaven remembered accurately details of the Lundy Granite Company and stated that 'The company took a large contract for supplying granite for the Thames Embankment, and sent up a specially-picked stone as a sample. This was accepted, and some of the stones from the island are in the foundations of Westminster Bridge today. They were pressed to supply stone according to sample, but they sent an inferior stone, and the contract was cancelled. The stone as a result got into bad odour in the market.'

The Times reported on 18 July 1867 that 'at the General Meeting of the Lundy Granite Company, summoned for yesterday, not a single member of the Board attended, and no business could be proceeded with'.

This unsatisfactory state of affairs must have continued as just over a year later, on 28 July 1868, the Heaven family were requesting that 'The contract be obtained from the Granite Company for limewashing Boundary walls, outhouses, etc. as hitherto', and an enthusiastic account of a visit in the following month described the quarries, the tramway, the steamer and the jetty and concluded with 'All that appears to be wanted is a good market and plenty of capital to make it a successful venture'.

The company was in severe difficulties and by the end of September 1868 had suspended operations and most of the remaining employees had returned to Bideford. Final winding-up took place in November 1868 when Sir Joseph McKenna and Messrs Lewis, Vanderbyl and Henshaw, directors who had been associated with the Lundy Granite Company, were obliged to resign from the board of the National Bank following a scandal over a share issue.[10]

On 30 January 1869 *The Times* reported that 'The Master of the Rolls has appointed Mr George Whiffin official liquidator of the Lundy Granite Company Ltd', and in the following August a committee was inquiring into the reported misconduct of A.K. Griffiths, a servant of the company and a 'medical certificate of his state of health' was sought.

Frederick Wilkins was appointed agent of the liquidators of the Lundy Granite Company in September 1868 and on 21 May 1869 made an arrangement with a Mr Henry Benthall to purchase. Three days later Wilkins was appointed manager of the new company, the Western Granite Company Ltd, while Mr Benthall entered into a partnership with a Commander Rivington, who in turn became the mortgagee who 'advanced the means to enable Mr Benthall to effect the purchase'.

Problems arose because the *Ogmore* continued to call at Lundy and was collecting salvage from the works of the defunct company to sell on the mainland to help reduce the company's debt while litigation was in progress, for although the company had been liquidated the island was still technically leased to Mr W.C. McKenna. Mr Heaven was anxious to remove both the company and his lessee from the island and to receive what he considered to be his true dues. But Mr McKenna was reluctant to leave and in November 1870 *The Times* reported that

[in] the Rolls Court Mr Swanson made an application on behalf of the official liquidator of the Lundy Granite Company for directions as to the manner in which he should act under certain difficulties which had arisen. . . . The property of the Company consisted of a lease from Mr Heaven, the owner of the island, it being transferred in the name of Mr M'Kenna, brother of Sir Joseph M'Kenna. The question now was what must be done with the leasehold interest of the company in the property. The official liquidator had been dealing with it but the parties alleged to have an interest were not satisfied with the manner in which matters stood . . . while a Mr Benthall had purchased the stock, Mr M'Kenna had agreed to assign, but was now unwilling to do so except on certain terms, in which the official liquidator could not acquiesce. Mr Heaven was not willing to assign the lease to Mr Benthall. Mr Roxburgh QC appeared for Mr Heaven, and Mr North on behalf of Mr M'Kenna.

Lord Romilly said he would not allow the company to pay more, and if Mr M'Kenna did not assign to Mr Benthall he must take the consequence of any proceedings which the latter gentleman might institute against him.[11]

On 6 February 1871 Mr Heaven levied distress for £1,050, a sum which equalled the rent and royalties due since 29 June 1869, but on 23 February 1871 the liquidators obtained an order restraining Mr Heaven from distress of the goods and a further order of 6 March 1871 refused Mr Heaven's application to proceed.

Mr Heaven duly appealed against these two orders and was heard on 10 March 1871. It was related that following the order of 19 November 1868 to wind up the company, the official liquidator did not remove the goods of the company from the island and paid the rent to Mr Heaven up to 24 June 1869,

> but apparently Mr Heaven seemed not to have recognised the Company as tenants. Some negotiations took place between the official liquidator, McKenna and Mr Heaven and some proceedings in Chambers as to the surrender of the lease and the grant of a new lease to one Benthall which, however, had no result. There was a considerable amount of property on the island belonging to the Company, and the official liquidator proposed to sell this and other property of the Company; whereupon Mr Heaven, having previously applied to McKenna for the rent, distrained for the rent due to 25.12.1870, McKenna being named in the warrant as tenant. The property under distress belonged to the Company and the Master of the Rolls 23.2.1871 made an order in the winding-up restraining Mr Heaven from proceeding. Mr Heaven then moved for leave to proceed, which was refused by the Master of the Rolls 6.3.1871.

As the property belonged to the company but was on land leased to another person the company was then not carrying on business or liable to rent, and so therefore no debt was due from them to the proprietor. According to law, when a company is wound up by the court any distraint made after such winding-up is void. The judgment was that Mr Heaven should prove against the company in the same way as any other creditors and that he ought to add his costs and prove the whole against the company. Mr Heaven appealed against both the orders.

On appeal, judgment was given by Sir J.M. James that the orders of the Master of the Rolls could not stand, and 'if the Company . . . for its own purposes . . . remains in possession of the estate, which the lessor is therefore not able to obtain possession of, common sense and ordinary justice require the Court to see that the Landlord receives the full value of the property, and if the Company chose to keep the estates for their own purposes, they ought to pay the full value to the landlord. I should have no hesitation in granting leave to a landlord to pursue his rights by distress for rent accrued during the time when the official liquidator chooses to leave the goods on the land.' Sir G. Mellish agreed and passed judgment that 'If the official liquidator for the convenience of the winding-up, does not surrender the lease, but continues to keep possession for the purpose of obtaining a better price for the goods, the landlord should not be deprived of his right to recover the rent'. The landlord is therefore entitled to take as security for his rent the goods upon his land 'whomsoever they belong to'. 'We must discharge the two orders. Mr Heaven will have his costs below, and the official liquidator will have his out of the estate.'[12]

As soon as this news reached the island the bailiffs left and on 22 April 1871 Mr McKenna arrived to hand over the farm keys to Mr Heaven and left three days later, after surrendering the original lease. All was not complete, however, as a Mr Saunders wrote offering to rent the farm and Mr McKenna requested such granite as the defunct company had quarried. Later in May prospective purchasers of the plant arrived.

Litigation, too, rumbled on. Mr Harvey Lewis was ordered to refund £135 which had been paid to him as remuneration for his services as a director of the Lundy Granite Company, and although judgment was given, it was reversed on appeal.

As late as 2 May 1872 the Lundy Granite Company, which still had a depot at Fremington Railway Station, applied for liberty to remove the cattle and sheep grazing on the island and for payment of £88 4s 9d recompense for stock sold ashore by Mr Heaven! In response, Mr Heaven counter-claimed the right to charge the company for the keep of the cattle on the island and, noting that the premises on the island were in a most dilapidated condition, also applied for compensation for damages.

Nothing more was heard of this and in August and September boats carried away 'old iron' from the quarries and Mr McKenna hired the smack *Acorn* to take away some hewn stone from the quarry jetty.

Following the end of this matter it is quite understandable that Mr Heaven refused to consider the quarrying of granite until the end of the century. However, in 1897 the Lundy Granite Quarries Ltd was floated but as only seven shares were taken up between registration on 15 December 1897 and 26 October 1900 the company was wound up.

A final effort at quarrying was made by the Lundy Island & Mainland Quarries Ltd which was initiated by the same seven shareholders as the former company and became amalgamated with Property Securities Company Ltd on 11 July 1907. The directors' report of 31 July 1909 stated 'that their efforts to start work at the quarries on Lundy Island had proved unavailing, and last autumn, previous to the offering of the island for sale at the Mart, the owner cancelled the lease held by the Property Securities Co. Ltd'. The company offered to buy the island but the asking price was too high and the company was finally dissolved on 10 February 1911. This was the last attempt by the Heaven family to develop quarrying on Lundy and, following the invention of Portland cement in 1905, the demand for building stone collapsed.

The next owner, Mr Christie, commissioned the civil engineer Mr G.B. Richards to compile 'Sundry Reports and Investigations'. Following a visit to Lundy in December 1921 he reported the following month that to avoid the problem that had arisen with the Lundy Granite Company trying to ship large stone, only small stones 'such as could be loaded down a shoot or similar apparatus' should be exported and that 'the only outlet for the material was seen to be for road material and similar purposes. . . . This entailed the installation of a crushing plant using gravity from the working level of the Old Quarry to the point of discharge.' After obtaining analysis of samples, surveyors' reports and capital estimates the author felt

John Harman's memorial tablet at V.C. Quarry

'the proposition appeared to be a promising one'. Having got this far the owners did not appear to be desirous of finding the necessary capital, probably the more or less dual-control at this time being considered detrimental. (Mr Christie was far from well, and his wife had to assume many of his responsibilities.)

Mr Richards estimated that the scheme would cost £4,300 and made several practical suggestions, first among which was that the advice of a professional geologist should be obtained.

Mr Harman's interest was aroused by this report, which he inherited on buying the island and in July 1939 H.C. Ryland proposed to Mr Harman that a company be set up to export granite for roadstone, the entire output to be taken by C.H. Broodbank, the building contractor, who was to have exclusive rights.

This embryonic scheme foundered when the Second World War broke out a few weeks later and the quarries have lain idle ever since.

Chapter Twenty-one

CLIMATE AND CULTIVATION

Climate on Lundy is affected both by the island's position in a tidal channel and by the prevailing westerly winds, which can at times be of such force that they uproot the surface vegetation and have been known to blow livestock over the cliff-edge. Although such severe gales are rare, the wind does have a permanent effect on the island vegetation and trees are to be found only on the sheltered East Side.

Records kept by Mr Heaven show that temperatures were generally seven to twelve degrees Fahrenheit higher in winter and correspondingly lower in summer than on the adjacent mainland, a fact he attributed to the modifying influence of the Gulf Stream.

Snow and ice are extremely rare and occur briefly only during exceptionally severe weather. The island does, however, experience a considerable amount of mist and fog and the fog-signal guns at the Battery once fired for a continuous period of seventy-two hours.[1] An unusual feature of the fog is that it frequently covers the plateau but leaves the beach and sidelands clear.

Rainfall is slightly less than on the mainland as the island appears to deflect the incoming Atlantic rainclouds so that often both North Devon and South Wales experience heavy rainstorms while Lundy remains under clear skies.

A certain amount of salt water spray is thrown up on the West Side, affecting the vegetation, and during strong winds clusters of sea froth, delightfully named Lundy Butterflies, are blown across and on to the plateau grass.

Except during prolonged dry spells the rainfall is adequate. The little streams which drain the plateau over the West Side are mostly dammed near the plateau edge to form drinking ponds for cattle and in 1975 the dam enclosing the western edge of Pondsbury was strengthened and raised to impound a larger body of water.

Domestic water supply depends on conservation and until 1969 all buildings had to rely on roof catchments, apart from the Old Hotel and Millcombe House which were fed from the covered reservoir just west of the Old Hotel which drained the Lighthouse Field. Golden Well ran a pipeline to Brambles and from the 1950s a tank on the summit of Castle Hill ran a pipeline to buildings around the castle. The Landmark Trust has since installed three large fibreglass tanks, two of 50,000 gallons capacity and one of 25,000 gallons capacity, which since 1981 have been fed

The rare sight of snow on Lundy, 1964 (unknown)

by electric pumps from streams and covered reservoirs. All the inhabited buildings on the island (with the exception of Tibbetts, which still relies on roof catchment) are gravity-fed from the fibreglass tanks through underground plastic pipes. Passive catchment was augmented in 1989 when a visiting female diviner discovered two sources which yield 150 gallons an hour. One of these is only a few metres north of the storage tanks themselves and the other is in the Tent Field to the west of the Black Shed. A third bore about 100 m east of the storage tanks was made in August 1990.

The more northerly parts of the plateau resemble the large West Country moors but the eastern sidings are sheltered, thickly overgrown by bracken in summer, and are uniformly steep, except where the valleys of Gannets' Combe, Millcombe and St John's Valley slope more gently to the water's edge.

Soil depth ranges from nil near the North End to almost 2 m in some deep gullies but is on average about half a metre of humus overlying silt. In hollows this forms marshes but towards the North End the soil more closely resembles peat. The barrenness of the North End has been caused by fires which have either been started deliberately or, as in the 1930s, have been caused by careless visitors.

Large transverse walls divide the island. The oldest, Quarter Wall, separated South Farm from North Farm. Halfway Wall when built divided North Farm into Middle Farm and North Farm, while Threequarter Wall, the most recent, further divides North Farm.

North of Quarter Wall the entire area is given over to free grazing by cattle, horses, sheep and wild animals. South of Quarter Wall as far as the lighthouse wall is permanent pasture except for the Tillage Field and the Brick Field, which are both enclosed and sometimes under cultivation. The main cultivated portion of the island, together with the village and farm, lies to the south of the lighthouse wall, but traces of ancient walls can be found all over the island, showing that cultivation was more intense than today.

Although the earliest mention of agriculture dates from 1225 when William de Marisco 'transported ten live does and two bucks from Mendip to Lundy',[2] the first detailed description of cultivation is that given in the inquisition made by a jury in 1274 which reported

> That there may be there twenty acres of arable land which may be sown with barley or oats; each acre is worth per annum two pence, whether tilled or not. There are also five acres of meadow, worth threepence an acre, also pasture for eight oxen and twenty cows with their offspring for two years. Also, that in all, the pastures can bear sixty-eight head of cattle also four mares and one stallion, with their offspring for two years, to wit, thirteen head. There is also there pasture for three hundred wethers and two hundred ewes with their offspring for two years, to wit, pasture for nine hundred sheep. Also the taking of rabbits is estimated at two thousand, and the estimate is at 5s 6d each hundred skins because the flesh is not sold; also the rock of Gannets is worth 5s; also other birds but they are not sold. There is also an eyre of butcher falcons, which have sometimes three young ones, sometimes four. This eyre the jury knew not how to estimate, as they build their nest in a place in which they cannot be taken. . . . In summer, even in time of peace it is necessary to have fourteen servants and a Constable to watch the defences of the island, and in winter ten servants.

The jury valued the island at £7 6s 2d. In the back of the inquisition is the following note:

> The jurors, being asked by him who made the extent, what the turf, gorse, brushwood, and the fresh water were worth to the King's benefit, answered that none of them could take value, as no man would buy them; but the auditing clerk perceives that all these things may be considered of such value to the keepers of the island as to lessen their wages to the extent of five shillings, and the fowls besides; although they cannot be sold, nor the keepers willing to eat them, yet he estimated them at forty pence. Of quarries, minerals, or timber none was found there. As for the flesh of the rabbits, what it is worth to the keepers of the island he leaves to the discretion of the King's Counsel to estimate. Be it mentioned however that for all these matters the keepers of the island have been wont to take nothing less in wages.

A subsequent inquisition held in 1321 valued the island at £11 3s 2d and found that Sir John de Wyllyngton had

> held the island with all its appurtenances, in which is a certain castle with a barton [a farmyard] for which they made no valuation, as the same was destroyed and burnt by the Scots.[3] There is a rabbit warren worth in ordinary years 11s., but this year destroyed in great part. Also a certain rock called the Gannets Stone with two places near it where the gannets settle and breed, worth in ordinary years 66s & 8d but this year destroyed in part by the Scots. Also eight tenants, who hold their land and tenements by a certain charter of Herbert de Mareis granted them for the term of their lives, who pay fifteen shillings yearly. Also one tenant, who should keep the said gannets during the whole of the season of their breeding, and for which services he will be quit of his rent of two shillings. Also pleas and perquisites of courts worth yearly four shillings. . . . There are in demesne forty acres of arable land worth yearly ten shillings; also, two hundred acres of pasture land worth 16s 8d per annum; also three acres of meadow worth 2s 6d; also waste land by estimation 200 acres worth yearly 8s 4d, so little because all the tenants in the island have common on it.

An inventory was made four years later, in 1325, on behalf of Edward II before his attempted flight to the island to avoid his wife and her supporters, and is quoted by Geoffrey Baker some years later.[4] He writes:

> The Isle of Lundy, which is in the mouth of the River Severn, two miles in length each way, abounding with pasture grounds and oats, very pleasant. It bringeth forth Conies very plentifully, it hath Pigeons, and other fowles, which Alexander Nechan calls Ganimedes Birdes, having great nestes. Also it ministreth to the inhabitants fresh springing waters flowing out of fountains, although it be on everie side environed with the salt sea; it hath onlie one entrance into it, in which two men together can scarcely go in front. On all the other parts there is a high hanging over of a great rocke, which letteth the passage to this Island as we have said. It aboundeth altogether with victualles, and is verie full of wines, oils, hony, corne, bragget, salt fish, flesh and sea or earth coales.

As *The Times* records: 'The Romans brought the vine to the beer-drinking Britons, and cultivated it as far north as Hadrians Wall. Domesday Book registered some 40 vineyards, and during the Middle Ages the number rose to more than 300, most of them run by monks from Rievaulx to Tintern. They were hit by the Black Death and the dissolution of the monasteries, and the Puritan revolution finished them off.'[5] So the somewhat surprising inclusion of wine as an island product is not as unlikely as it might sound. The slatey soil in sheltered parts of Millcombe Valley could well have been the site of a small Lundy vineyard.

William Camden, author of *Britannia*, was vicar of Ilfracombe in 1580 and, following a visit to Lundy, reported that 'there are about 500 acres of good land but the best part, for want of cultivation, is covered with furze and heath and the whole land swarms with rabbits and black rats. Sea fowl resort to it in summer, and in winter starlings and woodcocks. The rock is moorstone, covered with a soil formed from rotten vegetable matter – thickets at the south end.'

A Spanish reference – prepared for a Catholic invasion fleet – says that by 1597 'there were twelve people on Lundy with some cattle'.[6]

Apart from agriculture and fishing it is likely that the seals around Lundy's coast formed part of the island economy. A recent note mentions a verbal tradition, for which any records are now lost, of seventeenth-century exports from Hartland of seal skins. It further points out that Saxton's map of 1575 shows off Hartland the head of an aquatic creature 'doubtless the Sellus Magnus, the Greater Common Seal which was extinct from about the middle of the 18th Century'. Theophile Lebrun (*Le Grand Phoque*, Bordeaux, 1863) records that a cross-Channel trade flourished for 150 years and that Breton fishermen were partly responsible for the animals' extinction. 'There was almost certainly a link with Lundy, but its later involvement with the more profitable smuggling took the interest of the islanders away from the hard work of rendering the skins usable.'

Westcote, writing in about 1620, notes 'that it hath been tilled in former times the furrows testify yet plainly, but what commodities came thereof is not known, neither will any man try again; there is so little hope of profit. The most profit that is now made of it is by hogs, conies, and sea fowl. Trees it hath none, but stinking elders, which the stares [starlings] haunt in such multitudes that uneth [with difficulty] for their dung there, is any coming unto them.'

This barren picture is confirmed by Risdon, writing about 1630, who completes the picture by saying that 'horses, kine, sheep, swine, and goats it affordeth, with stores of conies; but their chief commodity is fowl, whereof there is a great abundance. I have seen their eggs so thick on the ground, that unless you look to your way they must needs have been troden on.'

Sir Bevill Grenville in a letter[8] gives a fascinating view of the farming and fowling in 1632. He writes:

I'm glad the gulls came safe to you and do humbly thank you that you pleased to accept so poor a present. I willed my man to carry half of his gettings to you, but wrote not because I knew not what would be brought. Mr Billing [Grenville's agent] tells me you have a mind for some knotts. There are some at Lu[ndy] but I could never yet light on them. I will try now again and if I can you shall have them. However I doubt not of some salt-birds for you, but I fear I shall not be able to send you a vast [any large amount] of any good butter from there this year. For since the departure of my old virgin, I have not had any from them that I liked, and though she was a black jade, yet she was the best about her dairy that ever I had, and I am now so destitute of a good dairy woman for that place as I would give anything for one. I am going thither this week to see my great works finished [the quay] which I hope will be within this month.

Thenceforth conditions must have improved. John Sharpe, a resident on Lundy from the 1690s until the 1740s, gave the population as 100 people who were engaged with cattle, the sale of feathers, eggs and skins, adding 'it bore exceedingly fine barley, potatoes and almost every kind of garden stuff in great abundance'. Much of this improvement might have been brought about by a Mr Richard Scores, a native of Hartland, who is known to have been the tenant farmer on Lundy about 1720.

The island stock in 1752 was 20 cows, 2 bulls, 30 bullocks, 7 sheep, 7 horses, 30 hogs, 16 deer and 7 goats, but a note was added that 'the flesh of the hogs bred on the island cannot be eat; the flesh is yellow and strong.'

Thomas Benson, during his short tenure, tried to improve farming by building walls, setting fire to overgrown vegetation and by introducing more deer, some of which still remained in 1777.

Sir John Borlase Warren's tenure was also short, but he was rich and had grandiose plans for the island. In notebooks to his agent he gives the following orders:

. . . discharge every person there at Lundy, except Capt. Wood, Lamb, and such others as shall be thought useful upon the island – those to be paid but not discharged. As soon as that is done, to send a proper husbandman to cultivate and improve the Land and stock the same with 60 head of Cow Cattle and 500 sheep, and more if the land will maintain them. A proper Farm Yard to be made and convenient building to be erected as such Farmer shall judge necessary. . . . Capt. Wood to go to Schetland to invite three or four families over to the Island to live, and each family to have a House and Acres of Land and to have the Use of Sir John's Boats for fishing upon paying one half of the Customary profit to Sir John. . . . The Husbandman must make the most profit of the Wool and by selling the Mutton: he will make the most of the Cattle by making Salt Butter and Cheese for the Bristol Market. The Young Fat Beef if there is not an opportunity of sending it fresh to Bristol Market is to be Salted and Barelled up. . . . Wood is to make the most of all the Rabbits and whenever . . . the Wind [is] favourable for Bristol he should collect all hands and in the Night kill as many as possible and send them to Bristol . . . he is also to make the most of all the Birds Eggs and Feathers . . . the Eggs should be sent to the Sugar Houses at Bristol.[9]

Whether these ambitious schemes were ever carried out is unknown although Warren is believed to have completed the walls left unfinished by Benson.

The Revd Thomas Martyn, Professor of Botany at Cambridge who had befriended Warren at university, visited Lundy in 1776 and reported that:

about 500 acres thereof, situate at the South End were covered with a coarse grass and might feed lean Welsh cattle; but that all the rest of the island was, in his judgement, incorrigibly barren, and bore little else to cover the rock but heath and moss; and that where there was any soil the staple was mostly very shallow and incapable, without very great expense, of any considerable improvement; and that the island was so very high, and so subject to winds, that it would be difficult to grow corn to much advantage; and that it was so overrun with rats and rabbits that any crops that might be produced thereof would, as he apprehended, be infallibly devoured by them; and that he was persuaded no trees had ever grown upon the said island, nor could be forced to grow thereon to any purpose, without great care, expense and difficulty; and that the said John Borlase Warren having caused many trees to be planted in the said island in the Spring of 1775, the deponant found that the same were all withered and dead; and that in his judgement the greatest advantage that could be made of the said island would be by agisting [care for/feed for payment] of cattle, but that there would be great drawbacks upon that advantage from the great expense which would necessarily attend upon carrying the cattle to and from the nearest land, which is about three leagues; and that the said island is distant eight leagues from Ilfracombe, which is the most certain port and place where proper vessels could be procured to carry passengers, cattle or goods; and that there was but one dwelling house and remains of an old castle on the said island, the said dwelling house being small, and in a very ruinous state and condition; and that he, the said Thomas Martyn, was better able to depose with respect to the soil of the said island, as he had made Natural History and Agriculture the chief study of his life.

A visitor on 19 August 1783 noted that 'the isle of Lundy is inhabited by two farmers and their families only who rent it for about £50 a year'.

A visit of inspection was made by Mr Cleveland, the then owner, with a party of friends in July 1787 when

the morning of Saturday, the 7th July, was appropriated by our traveller and Mr Cleveland to arranging disputes among the tenants, and swearing-in Mr. Hole Constable of the Island. . . . Discovered at a distance seven goats, all females, of various colours, white, black and brown; they were so wild that we could not get near them. . . . I saw the deer and goats browzing to the north part, on being disturbed they ran into the cleaves, where the ferns are so high that they were soon invisible. . . . The north part is now incapable of being improved, from Mr Benson's setting the heath and ferns on fire, while he was in possession, so that the earth continued burning for some days, till it came to the bare rock, and now nothing vegetable grows on it. . . . In this lowland are a few willows, about as high as brushwood, to which the woodcocks resort in the beginning of their flight.

Of the rabbits and other attributes it was said that

the inhabitants take about 1,000 couple yearly, principally valued for their skins; their flesh consumed on the island except a chance Ilfracombe boat comes by, to purchase a few. . . . The island was capable of great improvement; about 160 acres were then inclosed, in fields of seven, eight, and ten acres each; the produce wheat, barley and oats. The fields which were then in cultivation produced naturally a small three-leafed grass, like Dutch clover, and clover and Ever-grass grow very well, but the inhabitants sowed but small crops, trusting to their birds and rabbits to pay the rent [£70 per annum]

The birds were at this time a considerable source of income and the writer continues:

After dinner we walked to view the rocks on the western part of the island and saw vast quantities of wild fowl, (it being the breeding season) and the method of taking them in nets, which the inhabitants use, for the advantage of their feathers. The nets are made in the form of those commonly used for taking rabbits on warrens. They are fixed on the rocks, and sometimes on the ground, on sticks, in the breeding places. Every morning and evening the natives watch their nets and take out the birds that are entangled. They catch in a good season 1700 or 1800 dozen, and make one shilling per pound of their feathers. People from the neighbouring coast are hired to pluck them, at two pence a dozen, and pluck about four dozen a day. The birds usually taken are Muirrs, of which there are two sorts, parrots, and a small kind of gull. . . . The natives collect these eggs, and send to the Bristol sugar refineries. The Muirrs are the most profitable, twelve of them producing one pound of feathers. After being plucked they are skinned; these skins are boiled in a furnace for the oil they yield, which is used instead of candles; and the flesh is given to the hogs who feed on it voraciously. . . .

The visitors rowed to the north part of the island and there

saw vast quantities of birds, so tame we might shoot a dozen at a shot. The rocks, on which they laid their eggs, are wonderfully romantic and appear as if stones were piled on each other by art, looking like the ruins of some old fortification. There is one rock 200 feet high, which seems disjointed from the island where innumerable quantities of birds lay their eggs; the inhabitants fix their nets on various parts of the rock, and catch vast quantities as they fly forward and backward from the sea to their young. Their method of conveying them, when taken, to the island, is by means of a rope fastened at each end to the island and rock, on which hangs a basket to a pulley, which is drawn

occasionally backward and forward with the birds. The people run great
hazards in taking them out of their nets and sometimes lose their lives.[10]

In 1788, indeed, the Mr Hole mentioned above lost his life in this way. He was
buried in the same grave by the chapel ruins from which he had previously removed
bones which he thought, wrongly, to have been those of Lord Saye and Sele who
had in fact been buried at Broughton Castle.

At this time the tenant farmer was a Mr Budd who, on leaving in 1791, appears
to have been followed by a Mr 'J.S.'. This gentleman wrote in 1792, 'we increase in
black cattle prodigiously . . . we have a very great demand for feathers from London
and Bristol to the amount of one thousand pounds annually. Mackarel has been very
plenty; there were caught in one haul full 20,000 last week.'[11]

By 1794 stock had increased to 80 head of cattle, 400 sheep, 12 deer, with pigs
and poultry. There were 400 acres under cultivation, 300 acres of which were
arable, and the rest pasture: wheat was the main crop but potatoes and turnips were
also said to be good.[12]

By the time the Napoleonic Wars had ended in 1815 the whole of Middle Park or
Farm had been sown with grain and is believed to have been the largest single field
ever used solely for this purpose in the British Isles. Lundy had been visited by the
barrack master of Barnstaple during this time and he reported that 'there are
between five and six hundred acres of good pasture land and 300 acres of the best
are enclosed. Not above twenty acres of corn, very few sheep, mostly bullocks: the
milk being remarkably rich, more so than any in this Kingdom. Vegetables of all
kinds plenty.'[13]

Seabirds continued to be a source of revenue and Loyd says that 'in 1816, 379
pounds of feathers were plucked by the women, 24 puffins yielding one pound of
feathers'. Another source gives more detail:

> At Clovelly opposite Lundy Island there was a regular staff for preparing the
> plumes; and fishing smacks with extra boats and crews used to commence
> their work of destruction at Lundy Island by daybreak on the 1st of August
> [when the close time under the Sea Birds Preservation Act expired],
> continuing this proceeding for upwards of a fortnight. . . . On one day 700
> birds were sent back to Clovelly, on another 500, and so on . . . it is well within
> the mark to say that at least 9,000 of these inoffensive birds were destroyed
> during the fortnight.[14]

On buying Lundy in 1834 Mr Heaven forbad this slaughter of seabirds and made
great efforts to improve the farming. He leased the island farm to tenants and
reorganized the Celtic fields and medieval enclosures to form a field pattern very
much as it is today. Mr John Lee was a famous tenant in 1850[15] and remained until
1861 when he was followed by Mr Blackmore of Bishop's Lydeard. During Mr
Blackmore's tenure the Lundy Granite Company began operating and undertook

the management of the farm. Chanter, using information direct from Hudson Grosett Heaven, says that 'Improvement and cultivation received a severe check as during the existence of the granite works the Company took also on themselves the occupation and working of the farm, but sadly neglected them, deteriorating the land, and greatly reducing the stock, and in fact causing considerable damage generally by the rough and mischievous conduct of their quarrymen and labourers; so that on the closing of the works everything had retrograded, and it has taken years to restore things to their former position.'[16]

After the mid-nineteenth century, the fishing was let first at £10 per annum and then, from 1876, was let to a Mr Scovell for £21 10s per annum, when each season yielded over 2,000 prime fish for export including lobsters, crabs and crawfish with reported daily catches of 1,000 herring. An old seal gun which hung in the tavern was noted by a visitor in 1911 and could perhaps explain these excellent catches. An oyster bed was laid off the east coast but the poor results of its first sweeping in 1853 led to its abandonment.[17]

Malpractice did not end with the closing of the quarries. Quite apart from pilfering by visiting tugmen and other boatmen and examples of islanders smuggling goods off the island, the story is told of John Chapple, the gamekeeper, who did not turn much in and was accused of wasting shot. Some time after he had given notice and left with one of the fishermen's daughters, Bigwoods, the poulterers, wrote to ask in what way they had displeased the squire as no game had been received recently from the island! A market gardener also wrote to enquire why his sacks of peat had ceased to be supplied!

By 1875 some 280 acres were enclosed, drained and cultivated. Most of this was permanent pasture but there were 80 acres of barley, oats, potatoes, mangolds, turnips, rye and flax. The pasture carried 600 sheep and 70 cattle plus pigs, turkeys, geese, ducks and fowl.[18]

On the death of William Hudson Heaven in 1883 an obituary recorded that Lundy's chief products were 'Butter, Gannets and Granite'. When Thomas Wright took over in 1885 he leased the entire island except Millcombe House and its grounds. He had 900 sheep, 100 head of cattle, including 30 cows in milk, about 50 horses, also 3 mares for riding and carriage use, 6 draughts and a stallion besides pigs and poultry, fowl, geese, ducks, turkeys and guinea-fowl. Wright probably built the Threequarter Wall and had under cultivation land to the west side of the main path as well as all the land south of Quarter Wall. Beyond Threequarter Wall and between the Quarter and Halfway Walls he left wild.[19]

Wright continued until 1891 and was succeeded in the following year by Henry Ackland who took out a fourteen year lease. *Kelly's Directory* of 1893 recorded 50 acres under cultivation, with hay, oats, barley and roots; 800 sheep and 100 beasts and horses. Also 'an attempt is being made to cultivate flowers for cutting and exportation to markets on the mainland'.

A visitor the following year, 1894, wrote that 'wheat is now very rarely grown as it does not pay. Oats is the principal crop and [this year] was very abundant.

Rabbits were sold at 6d each. . . . The man came over, caught the rabbits, paid 6d a head.'

By the time Mr G.T. Taylor took over the farm in 1899, Mr Heaven had planted many fine trees in Millcombe and St John's Valleys and these have since matured to transform the valleys into perhaps the most delightful places on the island. Taylor leased the entire island, except for 80 acres, and he visited Lundy about once a month. His rent was £300 a year and he had 400 acres under cultivation. Stock was recorded as 150 bullocks and 60 sheep together with some goats and horses.

The encouragement of agriculture during the First World War led to intensive farming and by 1918 all of Middle Park was under wheat.

In 1926 Mr F.W. Gade succeeded R.G. Laws as Mr Harman's agent and, apart from a four-year break, remained on Lundy until his death in 1978. When he arrived there were 244 sheep, 83 cattle, 100 pigs, 80 hens, 2 geese, 18 ducks and 4 horses, but of the many grouse, partridge and pheasants that had been introduced for sport only a few pheasants remained.[20]

Mr Gade made an attempt about 1929 to provide shelter and prevent erosion by planting 2,000 Japanese larch trees on the sidings just south of Quarter Wall east, but these were soon destroyed by the rabbits and deer. As a lover of wild animals Mr Harman introduced a great variety of unusual breeds including squirrels, wallabies, peafowl and swans. Though few survived long, the 40 red deer and the 40 Japanese Sika deer that he imported in 1927 were more successful and the Soay sheep flock which developed from one ram and seven ewes survives to this day. The deer and goat population each numbered about fifty during most of the 1930s but when war broke out in 1939 home food production was intensified and the members of the Devon War Agricultural Committee who visited Lundy in March 1941 estimated that some 500 acres could be ploughed for potatoes and oats. As the island horse was then twenty years old and deemed inadequate for this task, a dismantled 2 ton Fordson tractor was brought across in a naval vessel and as in the First World War, members of the Womens' Land Army were sent over to help.

With wartime attention and fewer exotic animals the sheep population rose from 200 in 1955 to about 500 in 1959 before stabilizing at 430 in 1975. Stock was regularly sent ashore in the island boat and occasionally naval landing craft have carried large consignments. When the island had only air transport lambs had to be flown singly to the mainland!

By 1955 the wild animals had increased to 100 deer, 45 goats, 85 Soay sheep and a considerable number of wild horses and efforts were made to reduce these numbers. By 1957 there were only 30 deer, 12 Soay sheep and 27 goats while by 1975 the deer population had fallen to 16.

Regulations designed to eradicate bovine tuberculosis came into force in 1958 whereupon the last of the herd of red Devon cattle were shipped ashore. They were replaced later that year by an attested herd of 12 Galloway cows and 1 bull.

Attempts to provide fresh milk from pedigree goats proved unsuccessful. The introduction of a milking house-cow in 1984 produced an adequate supply of

Lundy ponies, a distinct but unrecognized breed

rich, but unpasteurized milk for several years. With the introduction of 'Long Life' milk, together with the frequent visits of the island ship bringing fresh milk which is then held in the island refrigerators, supplies of milk no longer present a problem.

By 1975 the Galloway herd had risen to thirty and cultivation centred on the growing of grass for winter feed – a record of 52 tons being cut in 1979.

Farming on islands has ceased to be profitable and when the island farmer left to take employment ashore in 1989 a decision was taken 'for economic reasons' to abandon 'aggressive farming'. The sheep population was reduced to 200 ewes and the Galloways were shipped ashore to be replaced by a few Devon cattle. The deer totalled 4 Sika bucks and 4 does; there were 9 goats, 91 Soays and 4 mares. These mares are all that remain of one of Mr Harman's successful introductions. A Welsh stallion and New Forest ponies gave rise to the distinct breed of Lundy pony and at one time a company was planned to develop this successful breed. None was ever registered but in 1972, following inspection and advice, the impure crosses were culled and the remaining animals carefully registered and branded. Sadly, European EC regulations refuse to recognize this as a distinct breed and so the Lundy numbers have declined.

Rabbits are first mentioned on Lundy in the thirteenth century and this is believed to be the earliest record in England. Causing great damage, they were unaffected by myxomatosis until 1982 when their numbers had been estimated at over 60,000. A more virulent strain of myxomatosis reached the island in 1991 and led to the virtual extinction of the rabbit population.

Black and brown rats are present as pests but the island has never harboured mice, moles, hedgehogs, snakes or other reptiles.

The Landmark Trust has undertaken a programme of tree planting in many sheltered spots on the East Side of the island and in 1986 planted over 300 trees, followed a year later by a further 500. In 1993 they decided, in view of the dramatic fall in the rabbit population and consequent improvement of grazing, to increase the number of sheep to a thousand and to intensify the use of farmland.

Chapter Twenty-two

LUNDY'S UNIQUENESS

The difficulty of enforcing mainland law on Lundy has led over the years to the enjoyment of certain island privileges which have been jealously guarded. Vikings, Mariscos and later pirates all enjoyed freedom from mainland control and Lundy's especial position was clearly recognized in correspondence between Queen Elizabeth I and Bishop Turnstall in 1559. The extra-parochial position of the island and the way in which possession has evolved from fee simple to outright ownership has also encouraged this unique position.

When Lundy was granted to John Wykes in 1479 its own fishing rights were clearly defined as extending 'for a space of 3 miles around the island'. Ralph Holinshead in his *Chronicles* mentions that 'of thys island the Parson is not onlye the captaine, but hath thereto waife distresse [i.e. flotsam and jetsam] and all other commodities belonging to the same'.

Mr Heaven was most concerned to maintain these rights and at an early date in his ownership told the Customs and Excise at Barnstaple, when claiming tax exemption, that 'in a Deed relating to the title to the island dated 14.6.1803 these exemptions are clearly referred to by covenant as being then existing'.

In 1858 the Poor Law Board appointed John Lee, the tenant, as 'Overseer of the Poor of the Parish of Lundy Islands'. This brought a quick response from Mr Heaven's solicitor explaining that the justices had no jurisdiction – the island was an estate and not a parish and that therefore the Act Victoria Cap 19 did not apply. This demand set off an intensive search to establish or support Lundy's claim.

Chanter in his book believed that these rights conferred upon 'the King of Lundy [had] the power of Knighting persons within his dominion, providing that they sat at the time of the ceremony on a particular "Castled Crag"'. On more than one occasion Mr Heaven confiscated guns which had been brought on to the island without his permission and he also refused certain parties of noisy steamboat excursionists to land.[1]

The owner's rights have, however, often been questioned. One such case occurred at the end of 1865 and seems to have concerned some of the employees of the Granite Company which was then itself in financial difficulties. A statement in Bideford County Court said that Lundy Island was characterized as a 'refuge for the destitute' and some of the islanders were 'the fag ends of society', they being opposed to paying their debts and objecting to the presence of county court bailiffs and police constables on the island. This resulted in an 'indignation meeting being held on the island, at which the name of the Bideford bailiff was freely blackened and the ancient rights of the Lundyites fully vindicated', a meeting perhaps initiated by William Hudson Heaven who feared the infringement 'of Island Rights, bringing it under Government jurisdiction'. Having expended this 'bottled wrath' a compromise was reached and the Granite Company undertook to use their ship to transport the bailiffs.[2] Accordingly at the end of June 1866 'Mr Willis Major under the instructions of the High Bailiff of the County Court visited Lundy Island and served the processes of the Court without delay or molestation. Mr Major states that he was most kindly and hospitably received and speaks highly of the hospital arrangements and of the medical care taken of the sick on the island.'[3]

The conclusion of this affair came the following year when 'as a result of the "Revolt" when Serjeant Petersdorff, the Judge of the Bideford County Court had threatened to indict the parties for conspiracy, the islanders seem to have come to their senses. The under-bailiff stated . . . that the "Governor of the Island" would not allow any person to remain there who would not pay his debts and that instalments were now paid through him.'[4]

Although legal disputes with the now defunct Granite Company continued into the 1870s they never threatened the independence of the island. This independence was, however, threatened when trouble was caused 'by unlawful sailors and pilots stealing from fishermen's pots. [They] actually landed on the island and fired at the fishermen. In consequence on the 30th June 1871 Mr Maxwell of the Devon Constabulary came by the *Ranger* about putting police on the island.' What actually followed is unclear but finally a letter reached the island on 4 August 1871 stating 'that while the Police were willing to assist, the Magistrates objected to the continued employment of their County Constables in that island, on the grounds that it is uncertain whether the island forms a part of the County of Devon, and because it makes no contribution to the County Rate'. They added that they would consider the provision of protection if the inhabitants 'provided for the expense of such protection'.

Before the year was out another unfortunate incident occurred when on 15 December a man was shot dead. Two sailors had come ashore and some hours later, when very drunk, had caused a commotion by committing wilful damage and using threatening behaviour. A party of islanders set out to bring them under control but, on meeting, a scuffle broke out during which one of the sailors, George Tibbets, pulled away the gun being carried by one of the islanders and in so doing discharged it into his own chest. The following day two policemen armed with a warrant to arrest the islander arrived from Ilfracombe. To their indignant astonishment Mr Heaven refused their authority to hand him the warrant, claiming Lundy to be a free island and outside jurisdiction. He did state, however, that he wished the matter to be cleared up, promising to travel with his men as witnesses but that the islander was to be free from arrest until they had all landed at Ilfracombe.

When the case came up, Mr Heaven got up in court and protested against the arrest as Lundy, being a free island, was outside the jurisdiction of the courts. The magistrate and the people in the court were thunderstruck for the moment but the magistrates, after conferring together, decided Mr Heaven was within his rights. When this conclusion was announced, Mr Heaven again rose and said: 'Notwithstanding, wishing to have all stigma of blame for this unhappy occurrence removed, we and the prisoner desire the case to proceed, and for that purpose I myself have come across, bringing eyewitnesses of the tragedy and request the case may proceed.' Again the magistrates conferred and then, announcing their compliance with Mr Heaven's request, while admitting they had no real jurisdiction, the case proceeded to the conclusion of 'Not Guilty – Accidental Death'.[5] There was some dissatisfaction with this verdict among the fishermen and pilots and murmurs of revenge may have led the islander, either voluntarily or under pressure, to leave for a new life in the West Indies soon after.

When in March 1888 one of the islanders died suddenly, the island doctor was telegraphed and he referred the case to the Hartland coroner. The following day the coroner replied that there was no need for a death certificate if the cause of death being from natural causes was not in doubt, as there was no resident doctor on the island. The lady in question was a Roman Catholic but as it was impossible for a Catholic priest to reach the island the lady was given an Anglican burial three days later.

There was a further firearms incident a few years later when two pilots from Bristol determined to fight a duel to the death. The men had already wounded each other when the Revd Mr Heaven heard of the matter and ordered them both off the island at once.

An undated newspaper cutting of about 1897 mentions that Mr Henry Ackland, the tenant farmer, 'is storekeeper, postmaster, and everything, no one else on the island being allowed to trade. . . . Mr Ackland brews beer, but there is no Customs Officer or taxgatherers to annoy. Everything is as free as the rocks themselves. There is only one master and that is Mr Heaven. Yet order is rigidly enforced though there are no representatives of the law.'

In spite of claiming to be extra-parochial, the widening franchise gave some islanders the right to vote. In 1885 they had to poll at Woolfardisworthy, a parish some miles inland but, in 1918 during the absentee ownership of Mr Christie, a polling booth was erected for the first time on the island and seven of those eligible cast their votes, the other three being ashore. There were eight voters on the list in 1921 when it was suggested at Bideford Revision Court that they should be put on an absent voters list and vote by post. The Chief Registration Officer for Devon was unsure if this could be done and sought advice, but at the election in November 1922 eight of the thirteen electors travelled to Instow to record their vote, and in January 1924 fourteen islanders crossed to Instow to vote. Matters were still confused until the end of 1950 when the Boundary Commission recommended the inclusion of Lundy in the Torrington electoral division[6] as Lundy had inadvertently been omitted from the First Schedule of the Representation of the People Act 1948, with the result that the inhabitants had been unable to vote at all during the previous two years. Mr Harman was very unhappy at this decision and noted in a letter to members of the Lundy Field Society in 1950, 'From the point of view of the islanders and of the Society I scent trouble for, if these people force the vote down the islanders' necks they might thereafter claim to be able to interfere in island policy.'[7]

Lundy's exact relationship with the mainland remained confused. The 1861 Census returns alleged that the island, though 'formerly extra-parochial has become a parish for the purpose of the Act of 20 Vic [i.e. 1857]'. In 1881 the island 'hitherto reported to be extraparochial has not yet been brought under the operation of the Poor Laws'. By 1901 Lundy was under the Hartland Registration Sub-District but was still 'extraparochial for civil purposes'. In 1906 it was in the petty sessional division of Bideford, and by 1921 although 'still treated as extra-parochial for civil purposes', had become 'included for convenience in Bideford Rural District'. The full description given in 1939 was: 'In Rural District and County Court District of Bideford, rural deanery of Hartland, Archdeaconry of Barnstaple and Diocese of Exeter.'

Meanwhile Mr May, the tenant farmer in 1921, sought counsel's advice over his proposal to import foreign wines without payment of duty. The advice was that this would be illegal as 'the Customs Consolidation Act 1876 and amendments . . . [restrict] importation of wines etc to "approved ports"'. Counsel also considered that Lundy was a part of the United Kingdom and subject to the general law and was not extra-territorial.[8]

There was no doubt in the mind of the Home Secretary in 1925 when Lundy was offered for sale, as he told the House of Commons that there was no danger of a sale to foreigners – 'No sale or transfer would affect British Jurisdiction over the island.'

Mr Martin Harman as purchaser was anxious to defend the island's unique status and was pleased to receive a letter from Mr May on 2 October 1925 saying that he had 'received no income tax assessment whatever regarding Lundy and there is no income tax payable by anyone living on the island'. Mr Harman was so keen to retain this situation that he asked the long-term lessee of one of the island properties to leave when he discovered her completing income tax returns, which had been sent to and were being sent from the island, for fear it would affect all islanders.

Martin Coles Harman was most insistent that no servant of the British government (other than those who had the right by agreement) should be allowed to land on Lundy without paying the landing fee. Felix Gade records that in 1929 a Royal Naval craft anchored in the Roads, and a party of four or five officers came ashore. When asked for landing fees the senior officer became indignant and stated that the Royal Navy went where they pleased in the king's domain. After an interview the senior officer grudgingly paid the dues – a useful admission on the part of the Royal Navy leading Mr Gade to have no hesitation in requesting and receiving landing dues from all other visitors who were members of the armed services in uniforms, except during wartime when they came only in the course of their duty.

When on 14 November 1929 Martin Harman issued two bronze coins, the 'Puffin' and 'Half Puffin', he made no secret of the fact. When he was subsequently summoned to appear before the Bideford justices charged that he had 'unlawfully issued as a token for money a piece of metal of the value of one halfpenny, contrary to section 5 of the Coinage Act 1870', he decided that he would not enter a plea of either 'Guilty' or 'Not Guilty' as he denied the right of the bench to try any case concerning Lundy. The facts of the case were not denied but, after retirement and consultation, the bench announced that Mr Harman had been found guilty and that he would be fined £5 plus 15 guineas costs. Mr Harman thanked the chairman of the bench and paid the fine 'under protest'.

Mr Harman was not satisfied with the belief of the Bideford magistrates that they had jurisdiction over Lundy and so he took the case to appeal which was heard in the King's Bench Division in the autumn of 1930, and the proceedings detailed in full in *The Times* of 14 January 1931. Mr Harman conducted his own case and contended that 'so long as it [Lundy] was reasonably well governed the mainland had not interfered. . . . Lundy pays no rates, taxes, or customs duties and that is right because it received nothing from the mainland. I claim that Lundy Island is a vest-pocket size self-governing Dominion. We are all loyal subjects of the British Empire, and desire that this case be referred to King George for His Majesty's decision!'

The facts admitted were that in 1321 the justices itinerant in Devonshire had heard and determined a dispute relating to ownership of the island. 'There was no evidence before the Justices of any subsequent fact ousting the jurisdiction.' In 1925 a coroner's inquest had been held on the island on a body found drowned. Mr Christie had protested, but the inquest took place. The 1871 affair concerning Charles Treleven was mentioned as well as a charge brought in 1897 against two men before the Devon justices of stealing copper from a wreck on Lundy, one of them being committed for trial to the Devon quarter sessions. The Register of Parliamentary Electors included islanders and Devon County Council had received applications for old age pensions from island residents. The appointment of a special constable for Lundy by the justices for the County of Devon on 19 November 1918 was also noted.

The Attorney General referred to the County Courts Order 1899; to the schedule to the Representation of the Peoples Act 1918; and to the Wild Birds Protection Order 1930. The Territorial Waters Act 1878 declared that Great Britain included the 'adjacent islands'. This seemed to be one point that the income tax collectors had overlooked – it might be that they would now put it right.

The Lord Chief Justice in giving judgment said that the appellant argued that he was the owner of Lundy, that it was situate outside the territorial waters of Great Britain and was not part of the body of the County of Devon. He thought there was much evidence to entitle the Bideford justices to come to the conclusion which they did indeed reach, and that this appeal must be dismissed.

Not mentioned in the 'coinage' case was the recent legal advice given in 1927 concerning Mr Harman's Right of Wreck. Advice was that the Receiver of Wrecks has jurisdiction over all wrecks, regardless of ownership of foreshore, and it is only if the owner fails to claim his vessel that the owner of the foreshore has any rights.

Although the High Court judgment obliged Mr Harman to sell the remaining puffin coins on Lundy as souvenirs, the island postage stamps continued to be issued in 'puffin' values until decimalization in 1971, and Mr Harman remained vigilant to protect Lundy's independence. For example, the military authorities decided in 1934 to survey various places around the coast with the intention of building a chain of coastal defences. A group of officers and advisors planned to visit Lundy by launch on 26 April and although a warning of their intentions was telegraphed to Lundy with the instruction that the island should 'oppose landing at all costs', the visitors did succeed in landing, although nothing more was heard of their plans.

When war broke out in 1939 the agent wrote: 'I wish here to state on behalf of the owner of Lundy, Mr Martin Coles Harman, that he denies the right of any dept. of H.M. Govt. to requisition any material or building or land on Lundy. At the same time I wish also to state, on behalf of Mr Harman, that in the present state of National Emergency, he is ready to lend his whole-hearted cooperation.' Following this, the Old Light was leased at a rent of £400 a year to the Admiralty for the duration of the war.

Some measure of Mr Harman's fierce defence of Lundy's independence can be gauged by his response to the protest lodged by the RAF in 1941. It appears that the Royal Naval personnel based on Lundy reported that islanders were helping themselves to duralumin from the remains of the fuselage and wings of the German aircraft which had crashed into the West Side. Mr Harman disputed the right of the RAF to claim any portion of the aircraft, arguing that any plane that crashed on Lundy became his property. The dispute led to some 'heated exchanges' until Mr Harman wrote: 'As you claim this aircraft to be the property of the RAF, will you please remove it from the island without delay.' The result was that a party of aircraftmen, led by a corporal, was sent to the island with instructions to throw every remaining part of the Heinkel over the cliff-edge into the sea. They did their work well and today only the remains of the engines can be found rammed into the cliff-face.

The Isles of Scilly became subject to income tax in April 1954 leaving Sark and Lundy as the only places in the British Isles where this tax was not levied. No attempt had been made to collect revenue on Lundy since the days of Sir John Borlase Warren when a revenue officer spent seven years there and collected no more than £5 in all. In October 1973 the government decided that this anomaly should end and so mainland rules of taxation were extended to include the island, though local rates were still not collected and licences for dogs, guns or road vehicles were still not required. Islanders do, however, pay the national contribution to the National Health Service and Insurance benefits, as do all the inhabitants of the British Isles.

In 1959 the skipper of a French fishing vessel had been fined for fishing within 3 miles of Lundy. Mr Albion Harman had given permission to the Frenchman under the impression that he was so entitled. The chairman of the court was of the opinion that Mr Harman did not possess the exclusive fishing rights of the island whereupon, having lost the case, the island applied to be classified by the Ministry of Agriculture as a hill farm and thereby become eligible for certain grants and subsidies.

Devon County Council submitted a memorandum to the Boundaries Commission in December 1959 saying that the position of Lundy should be clarified in matters affecting crime and local government and this eventually led to Lundy becoming part of the County of Devon with effect from 1 April 1974, when local government was reorganized throughout the country.

The consequences of this reorganization were widespread. Mr Gade, writing in 1973, said:

What the National Trust has permitted in the way of incursions into these rights and privileges, is to admit that Lundy is in the County of Devon, which makes it possible for the County Council to insist upon such things as the obligation to seek planning approval for all kinds of buildings and even alterations to existing buildings. . . . I'm sure that the late Mr Martin Coles Harman made no enquiries about the right which he gave himself to have coinage minted solely for use on Lundy, because he knew very well that he would be warned that to utter coinage would be contrary to the law of Great Britain. He went ahead with the minting of the coins intending to argue the point later if obliged to.

Grants were received in the 1970s for repairs to the Beach Road and the final act came in June 1980 when the island was assessed for a general rate of £1,250 per annum by the local authority.

Lundy may have lost almost all of its former privileges through erosion or through legal decision, but dogs and guns are still unlicensed, the tavern keeps its own hours of opening and the now world-famous Lundy stamps still emphasize the unique quality of the place.

Chapter Twenty-three

COINAGE, MAIL SERVICE AND STAMPS

Many people who have never visited the island have heard of, seen or collected Lundy stamps or coins. There are so often assumed to be a recent innovation and few realize that coins are believed to have been minted on Lundy over three hundred years ago, during the Civil War.

Lt.-Col. H.W. Morrieson in a lecture to the British Numismatic Society entitled 'The Coinage of Lundy 1645–6',[1] described the circumstances of the time and pointed out that Thomas Bushell, who had interests in both South Wales and in Combe Martin, would have found Lundy an ideal situation for his mint following the fall of Bristol to the Parliamentarians on 11 September 1645. When in July 1646 Bushell stated his terms for the surrender of Lundy he included his mint, which he must have had with him on the island as Oxford, the site of the last mainland royalist mint, had already fallen.

All the coins under discussion bear the mint mark A for 1645, or B, or a plume in 1646, and resemble those known to have been made at Bushell's Bristol mint. It has been argued that the A and B coins were struck at Appledore and Barnstaple respectively, as both these towns held out for the king until 1646 and were accessible for over six months after Bristol had fallen. This theory is unlikely as the privilege of erecting mints in Devon and Cornwall was vested in Sir Richard Vyvian who, had he struck coins at Appledore and Barnstaple, would have used his own dies from Exeter. Lundy, being a natural fortress would have offered the most secure site for a royalist mint and, as the island does not seem to have been blockaded, it would have been possible for bullion to have been taken there and for coins to have been brought away.

The coins considered by Lt.-Col. Morrieson to have been minted on Lundy are as follows:

Halfcrowns:	1645	obverse, one pattern known
		reverse, three patterns known
	1646	obverse, two patterns
		reverse, six patterns
Shillings:	1645	obverse, two patterns
		reverse, two patterns
	1646	obverse, two patterns
		reverse, three patterns

Sixpences:	1645	obverse, one pattern
		reverse, one pattern
	1646	obverse, two patterns
		reverse, two patterns
Groats:	1645	obverse, one pattern
		reverse, one pattern
	1646	obverse, one pattern
		reverse, two patterns
Threepence:	1645	obverse, one pattern
		reverse, one pattern
	1646	obverse, one pattern
		reverse, one pattern
Half groat:	1645	none
	1646	obverse, one pattern
		reverse, one pattern

At a subsequent meeting, attended by Mr Martin Coles Harman, Lt.-Col. Morrieson again discussed the Lundy mint and although some objections were raised, his theory has subsequently been widely accepted.

Lundy coins, 1929 (unknown)

In 1929 Mr Harman decided to have some coins minted for use on Lundy, equivalent in value and size to the one penny and halfpenny and these he called puffins and half puffins. The coins were minted in the same bronze alloy as imperial bronze coinage by Ralph Heaton & Sons of Birmingham.

On the obverse of the coins is a profile of Mr Harman and the words 'Martin Coles Harman 1929'. On the reverse of the one puffin coin is the legend 'Lundy One Puffin' with a puffin bird, while on the reverse of the half puffin is the legend 'Lundy Half Puffin' with the profile head of a puffin bird. The coins are not milled but are inscribed around the edge 'Lundy Lights and Leads'. There were 50,000 of each value struck and supplied at £2 10s 9d (£2.55) and £1 6s 6d (£1.33) per thousand respectively, with a charge of £100 for designing and sinking the dies.

The coins were issued on 14 November 1929 and were current on Lundy where English silver and Lundy copper were used concurrently. Arrangements were made by Mr Harman with the Bideford banks to exchange English copper for Lundy copper, an arrangement that continued until the High Court ruling of 1931, since when the coins have been sold only as souvenirs.

In 1965 the original dies were acquired by a company known as Modern World Coins who issued a double commemorative proof set of coins to mark the 40th anniversary of the purchase of Lundy by Mr Harman. Minting of the four specimens was undertaken by John Pinches Ltd of London, who had designed the original 1929 engravings and dies. A limited 3,000 proof sets were struck in imperial bronze and in nickel brass. These coins are identical to the 1929 issue except that they are not inscribed around the edge and they have the year 1965 in place of 1929.

Written messages must have been transported to and from Lundy for centuries, being carried by a trustworthy person and with private arrangements for any costs involved.

Following the establishment in 1840 of the Penny Post by Sir Rowland Hill and the use of adhesive stamps, the mainland national system developed quickly, but it was nearly half a century before the General Post Office established a service to Lundy. Until this time islanders' mail was carried free to and from the mainland post office and presumably Trinity House staff's mail was carried by their tender. Between 1863 and 1868 the employees of the Lundy Granite Company would have sent and received their mail on the company's ships. At other times visiting ships probably agreed to post mail on the mainland and the Heaven diaries mention as late as 1875 that 'Pilot Alfred Ray came ashore – and bound up channel took letters to post', implying that this was not an unusual service to the islanders. Finally, official interest was aroused and the following minute was sent to the Postmaster General on 15 April 1886 by the Secretary to the Post Office, Sir S.A. Blackwood:

Representation has been received from the Trinity House and the Committee of Lloyds in support of an application from the lessee of Lundy Island, on the

North Devon coast, for the establishment of a Postal Service to and from that Island, which is dependent upon trading vessels for the receipt and dispatch of letters.

This question has been considered on former occasions, and the paucity of the letters, as compared with the cost of a Postal Service, has hitherto precluded the Department from coming to any arrangement: but it now appears that by means of one of the steam tugs which ply between Cardiff and Lundy, a service once a week might be afforded with a fair degree of regularity, Mr Button of Cardiff having offered to make the trip from that port on Wednesday in each week with letters for delivery, and to return as soon as possible with letters for dispatch, provided he be paid for this conveyance at the rate of 1d for every letter, newspaper packet or parcel. It is estimated that there are 140 letters etc and 13 parcels a week for Lundy; but it is difficult to say how many there would be for dispatch. Under ordinary circumstances, the Revenue available for a Postal Service is computed at $\frac{1}{2}$d for each letter etc for delivery, i.e. in one direction only, but the acceptance of Mr Button's offer would more than absorb the whole payment of 1d, seeing that his stipulation is for payment at the rate of 1d for every article conveyed in either direction, even if it bear postage of $\frac{1}{2}$d only. On such terms the Service would of course entail some loss, but the case is exceptional, and is, I think, as much entitled to exceptionally liberal treatment as has been accorded to several islands on the West Coast of Scotland. I recommend therefore that a service once a week to and from Lundy may be established on the terms proposed, in the hope that it will not only develop the resources and promote the convenience of the island, but also lead to such an increase of correspondence as may, before long, admit of adoption of an arrangement which will be self-supporting.

Without a Post Office in the islands, the proposed service could scarcely be maintained in a satisfactory manner, and the carrying out of the measure should, therefore, be contingent on suitable provision being made for an Office. The Surveyor anticipates some difficulty in this head, but the difficulty would probably not prove insuperable.

The GPO undertook to pay half the expenses of the weekly mail and the rest was to be borne jointly by the proprietor and the lessee, Thomas Wright. Wright was most anxious to develop Lundy as a tourist attraction, emphasizing the sporting opportunities. Anticipating demand, he opened the hotel and seems to have been the driving factor in requesting a GPO service. After other feared difficulties had been overcome the post office opened on 4 March 1887 on which day eighty-seven letters were sent to Cardiff. The first chartered ship was *Queen of the Bay* but was soon superseded by *Lord Derby*.

The post office was established in the store (the present-day Marisco Tavern), where it remained until 1896. Mr Allday was then appointed postmaster and the office transferred to the telegraph office, which occupied the downstairs front room of the southernmost of the semi-detached houses that had been built in 1885 near the castle to house Lloyd's signallers. This arrangement lasted until 1906 when a small lean-to hut was built against the castle wall to house both the telegraph office and post office and to provide quarters for visiting GPO officials.

Prior to the GPO's involvement, Lundy mail had been routed via Instow post office and so confusion and delay resulted when, under the new arrangement, mail for Lundy arrived at Instow, only to be forwarded to Cardiff where it might be stowed on a ship which itself might be delayed on a fishing trip before putting in at Lundy. The system became so unreliable that on 20 April 1888 a regular service was started to and from Instow every Thursday, using the *Gannet* (Capt. W. Dark) which for the previous nine years had been providing a reliable service as the island supply boat, and in May 1888 the mail service via Cardiff was closed.

Incoming mail was distributed free and was not marked but outgoing mail for which mainland postal rates applied was stamped and cancelled 'Lundy Island' as in mainland practice.

The service had run so smoothly for twenty-three years that the Postmaster General was surprised when, in 1911, Capt. Dark requested the termination of his contract, feeling unable to continue at the unaltered fee originally agreed in 1888. In his efforts to make the service more effective Dark had in 1909 spent £200 to install a motor and now, with added running costs and the £10 per annum required by the new Workman's Compensation Act to cover his crew of three, could no longer operate at the existing fee.

Before inviting new tenders the Post Office costed the Lundy service and discovered that the average 139 letters and 5 parcels from Lundy and the 189 letters and 16 parcels to Lundy produced a revenue of £23 18s 10d to be set against an expense of £74 10s 10d. This trading loss obliged them to accept the lowest tender of the three which came in August.

J.R. Hocking of Appledore quoted the £57 per annum compared with Fred Dark's £125, and William Dark's £150. Hocking soon found with his *Morning Star* that the duties were not as easy as he had anticipated and after five months he asked to be released from his contract.

A solution appeared in sight as in November 1911 Mr Tucker, Secretary of the Bideford and Bristol Steamship Company, had written to the GPO to ask if he could be notified if the mail contract with Lundy should be open at any time. The Bideford and Bristol Steamship Company founded by a cooperative of local traders in 1894, ran their 99 ton packet the SS *Devonia* (Capt. Francis Beer) between Bristol Channel ports and, in a tender dated 7 March 1912, offered to carry mail from Instow post office to Lundy once a week on an outward voyage to Bristol on Mondays and carry the mail from Lundy to Instow on their return journey later in the week – this for a sum of £75 per annum., on the understanding that the post office agent on the island would collect or deliver the mail to the beach on both occasions.

This quotation seemed admirable and Mr Saunt, the island lessee, agreed that this was an improvement as it allowed a longer time for letters to be answered. Dark must have heard of this scheme as he tendered his services again, this time for £72 per annum only four days before the *Devonia* began its contract, on 18 March 1912.

Within a few months of opening the service, the B&BSSC agreed to alter the service to allow the Monday trip from Instow not only to deliver mail but also to collect islanders' correspondence and take it on to Bristol. Similarly the return Thursday trip would bring mail from Bristol and collect from the island to take back to Instow. This arrangement continued throughout the First World War, augmented occasionally by Admiralty patrol vessels from Milford Haven or by the Admiralty trawler *Robert Davidson* from Ilfracombe.

In April 1920 Mr A.L. Christie, as new owner of the island, bought a North Sea drifter, the *Lerina*, to serve as the island's transport and a contract was made with the Admiralty and Post Office under which mails and stores for the lighthouses and signal station were carried between Instow and the island once a week for £208 per annum. When Mr Harman bought Lundy in 1925 he took over the boat and, with it, the mail contract.

Lundy postmasters were appointed by the head postmaster of Bideford subject to the approval of the owner of the island. The longest serving of these was Mr F.W. Allday, who went to Lundy in 1896 and did not leave the island at all until he went ashore to consult a doctor in 1920. When he finally left in 1925 his place was taken by Mr Harry Lang, who resigned after a year to be followed by Mr R. Mien.

When Mr Mien in turn left Lundy at the end of 1927 Mr Harman was already finding that the cost of carrying and distributing mail was uneconomic and he gave notice to terminate his mail-carrying contract and asked for higher rates. 'This was not agreed to and he then made an intriguing suggestion. He offered to perform the service free of charge, provided letters posted on Lundy were forwarded to all parts of Great Britain and Northern Ireland without payment of postage.'[2] The GPO could not agree to this and as there was no alternative transport, the GPO closed their post office on Lundy on 31 December 1927. From then until November 1928 Mr Harman carried mails to and from Instow post office at his own expense – incoming mail being delivered free, with outgoing mail (carrying King George V postage stamps) being franked at Instow for forward transmission. The GPO incidentally had been paying Mr Harman £104 per annum at the time the contract ended to carry the mails 'once a week', although of course they were carried on every sailing.

Sometime in 1927 Mr Harman was the invited guest to a meeting of the British Numismatic Society to hear a lecture by Lt.-Col.. H.W. Morrieson on the coinage of Lundy during the period of the Civil War. Mr Harman, a great individualist and fierce defender of Lundy's independence, was that evening inspired to produce his own coins and it followed quite naturally that by issuing his own stamps he could defray his costs in transporting mail to and from the mainland, outgoing mail to be surcharged by a Lundy stamp by the sender and incoming mail to have a Lundy stamp affixed before distribution, for which the recipient was charged.

The Lundy letter box, 1992

At first both English and Lundy stamps were placed together at the top right-hand corner of the outgoing envelope, but as this caused confusion the Lundy stamp had to be placed elsewhere. Then in 1930 the GPO drew attention to the regulations which prohibit the affixing of any stamp on the same side as the English stamp and so, from then until 1992, all outgoing Lundy mail carried the Lundy stamp on the back of the cover, although from 1962 the regulations were eased to allow both the English and the Lundy stamps to be affixed on the same side of postcards only. These rules were all superseded in 1974.

Lundy stamps were issued in 'Puffin' values – one puffin equalling one penny. The initial rates for 'puffinage' were: first 2 oz, ½ puffin; subsequent 2 oz, 1 puffin.

1929 initial issue: ½ puffin, 1 puffin
1930 issue: 6 puffin, 9 puffin, 12 puffin

The experimental air mail service started by R.T. Boyd on 1 June 1934 laid the foundation for the regular, but private, service which began as Atlantic Coast Air Services on 1 April 1935. An additional charge for carriage by air was made by the airline who issued their own stamps. All values were in sterling and the first issue, an adhesive printed label, was aptly known as the 'Tramticket' issue.

1935 Atlantic Coast Air Service issue[3]
First printing: $\frac{1}{2}d$.
Second printing: $\frac{1}{2}d$, 1d, 3d.

1936 Atlantic Coast Air Services issue ('Large Map')
$\frac{1}{2}d$, 1d, 2d, 3d, 6d, 1s.

1937 Lundy and Atlantic Coasts Air Lines Ltd issue ('Small Map')
$\frac{1}{2}d$ violet. (These were hastily withdrawn as Mr Harman did not want it to be thought that Mr Boyd's air service was owned by the Lundy island authority. They reappeared in 1938 overprinted 'Lundy and Atlantic Coasts Air Lines Ltd'.)

1939 Lundy and Atlantic Coasts Air Lines Ltd issue
$\frac{1}{2}d$ bright red, 1d black.

1939 Additional values issue [p stands for puffin; see p. 212]
2p grey-blue, 3p black, 4p pink.

1939 Tenth anniversary overprint
$\frac{1}{2}p$, 1p, 6p, 9p, 12p.

1940 Red Cross overprint
$\frac{1}{2}p$ 1p, 2p, 3p, 4p, 6p, 9p, 12p.

1942 Victory overprint
$\frac{1}{2}p$, 1p, 2p, 3p, 4p, 6p, 9p, 12p.

1942 Tighearna sheet issue
Miniature sheet of two $\frac{1}{2}p$, one 2p, and one 9p stamps.

1943 Ninth anniversary overprint
$\frac{1}{2}p$, 1p, 2p, 3p, 4p, 6p, 9p, 12p.

1943 Additional values overprint
$1\frac{1}{2}p$ on 12p, $2\frac{1}{2}p$ on 6p.

1943 Wright Brothers overprint
$\frac{1}{2}p$ on 12p; 1p on 6p; $1\frac{1}{2}p$ on 9p; 2p on 6p; 3p on 9p; 4p on $\frac{1}{2}p$; 5p on 12p; 6p on 1p; 7p on 6p; 8p on 12p; 9p on 1p; 12p on $\frac{1}{2}p$.

1950 'By Air' overprint
$\frac{1}{2}p$, 1p, 2p, 3p, 4p, 6p, 9p, 12p.

1951 issue
$\frac{1}{2}p$, $1\frac{1}{2}p$, $2\frac{1}{2}p$, $3\frac{1}{2}p$, 5p, 7p, $7\frac{1}{2}p$.
8p overprinted on 12p.

1953 Coronation overprint
$\frac{1}{2}p$, 1p, 2p, 4p, 6p, 9p, 12p.

1954 Jubilee issue
Surface: $\frac{1}{2}p$, 1p, 2p, 4p, 6p, 9p, 12p.
Air mail: $\frac{1}{2}p$, 1p, 2p, 3p, 6p, 12p.

1954 Air mail pictorials issue
Similar design and values to Jubilee issue, but with colours reversed

1955 Millenary issue (triangulars and rhomboids)
$\frac{1}{2}p$, 1p, 2p, 3p, 4p, 6p, 9p values (surface and air mail).

1957 issue
1p, 2p, 3p, 4p, 6p, 9p.
1961 Europa overprint
'Europa 1961' overprinted on the nine millenary values
1962 Anti-malaria campaign issue (large diamond shape)
½p, 1p, 2p, 3p, 6p, 12p.
1962 Europa issue
1p, 2p, 6p, 9p.

Puffinage rates were changed from 1 April 1964. Postcards remained at 1p but letters up to 8 oz were charged at 2p.

1964 Shakespeare Quartercentenary issue
2p, 10p, 18p.
1965 'One Puffin' overprint
1p overprinted on 3p of 1957.
1965 Churchill commemorative issue
2p, 10p, 18p.
1967 'Help Save Seabirds from Oil' issue
Block of four 6p stamps in four languages.
1969 'One Puffin' overprint
1p overprinted on 9p of 1930.
1969 Appeal overprint
'Appeal' and '1p' on 9p of 1930.
1969 Postal anniversary issue
1p, 2p, 6p, 9p, 12p.
1970 'One Puffin' red overprint
Second overprint of 1p on 9p of 1930. Accidentally done in red and never used postally.
1971 Decimal issue
½p, 1p, 3p, 3½p, 4p.
1972 St Helena's church anniversary issue
1p, 2p, 3p, 5p, 10p.
1972 Trinity House issue
1p, 2p, 3p, 5p, 10p.
1974 Definitive issue
2p, 4p, 4½p, 5p, 5½p, 10p, 20p.
1974 Royal National Lifeboat Institution issue
1p, 4½p, 5½p, 10p.
1975 Architectural Heritage issue
1p, 6½p, 8p, 10p.
1976 New value issue
7½p (to align with increased mainland rates).

1976 American Bicentenary issue
  7½p, 9½p, 12p, 15p, 20p.
1976 Christmas issue
  7½p, 9½p, 16p.
1977 Silver Jubilee issue
  2p, 5p, 8p, 10p, 25p, 50p.
1977 Royal visit overprint
  Silver Jubilee souvenir sheets overprinted to commemorate the visit of
  HM Queen Elizabeth II to Lundy on 7 August 1977
1978 Coronation Jubilee issue
  8p, 10p, 12p, 20p.
1978 Marine Reserve issue
  8p, 10p, 11½p, 20p.
1978 New value issue
  ½p.
1979 '50th Anniversary of Lundy Stamps' issue
  8p, 10p, 11½p, 19½p, 22p.
1982 New values issue
  10p, 14p, 15p, 16p, 17p, 18p, 19p, 20p, 21p, 22p, 23p (to coincide with
  increased mainland rates).
1985 'First Balloon Flight' overprint
  Overprint in red on 20p of 1974.
1989 RSPB Centenary issue
  3p.
1989 Lundy Philatelic Bureau 'Bureau Mail' overprint
  '3' overprinted on 10p of 1982.
1989 60th Anniversary overprint
  '1929–1989' overprinted on 1982 values: 10p, 14p, 16p, 17p, 18p, 19p,
  20p, 21p, 22p, 23p.
1990 New provisional overprints
  Mainland postal charges increased on 17 September 1990: 5p on 17p; 22p
  on 14p; 27p on 16p; 31p on 19p; 45p on 21p.
1991 New definitive issue
  5p, 10p, 22p, 24p, 25p, 26p, 27p, 28p, 29p, 30p, 31p, 32p, 33p, 100p.
1992 'Discover Lundy' issue
  23p, 29p, 33p, 49p, 75p.

The above list of issues and values gives an outline of the variety of Lundy's stamps.
Full details of the issues together with their present values are given in an illustrated
book[4] which has been followed by a similar handbook illustrating the postmarks and
cachets used on Lundy mail.[5]

Chapter Twenty-four

FLORA AND FAUNA

Lundy has an extremely rich and interesting flora which has been closely studied since the inception of the Lundy Field Society in 1946. Prior to that, investigations had been published by Chanter, by Loyd in 1925, by Dr F.R. Elliston Wright[1] in the 1930s and by Mervyn G. Palmer in 1946.[2]

In 1971 Mrs E.M. Hubbard undertook 'A Survey of Trees on Lundy'[3] and in the following year published a list of flowering plants[4] which included all previous recordings. She writes:

> The composite floral list which embraces the ordinary flowering plants appears impressive in its number and diversity. Within the confines of a bleak, rocky island of but 1100 acres no less than 413 species have at some time been recorded and this total excludes ferns, grasses and sedges . . . and this apparent richness is even more remarkable if one considers how specialized the flora must be in such a generally hostile habitat. Not only do plants have to contend with high salt-laden winds, strong ultra-violet light, and violent storms, but the peaty soil itself is thin, highly acidic, subject to great variation in water content, and poorly supplied with mineral salts and clay constituents. Moreover there are large areas covered by such species as rhododendron, heather, and bracken which dominate their own particular habitats to the virtual exclusion of other plants. Against this must be set the good fortune Lundy has enjoyed in being farmed by traditional methods which conserve the existing flora . . . the botanical picture which emerges is a dynamic one of a basic stable flowering-plant population diligently recorded by naturalists, but enjoying but an ephemeral single generation existence.

Apart from Mrs Hubbard's survey of trees on Lundy which recorded no fewer than 433 trees and her definitive list of flowering plants which recorded 413 species, the annual reports of the Lundy Field Society contain lists of other flora recorded on the island, and these include gramineae,[5] lichen,[6] hepatics,[7] and fungi,[8] as well as other papers of botanical interest to which students should refer.

Lundy is perhaps best known for two species. The first is the Lundy cabbage (*Rhynchosinapsis wrightii*) named after Dr F.R. Elliston Wright who first noticed it in

1933. After specialist examination it was confirmed to be unique to Lundy and named after its discoverer in 1936. The plant, a primitive member of the cabbage family, grows on the cliffs and slopes of the eastern side of Lundy to a height of almost a metre and produces a bright yellow flower. It appears to thrive on newly disturbed soil and following the rockfalls and earth slips on the Beach Road between the beach and Millcombe Valley in the 1960s and '70s, its range has extended greatly and it is now found on the sidings above the Miller's Cake and the Sugar Loaf.

This region marks the southernmost limit of the second well-known Lundy plant, the rhododendron (*Rhododendron ponticum*). This is a Himalayan plant unknown in the west until late Victorian times and was introduced to Lundy in the late 1920s, with disastrous results. The highly acidic soil and the shelter offered by the eastern sidings has allowed the plant to spread along the entire East Side from the Sugar Loaf to Gannets' Combe. Although it produces an attractive flower, its dense vegetation prevents light reaching other plants and effectively sterilizes the soil on which it grows. It spreads relentlessly and working parties are now engaged every year to attack young plants at the edge of the 'rhododendron forest' to try to limit the spread and prevent it from engulfing the entire island.

A similarly dangerous plant, Alexanders (*Smyrnium olusatrum*) has recently been observed near Millcombe Gates and vigorous attempts are being made to eliminate it. It, too, has the power to spread relentlessly and until recently the small Bristol Channel island of Steep Holm was completely overrun by it.

Lundy – 'Puffin Island' – is predominantly a bird island. It serves as a nesting site for Atlantic seabirds, as an important link in the chain of landfalls used by migrating species and it also has many resident breeding species of its own.

References to its bird life occur in the earliest written references to the island, but it is only since the explosion of interest in the twentieth century, and especially since the formation of the Lundy Field Society in 1946, that close observation has revealed the true importance of the island for both migrating and nesting species. These observations were fully documented and analysed in a 1980 publication[9] that shows that Lundy has, at various times, been visited by almost every bird known to occur in north-west Europe.

Records reveal wide variations in the population of certain species over the years. The factors responsible range from alterations in the food supply, pollution, the weather at nesting times, disease and harrasment, both by predators and by man. Auks appear to have suffered most. They were caught in their thousands in the early nineteenth century and as late as 1939 Perry estimated the population of guillemots to be 19,000 pairs, of razorbills to be 10,500 pairs and of puffins to be 3,500 pairs.[10] By 1973 the totals for individual birds were 1,744 guillemots, 1,250 razorbills, and in 1990 a maximum of only 26 puffins were recorded.

That other birds have nested on Lundy in the past is beyond doubt. Gannets are still to be seen close to the island and fishing inshore, but although there were still

Puffin (R. Britton)

Razorbill (R. Britton)

fifteen pairs nesting on Gannets' Rock in 1883, the bird was being persecuted and the last colony on Lundy at the North West Point suffered from the disturbance caused by the building of the North Light and by the subsequent boom of its foghorn. Nevertheless five pairs hung on until 1903, in which year all their eggs were taken. It was about this time that a new gannetry was established on Grassholm, an uninhabited island off the Welsh coast, whence the Lundy gannets presumably fled. It is to be hoped that now nesting birds are protected by law, that Grassholm has become successfully overcrowded, and Lundy North Lighthouse has gone silent, that gannets may return to nest on Lundy.

Another former breeding bird would appear to be the now-extinct great auk which, being flightless, would nest close to sea-level, away from the attention of hunters. There appear to have been one or two couples nesting irregularly on the north-west coast of Lundy until the 1830s. The last surviving pair of great auks was killed in Iceland in 1844.

Lundy has also been the landfall for rare American, African or Asiatic birds blown off course, when strong winds occasionally blow for many days from one

Manx Shearwater (R. Britton)

particular quarter. Among these rarities are: little egret; American robin (1952); Spanish sparrow (1966); Rufous-sided towhee (1966); northern oriole (1958); harlequin (1991); blue-winged teal (1987); ancient murrelet (1990); eastern phoebe (1987); great spotted cuckoo (1990); olive-backed pipit (1989); Swainson's thrush (1985); gray-cheeked thrush (1985); black-poll warbler (1985); collared flycatcher (1990); red-eyed vireo (1989).

Marine mammals include frequent sightings of dolphins and porpoises, and the Landing Bay was visited by a killer whale in 1980 and by a long-finned pilot whale in 1991. The grey Atlantic seal is a popular sight as up to 100 pairs regularly breed in sea caves around the island.

Among the land-based feral animals are bats, both pipistrelle and long-eared, and the pigmy shrew which is common but rarely seen. One or two mice have been recorded and the black (ship's) rat and the brown rat uniquely coexist, though their numbers have declined recently.

Of the introduced mammals the rabbit and the goat have had the greatest influence. Rabbits were introduced in the thirteenth century, probably by returning crusaders, who established warrens on off-shore islands, where the animals were bred for their fur. Martin Harman estimated their numbers in the 1930s to be as high as 20,000 because in one season 11,000 had been trapped. Myxomatosis reached Lundy in 1983 leaving only 800 survivors, but a further severe outbreak in 1992 virtually eliminated those remaining, leaving perhaps less than a dozen survivors near the North End. The effect on the grazing has been dramatic and the island is now able to support double the number of sheep than previously.

Goats were probably left on the island by sailors, as was their practice a few centuries ago, to provide a source of meat for future shipwrecked mariners. Goats, and to a lesser extent rabbits, are probably the reason why the island vegetation has changed from the near-impenetrable thicket towards the North End recorded in the 'Journal of 1752', to the balding turf of today. Goats had become extinct by 1914 but when Martin Harman bought Lundy in 1925 he set about introducing various animals, among which were goats in 1926. These bred to such an extent that the herd of sixty had to be culled in 1973 and there now seems to be a stable population of about ten.

Mr Harman introduced 8 Soay sheep in 1942 and these hardy animals have been most successful. He also introduced fallow deer, Japanese (Sika) deer and red deer in 1927. The fallow and red varieties are now extinct, but about a dozen Sika deer remain hiding for much of the time on the eastern sidings where they do tremendous damage, especially to trees.

Mr Harman also introduced more exotic animals from time to time, but without success. Three wallabies survived a short while, but two swans, destined to decorate Pondsbury, flew off within an hour back towards the mainland.

Horses have been on Lundy as riding and as draught animals for many centuries. Mr Harman introduced fifty animals of mainly New Forest stock in 1928 in an attempt to establish a new breed of Lundy pony. Careful breeding has produced a distinctive breed which numbers about twenty. The number of cattle and sheep carried on the island varies from year to year and is dealt with in Chapter Twenty-one above.

Other island fauna has been studied in great detail by members of the Lundy Field Society and reports on insects,[11] *lepidoptera*,[12] non-insect invertebrates,[13] *coleoptera*,[14] and fishes[15] are recorded in the society's annual reports.

Appendix 1

POPULATION

Lundy has been inhabited from the earliest times and its population has varied because of climatic, economic and political changes. Figures given by various former authors were often at least second-hand, but the first national census of 1851 produced accurate figures.

The fluctuations in the population level shown in the list below must also be studied alongside the general history of the island, bearing in mind the degree of commitment of the owners of the time.

The earliest figure dates from the time of the de Mariscos:

Date	No.	
1242	17	Outlaws. William de Marisco and confederates.
1243	50 +	The king's constable, garrison and farm workers.
1597	12	
1647	21	24 Feb. Thomas Bushell and garrison.
1655	100 +	Probably exaggerated.
1694	23	Grose. 'Housed in seven houses'.
c.1795	20	Estimated (report to barrack master, Barnstaple).
1813	30	Estimated.
1833	6 ?	'One family'.
1851	34	(16m. + 18f.) First official census. 'In five houses'.
1858	19	Including labourers. All housed at farm (number is exclusive of Trinity House personnel or visitors).
1861	35	(22m. + 13f.) 'In five houses'. One new house uninhabited.
1865	240	Estimated. The quarries in full operation.
1871	65	(31m. + 34f.) In ten houses. Also thirty-three uninhabited houses and four under construction.
1881	61	(31m. + 30f.) In eleven houses. Sixteen houses uninhabited and four under construction.
1883	67	*Kelly's Directory*.
1885	61	
1886	40	Estimated.
1887	43	Chanter. 'Mr Heaven, his family and establishments, farm

Date	No.	
		manager and his family and servants, a few labourers, and Trinity House officials & families'.
1889	56	*Kelly's Directory.*
1891	53	(26m. + 27f.) In twelve houses. Sixteen uninhabited houses.
1893	67	*Kelly's Directory.*
1895	60	Estimated.
1897	116	*Kelly's Directory.*
1901	94	(78m. + 16f.) Figure includes fifty-nine men on board vessels. Islanders in eleven houses + four houses uninhabited. This total of fifteen houses compares with twenty-eight in 1891 and shows that thirteen houses at Quarter Wall were demolished to build St Helena's church.
1902	25	*Kelly's Directory.*
1906	25	10 employees of tenant; 5 Trinity House; 4 post office; 6 'Mr Heaven's people'.
1910	44	
1911	49	(23m. + 26f.) In eleven houses.
1916	8	(3m. + 4f. + one baby).
1921	48	(35m. + 13f.) In eleven houses.
1925	23	Parish register of 27 December 1925.
1926	25	
1927	14	
1929	18	
1931	21	(13m. + 8f.) In five houses.
1933	13	
1944	8	Agent, his wife, and 6 lighthousemen.
1950	15	Incl. 6 lightkeepers.
1956	20	Incl. 6 lightkeepers.
1963	28	Incl. 6 lightkeepers & 5 seasonal workers.
1966	22	Incl. 6 lightkeepers & 5 seasonal workers.
1970	40	Incl. 6 lightkeepers & 11 seasonal workers.
1971	41	Incl. 6 lightkeepers & 5 seasonal workers.
1975	46	Incl. 3 lightkeepers & 10 seasonal workers.
1977	39	Incl. 3 lightkeepers & 10 seasonal workers.
1980	20	Incl. 3 lightkeepers & 3 seasonal workers.
1986	24	Incl. 3 lightkeepers and warden.
1993	14	Incl. 3 lightkeepers.

Appendix 2

OWNERS, ADMINISTRATORS AND TENANTS OF LUNDY

*c.*1140–*c.* 1150 Henry de Newmarch.

*c.*1150–   Jordan de Marisco.

1160–1220   The Knights Templar granted Lundy by Henry II, but the Mariscos did not yield possession.

1194–1225   William de Marisco (son of Jordan).

1225–34   Sir Jordan de Marisco (son of William).

1234–42   Sir William de Marisco (son of Sir Jordan). Dispossessed in 1242 when Lundy declared forfeit to the Crown due to the piracy of his father's cousin William de Marisco (son of Geoffrey), who had installed himself on the island since 1235.

1242–54   Forfeit to the Crown (Henry III).

1242–3   William de Rummare, constable.

1243   Richard de Especheleg, constable.

1244   William de Cantilupe, constable.

1245–50   Henri de Traci, constable.

1250–1   Robert de Walerond, governor.

1251–   William la Zuche, keeper.

1254–81   Prince Edward (eldest son of Henry III) (became King Edward I, 1272); William la Zuche still there October 1254.

1264   Mauger de Sancto Albino, keeper.

1264   Sir Ralph de Wyllyngton, keeper, July–Sept.

1264–5   Humphrey de Bohun the Younger, keeper.

1265   Adam Gurdon, keeper, June–Nov.

1265–6   William, Earl of Pembroke (the king's brother), keeper.

1266–72?   Prince Edmund (the king's second son), keeper.

? 1272–?4   Sir Geoffrey Dinan, Baron Dinan.

? 1274–5   Oliver de Dinan, his son (possessor without authority).

1275   Geoffrey de Shauketon, keeper, May–July.

1275   Oliver de Dinan, lessee.

1281–4   Sir William de Marisco, restored.

1284–9	Sir John de Marisco (his son).
1289–90	Hebert de Marisco, a minor (son of John).
1290	Rotheric de Weylite appointed custodian by the king. Olivia de Marisco (Sir John's widow) claimant.
1300–21	Olivia de Marisco.
1321–6	Herbert de Marisco, held title but not possession (d. 1326).
? 1321–2	Sir John de Wyllyngton (whose lands forfeit to Crown in 1322).
1322–6	Hugh, Lord Despencer the Younger (d. 1326). Granted by Edward II who was deposed 1326.
1326–7	Prince Edward, later Edward III.
1326	William de Kerdestan, keeper, Nov.–Dec.
1326–7	Otto de Bodrigan, keeper.
1327–	Sir John de Wyllyngton – estates restored (d. 1332); Stephen de Marisco (brother of Sir John de Marisco) claimant.
1332	Sir Ralph de Wyllyngton (son of Sir John de Wyllyngton).
1332–44	William de Montacute, 1st Earl of Salisbury (purchased from Ralph de Wyllyngton, with financial settlement to all other claimants).
	John Luttrell (d. 1337–8) ?lessee.
1344	William, 2nd Earl of Salisbury, a minor. Inheritance in the protection of King Edward III. Katherine de Montacute (widow of 1st Earl) claimant to one third.
1349–50	William, 2nd Earl of Salisbury (came of age 1349, the year his mother died).
1350–90	Sir Guy de Bryan (who married Elizabeth, daughter of the 2nd Earl of Salisbury).
1390	Elizabeth de Bryan, a minor (granddaughter of Sir Guy). Inheritance in the protection of King Richard II.
1391–3	John Devereux (brother-in-law of Elizabeth de Bryan) appointed keeper by the king. Died 1393 when keeper.
1393–1400	John de Holand (the king's half-brother).
1400–34	Elizabeth Lovell (née Bryan, came of age 1400).
1434–6	Maud Stafford (née Lovell) (her daughter).
1436–8	Humphrey Fitzalan, Earl of Arundel (her son), a minor (d. 1438).
1438–57	Avice Butler, Countess of Ormonde (née Stafford) (his half-sister).
1457–61	James Butler, 5th Earl of Ormonde (her husband). Executed 1461 when lands forfeited to Crown.
1462–3	William Neville, Earl of Kent. By gift of his nephew, the new king, Edward IV.
1463–78	George, Duke of Clarence, the king's brother (d. 1478).

1478	Forfeit to the King, Edward IV.
1479–88	John Wykes, 'Gentilman', by grant of the king.
1488–1515	Thomas Butler, 7th Earl of Ormonde, restored to his brother's estates.
1515–32	Anne St Leger (née Butler) (his eldest daughter).
1532	Sir George St Leger (her son).
1577	Sir John St Leger (his son).
1577–91	Mary St Leger (his daughter), who married Sir Richard Grenville.
1591–1619	Sir Barnard Grenville (her son). Leased to tenants, of whom Robert Arundell held a fourth of the island until 1600.
(1601–3)	Seized by Sir Robert Basset, Catholic Pretender to the throne.
1619–43	Sir Bevil Grenville (son of Barnard).
1643–1701	John Grenville, later 1st Earl of Bath (his son).
1643–7	Thomas Bushell, appointed governor by the king during the Civil War.
1647–60	William, 1st Viscount Saye and Sele, by grant of Parliament (John Grenville, Royalist, still claimant).
1658–9	Sir John Ricketts, Commonwealth governor.
1660	John Grenville, now 1st Earl of Bath, restored.
1701	Charles Grenville (his son).
1701–11	William Grenville (his son) (d. without issue).
1711–54	John Leveson, Lord Gower (Jane Grenville, daughter of 1st Earl of Bath married Sir William Leveson Gower).
1715	17 March. Island leased to Mr Morgan.
c.1720	Mr Scores, tenant farmer ('illegal practices').
1748–54	Thomas Benson MP, lessee.
1754–75	Administered by executors of Lord Gower (d. without issue).
1775–81	Sir John Borlase Warren, by purchase.
1781	W. Clayton, lessee.
1781–1802	John Cleveland, by purchase; (island leased to tenants under owner's supervision). Mr Hole, tenant farmer (d. 1788); Mr Budd, tenant farmer, left 1791; 'J.S.', tenant farmer 1792; Hugh Acland, tenant farmer, 1797–1817.
1802–18	Sir Harry Vere Hunt Bt., by purchase.
1805–7	Island leased to Mr H. Drake.
1818–30	Sir Aubrey de Vere Hunt (his son).
1830–4	John Matravers and W. Stiffe (his creditors).
1834–83	William Hudson Heaven, by purchase. Resided on Lundy.
1847–61	Mr John Lee, tenant farmer.
1861–2	Mrs Blackmore, tenant farmer on fourteen year lease.
1862–71	W. McKenna, leaseholder, who sub-let farm to Lundy Granite Co., lessees of the granite workings.

1883–1916	The Revd Hudson Grosett Heaven (son of W.H. Heaven).
1885–91	Mr Wright, tenant farmer.
1892–9	Mr Henry Ackland, tenant farmer; Mr Dickinson, storekeeper and postmaster.
1899–1908	Mr G.T. Taylor, tenant farmer on twenty-five year lease.
1908–12	L. and W.F. Saunt, lessees of the island, except Millcombe.
1912–16	Walter C. Hudson Heaven (nephew of Revd H.G.H.), manager.
1916–17	Walter C. Hudson Heaven (nephew of Revd H.G.H.).
1917–20	Mr S.T. Dennis, manager.
1918–25	Augustus Langham Christie, by purchase.
1919	Charles Hill, bailiff.
1920–5	Mr C. Herbert May, lessee.
1925–54	Martin Coles Harman, by purchase.
1925–6	R.G. Laws, agent.
1926–46	Felix W. Gade, agent.
1940–Feb. 1942	Mr Van Os leased Lundy (apart from Millcombe House).
1946–9	D. Heaysman, agent.
1949–70	Felix W. Gade, agent.
1954–68	Albion P. Harman, Ruth Harman-Jones, Diana P. Keast, children of, and heirs to M.C. Harman: joint owners.
1968–9	Kathleen Harman (widow of A.P. Harman), Ruth Harman-Jones, Diana P. Keast: joint owners.
1969–	National Trust.
1969–	Landmark Trust, lessees.
1970–7	I.G. Grainger, agent.
1978–83	Col. R. Gilliat, agent.
1983–	John Puddy, agent.

Appendix 3

LUNDY COMPANIES

Several companies have been associated with Lundy, both directly and indirectly, over the past century or so. Details of these companies are freely available at the Companies Register and are given below.

Lundy Granite Company Ltd (No. 544c)

Registered 18 July 1863. Objects:

> To purchase the lease, quarries, rights and interests of William Columban McKenna of 8 Colville Terrace West, Bayswater, in the County of Middlesex, in and about the island of Lundy in the Bristol Channel, agreeable to a contract bearing the date 10.7.1863, between the said William Columban McKenna and Francis Costelloe of Kingsland, on behalf of this company. Also to open granite quarries on the said island and to work the same, and to transport the said granite. Also to cultivate the said island. Also to purchase or hire any land or buildings or any docks or wharves in London or elsewhere, which may be considered desirable for the purpose of selling the granite or other productions of the island, and generally to do any act which may be necessary for, or may tend to the development of the resources of the island.

Capital stood at £25,000, being 5,000 shares at £5 each. The capital was afterwards increased to £100,000 divided into 20,000 shares, of which 15,480 had been taken up. The capital was spent in opening up the quarries and in building accommodation, and the Quarry Beach jetty etc. The company, was, however, wound up on 19 November 1868 and on 29 January 1869 an order of official liquidation was made. (A company calling itself the Western Granite Company Ltd was writing to the Devon press from Lundy in July 1870. This company was never registered and does not appear in the Companies Register. It seems likely to have been a desperate attempt by Frederick Wilkins, Henry Benthall and Commander Rivington to prolong the life of the Lundy Granite Company and to reap whatever rewards they could.)

Lundy Island Floating Breakwater Company Ltd (No. 855c)

Registered 23 December 1863. 'The objects for which the company is established are the construction of a floating breakwater within the roadstead on the eastward side of Lundy Island. Also to provide for the maintenance of the structure and the purchase of a steam tug vessel.' Capital was £2,000 as 400 shares of £5 each, and it was intended to levy tolls from vessels within the harbour. Among a list of subscribers was Capt. Christopher Claxton, of 11 Park Road Villas, Brompton, S.W., to whom all official notices were sent but were all returned marked 'Not known at this address'. In the absence of any returns, or directors, the company was dissolved by the Registrar of Joint Stock Companies in 1882.

Lundy Cable Company Ltd (No. 19296)

Registered 11 January 1884. Objects: 'To lay one or more cables between Lundy and Hartland Point or to other places in England or Wales. To lay telegraphic land lines between a signal station on Lundy and a mainland post office in England or Wales. To erect a signal station on Lundy etc., etc., and things relating thereto.' Capital of £10,000 with 1,000 shares at £10 each.

Lloyd's agreed to provide all signal stations for ten years, to defray working expenses, and to pay the company royalty of 2s per message, to owners and others, plus an annual subsidy for duplication of such messages to their London offices.

It was estimated that 80,000 vessels passed Lundy annually and if one tenth were to use the company's line it would generate an income of £880. A licence was thus obtained without difficulty from the Board of Trade. Rogers, telegraphic engineers of London, was contracted to lay the 10 mile cable, and Legg of Swansea to construct 4 miles of land line from Hartland Point to the post office.

Despite a promising start the venture proved unprofitable and the company went into liquidation in 1887.

Lundy Granite Quarries Ltd (No. 55273)

Registered 15 December 1897. Objects: 'The company was to have exclusive right of quarrying granite and other stone for a period of 21 years from 21.12.1896, with the option of continuing the term for a further period of 21 years at a rent of £200 as therein mentioned and subject to royalties.' Among the objects were the purchase of machinery, cranes, tools, etc., and the proposal to manufacture 'granolithic' or other artificial stone. Further, 'To construct dwellings, temporary or otherwise, for the use of workmen on the island and to construct a breakwater, floating or otherwise, within the roadstead on the eastern side. To purchase or charter vessels for conveyance, and to construct, erect and maintain gas works, water works and electric light works.'

Capital was £30,000 as 30,000 shares at £1 each. By 2 May 1898 only seven shares had been taken up, and the company was therefore wound up on 26 October 1900.

The Lundy Island and Mainland Quarries Ltd (No. 64458)

Registered December 1899. Objects: Similar to those of Lundy Granite Quarries Ltd but including the construction of breakwaters 'or aerial cableways'.

Capital was £80,000 as 80,000 shares at £1 each. The company was initiated with the same seven shareholders as for Lundy Granite Quarries Ltd. On 14 March 1902 the name was changed to Lundy Island Granite Quarries Ltd.

Lundy Island Granite Quarries Ltd

Trading under its new name this company's management decided that royalties should be paid at 4*d* a ton.

By 31 December 1905, 4,013 shares had been taken up. On 11 June 1907 the company was amalgamated with Property Securities Co. Ltd. The director's report dated 31 July 1909 stated 'that their efforts to start work at the quarries on Lundy Island have proved unavailing, and last autumn, previous to the offering of the island for sale at the Mart, the owner cancelled the lease held by the Property Securities Co. Ltd'. The company offered to buy the island but the price was too high.

The company was dissolved on 10 February 1911.

Lundy and Atlantic Coast Air Lines (No. 327241)

Formation of this company was proposed by R.T. Boyd and F.W. Gade on 17 April 1937 with a share capital of £10,000 as 10,000 £1 shares and with a registered office at Bridge Buildings, Barnstaple.

A certificate entitling the company to commence business was issued on 29 April 1937, and on the following day Mr R.T. Boyd sold his business, the Barnstaple and North Devon Aerodrome, to the new company completely except for one Moth airplane (No. G–ABBK).

On 22 May 1937 the company raised a mortgage of £1,000 and used this sum, plus 1,250 £1 shares, to buy a Short Scion airplane (No. G–ACUW), and for a further £400 cash plus 750 £1 shares acquired from Frank Janes Perrin his Monospar S.T.4 airplane (No. G–ACCP) and D.H.60 Moth airplane (No. G–AAIM). Mr Perrin gave his time to the new company for which he received £30 per calendar month as manager while agreeing to give his services as pilot and instructor without charge.

By 28 May 1937 a total of 4,358 shares had been allotted. The balance sheet for the year ending 30 April 1938 showed the fares and sales as £1,649, but the balance showed a net loss of £393 10s 1d. The balance sheet a year later again showed a net loss – this time of £354 3s 6d.

On 3 March 1941 the name of the company was changed to Atlantic Coast Air Lines Ltd, and although civil flying was curtailed by the war, the airfield was taken over by the Air Ministry which paid rent to the company.

The balance sheet for 1944 showed a profit of £2,750. The company ceased trading on 28 March 1947 and was finally wound up on 31 March 1953 when all the record books were destroyed.

Devonair Ltd

Registered on 6 December 1952 with a nominal capital of £2,000 as 2,000 £1 shares. Three directors were appointed one of whom was Capt. Maurice L. Looker, the pilot. The company's registered office was at Bridge Buildings, Barnstaple.

By 12 January 1953, 845 shares had been sold, of which the late Martin Coles Harman had taken 250. By March 1954, 1,351 of the 2,000 shares had been sold. The company had no debts and paid no dividend.

On 21 October 1954 the registered address was altered to Wrafton Gate and five days later all the assets were mortgaged. Permission was obtained to increase the capital to 5,000 shares on 4 November 1954.

Gannet Fishing Company

Registered on 11 February 1956 with a nominal capital of £100 as 100 £1 shares. The registered office was 24, Broad Street Avenue, London, EC 2. In a return dated 23 February 1956, five ordinary shares had been allotted, one each to the first two directors and one each to A.P. Harman and his two sisters. At an extraordinary general meeting on 12 March 1956 the capital was increased from £100 to £5,000.

On 1 September 1958 the *Lundy Gannet*, owned by the company, was mortgaged for £2,500. After the ship was sold in 1976 the company went into voluntary liquidation without liabilities or assets.

The Lundy Company (Certificate No. 960421)

Registered on 18 August 1969 with a nominal capital of £100 as 100 £1 shares. This private company has among its objects: 'To acquire, undertake, carry on and execute on the island known as Lundy any business, undertaking, transaction or operation whatsoever, including but without prejudice to the generality of the foregoing farming and the provision of hotel and other facilities for visitors, and to establish and maintain such means of communication and such transport facilities between Lundy and elsewhere as may seem to the Company desirable.'

As a private company 'two persons present in person or by proxy shall be a quorum at any General Meeting' and the directors 'shall not be less than two nor more than five in number'. Mr J.L.E. Smith and Mrs C.M. Smith were directors in 1969, but in 1972 two solicitors were appointed as alternative directors to Mr and Mrs Smith.

White Funnel Steamers (No. 1458817)

Registered on 11 October 1979 with nominal capital of £100 as 100 £1 shares. Objects: 'To operate, establish, maintain and administer and carry on all or any of the businesses of manufacturers, designers, repairers, operators, hires and letters of hire, distributors, charterers, and agents for the sale of, and dealers in pleasure steamers.'

There were two subscribers, Michael Richard Counsell and Christopher Charles Hadler, both of 15 Pembroke Road. Every director was to be a permanent director. The registered office was at Alliance House, Baldwin St., Bristol BS1 1NQ. The directors were John Lindsey Eric Smith, banker, 21 Deans Yard. Other directorships were listed as: Abacus Securities Ltd; Coutts & Co.; Cumulus Finance Co. Ltd; Cumulus Investment Trust Ltd; Cumulus Systems Ltd; The Lundy Company; Manifold Trust Co. Ltd; Ottoman Bank; Rownsmoss Ltd; Smith St Aubyn & Co. Ltd; Sterling Trust Ltd; Strand Nominees Ltd; CCST Commodities Ltd; Sidney Clifton Smith-Cox, Alliance House, Bristol. The Secretary was Roger Frank Lucas, address given as Alliance House. The certificate of incorporation was dated 2 November 1979. (The company incurred a loss of £60,000 during its brief existence.)

Lundy Services Limited (No. 1540558)

At an extraordinary general meeting at Wishlynn Limited held on 15 June 1981 a special resolution was passed to change the company name to Lundy Services Limited. This was incorporated on 7 August 1981.

The nominal capital is £100 divided into 100 shares of £1 each. The objects for which the company is established include: 'To acquire, undertake, carry on and execute on the island known as Lundy any business, undertaking, transaction or operation whatsoever, including but without prejudice to the generality of the foregoing farming and the provision of hotel and other facilities for visitors, and to establish or procure and maintain such means of communication and such transport facilities between Lundy and elsewhere as may seem to the company desirable.

Notes

Chapter 1 Early History

1. G.R. Mitchell, 'Glacial Gravel on Lundy Island' in *Transactions of the Royal Geological Society of Cornwall*, XX, pt 1 (1965–6).
2. A.J. Schofield and C.J. Webster, Lundy Field Society, 40th Annual Report (1989), pp. 34 ff.
3. A.T.J. Dollar, 'Abbreviated Report of Investigations up to and including June 1932 – Neolithic Man on Lundy Island', unpublished ms.
4. Peter Levi, *The Flutes of Autumn* (Harvill, 1983), p. 183.
5. S.M. Pearce, *The Kingdom of Dumnonia* (Padstow, Lodenek Press, 1978), p. 70.
6. Geoffrey Ashe, *A Guidebook to Arthurian Britain* (1980), pp. 8, 149.
7. Rachel Bromwich, *Tricedd Ynys Prydein* (1978), Triad 52, pp. 140–1, p. 377.
8. H.R. Smith, *Saxon England* (1953), pp. 576–7.
9. R.H. Hodgkin, *History of the Anglo-Saxons*, Vol. 2, p. 476.
10. Four possible sites have been suggested for Cynuit: at Clovelly; near Countisbury; near Cannington; near Bideford. Of these, Kenwith near Bideford, where the castle mound and earthworks can still be traced, best fills the description given in reputable sources.
11. K.S. Gardner, *Lundy, An Archaeological Field Guide* (Landmark Trust, 1971).
12. 'Holdboldi Hundason – a Chieftain of Tiree' in *Orkneyinga Saga* (Harmondsworth, Penguin, 1978), p. 233.
13. D.C. Capper, *The Vikings of Britain* (1937), pp. 187–8; quoting Icelandic saga translated by Sir G.W. Basent, HMSO (1894).
14. E. St John Brooks, *Journal of the Royal Society of Antiquaries of Ireland*, LXI, p. 29.
15. Smith, op. cit.
16. Deacon, *Madoc and the Discovery of America* (1969), pp. 41, 94; quoting 'Devonshire Records, Exeter. 1893' (these have so far proved to be untraceable).

Chapter 2 The de Mariscos

1. *Burke's Landed Gentry* (1952); see entry for the De Marris family.
2. *Notes and Queries* (21 June 1930), p. 440; *The Complete Peerage* (1949), Vol. II, Appendix D, pp. 107–8.
3. *Somerset Pipe Roll 1194 and 1195*.
4. *Pipe Rolls*.
5. George Oliver, DD, 'Monasticon Dioecesis Exoniensis' (Exeter, 1846), p. 208 quoting deed in *New Monasticon*, vol. 6, fol. 842; and see Cart. Rot. 1 John, pt 1.22.
6. *Oblate Roll 1200*.
7. *Somerset Pipe Roll 1202*.
8. *Pipe Rolls*. William owed 120 marks for having Lundy in 1204. In 1205 and 1206 he still owed 120 marks, and in 1207 and 1208 he owed 108 marks. In 1209 he owed £53 7s 4d; in 1210 he owed £43 7s 4d and in 1211 he owed £22 8s.
9. *Pipe Roll 1202*.
10. Lyson's, *Magna Britannia*, vol. 6 (Devonshire), pt 2, p. 587.
11. *Liberate Rolls*, 2 May 1204.
12. Revd Joseph Stevenson, *The Church Historians of England containing the Chronicle of Melrose* (1856), vol. 4, pt 1, pp. 162–9.
13. *Letters Patent*, 7 November 1217.
14. Camley was the dower of his wife Lucie de Alneto who is buried with her son Jordan and grandson

William in Bath Abbey; see J. Collinson, *History and Antiquities of the County of Somerset* (1791), vol. 2, p. 392.

15. Matthew Paris, *Chronica Major* (J. Stow, 1571).
16. William, son of Jordan, inherited Lundy on the death of his father in 1234; see *Calendar of Inquisitions Post Mortem*.
17. Geoffrey's castles of Killorglin in Desmond, and Holywood in County Dublin; and William's castle in Coonagh, County Limerick.
18. Probably Reginald de Marisco.
19. A. Leslie Evans, *Margam Abbey* (1958), pp. 71–2.
20. *Calendar of Close Rolls*. Henry III (1237–42), p. 443.
21. John Lawrence, *A History of Capital Punishment* (Sampson Low, nd), p. 6; 'Hanging, Drawing and Quartering was invented for the express benefit of a William Maurice, the son of a nobleman who was convicted not of treason but of piracy. He suffered in 1241.'
22. Heraldic evidence supports this as the arms of the Marisco family were 'Gules, a lion rampant argent' and that of William de Marisco (d.1242) were 'Or, a lion rampant sable, langued Gules'; see G. Steinman Steinman, 'Some Account of the Island of Lundy' in *Collectanea Topographica et Genealogica* (John Bowyer Nichols & Son, 1837), vol. 4, p. 75; a lion rampant suggests royalty.

Chapter 3 Early Middle Ages 1243–1485

1. *Liberate Rolls*, 12 June 1242.
2. Ibid., 15 June 1242.
3. Ibid., 23 June 1242.
4. Ibid.
5. *Close Rolls 1242*, p. 446.
6. *Liberate Rolls*, 22 July 1242.
7. Ibid., 6 October 1242.
8. Ibid., 8 November 1242.
9. Ibid., 11 November 1242.
10. Ibid., 5 February 1243.
11. Ibid.
12. Ibid., 3 March 1243.
13. Ibid., 29 April 1243.
14. Ibid., 15 April 1244.
15. *Patent Rolls*, 23 May 1244.
16. *Liberate Rolls*, 26 May 1244.
17. *Close Rolls 1244*.
18. Ibid., p. 194. (St Briavels is in South Wales.)
19. Ibid., 1 July 1245.
20. *Patent Rolls*, 8 August 1250.
21. *Liberate Rolls*, 27 September 1250.
22. *Patent Rolls*. A passage in H.W.C. Davis, *England under the Normans and Angevins* reads: 'Henry III gave to his son, at the time of the marriage, an extensive appendage, which in fact comprised all the outlying possessions of the Crown.'
23. On 8 October 1254, this would appear to be a misnomer.
24. *Patent Rolls*, 12 July 1264. Richard de Walerond gave a notification that the commitment of Lundy to his keeping gave him no rights therein.
25. Ibid., 15 September 1264.
26. Ibid., 14 June 1265.
27. Ibid., 2 June 1266.
28. This term almost certainly means 'by honour of baronage', as the Dynhams were the Barons Dynham. It has been suggested as a mis-spelling of 'per ballium' which means by bailment, i.e. life interest only.
29. *Hundred Rolls*, 3 Edw. I, vol. 1, pp. 73, 93.
30. *Fine Rolls*, 28 May 1275.
31. *Close Rolls*, 29 May 1275.
32. *Patent Rolls 1275* (exact date not given).
33. *Fine Rolls*, 9 July 1275.
34. Madox, Formulare Anglicanum 601. m21.
35. *Charter Rolls*, 28 October 1281.

36. *Patent Rolls*.
37. *Close Rolls*, 13 April 1291 (Roderic is almost certainly the Rotheric mentioned above).
38. Ibid., 16 July 1300.
39. J.R. Chanter, *Lundy Island* (Cassell, Petter & Galpin), p. 69.
40. *Calendar of Inquisitions*, 18 May 1322.
41. *Charter Rolls*, 16 June 1322 (similar entry in *Patent Rolls*, 20 July 1322).
42. T. Westcote, *View of Devon 1630* (Exeter, 1845).
43. *Fine Rolls*, 2 December 1326.
44. *Close Rolls*, 7 February 1327 and *Fine Rolls*, 3 December 1326.
45. *Patent Rolls*, 18 February 1327; *Calendar of Patent Rolls*, Rich. II (1905) 82.
46. *Close Rolls*, 26 February 1327.
47. The son of Herbert, Stephen de Marisco died in 1374 without issue, see *Calendar of Ormonde Deeds*, 26 April 1331.
48. *Rolls of Parliament*, vol. 2, p. 64; *Patent Rolls*, 28 October 1332.
49. Devon *Feet of Fines*, vol. 2. Devon and Cornwall Record Soc. (1939), Extract No. 1242.
50. *Close Rolls*, 24 November 1346; confirmed in *Cal. Inqu. Post Mortem* 1338.
51. *Fine Rolls*, 19 April 1391.
52. *Patent Rolls*, 4 February 1392.
53. Ibid., 24 February 1393.
54. *Close Rolls*, 17 March 1400, repeated in *Fine Rolls*, 28 May 1400 and in *Close Rolls*, 15 June 1400.
55. *Patent Rolls*, 1 August 1462.
56. Ibid., 25 January 1463, repeated 2 July 1465, 18 July 1474.
57. John Pinkerton, *The History of Scotland* (1797).
58. Anna Blair, *Scottish Tales* (Glasgow, Drew, 1987), pp. 70–3.
59. *Patent Rolls* and *Calendar Patent Rolls*, Ed. IV (1901) 155.

Chapter 4 Late Middle Ages 1485–1636

1. 8 August 1515.
2. *Calendar of Letters and Papers Henry VIII*, VII (1883), no. 148.
3. Ibid., XII, 2 (1891), no. 159.
4. *Calendar of Letters, Dispatches and State Papers, Spain, Henry VIII*, VI, 2 (1895), no. 41, and James Froud, *History of England*, vol. 4 (New York 1871), p. 158.
5. *Calendar of State Papers Henry VIII*, V (1849), no. 172.
6. Acts of the Privy Council, N.S. II (1890) 253.
7. Public Record Office LR6/15/6.
8. Ibid., S.C. 6/Hen VIII/3127 membrane 12.
9. *Calendar of State Papers, Foreign*, Series No. 668, 12 May 1559.
10. Ibid., No. 693, 16 May 1559.
11. A.L. Rowse, *Sir Richard Grenville of the Revenge* (Cape, 1937), p. 149; quoting *Close Rolls* 20 Eliz. pt.1 (C54/1024).
12. John Strype, *The Annals of the Reformation (1820–40)*, vol. 2, pt 2, pp. 616–17.
13. Roger Granville, *History of the Granville Family* (1895).
14. Neville Williams, *Captains Outrageous* (Barrie, Rockliff, 1961).
15. Rachel Lloyd, *Elizabethan Adventurer* (Hamish Hamilton, 1974); quoting High Court, Admiralty 1/42.
16. Percy Russell, 'Fire Beacons in Devon', *Transactions of the Devon Association*, LXXXVIII (1955), p. 269 quoting Duke of Somerset's Papers in Hist. MSS Comm. 15th Report, App. VII.
17. W. Cotton, 'An Expedition against Pirates' in *Transactions of the Devon Association* (1886), and reprint of the Barnstaple Records – extract from the receivers accounts for 1578–88.
18. R. Pearce Chope, 'New Light on Sir Richard Grenville' in *Transactions of the Devon Association* (1917), Appendix A.
19. Reply from the council (9 May 1596) in Acts of the Privy Council N.S., XXV (1901), 237 & 380. Also Hist. MSS Comm. Marquis of Salisbury VI (1895), 35.
20. *Calendar of State Papers Ireland*. Eliz. V (1890), 293–4.
21. Hist. MSS Comm. Marquis of Salisbury, pt 8, (HMSO 1899), p. 58.
22. A.J. Loomie in *Mariners Mirror*, November 1963.
23. Hist. MSS Comm. Marquis of Salisbury, pt 8, p. 60.
24. St Mary's church guidebook, Atherington, Devon.
25. List of proceedings in the Court of Requests. 1, Lists & Indexes 21 (1906, rep. 1963), 327 (Public Record Office ref: REG.71.68).

26. Hugh Trevor-Roper, *Catholics, Anglicans and Puritans* (Martin Secker & Warburg, 1989), p. 20.
27. Ibid., p. 21.
28. *Calendar of State Papers*, 18 January 1600 and PRO SP 12/274/20. Printed in H. Foley, 'Records of the English Province of the Society of Jesus' (1877–84) IV, pp. 646ff.
29. *Calendar of State Papers Domestic* (1591–4), pp. 209, 246; (1598–1601), p. 181.
30. Public Record Office State Papers 14/6/1 (examination of Richd. Bellew and Nathaniel Austin, servants of Sir Robt.Basset); Hist. MSS Comm. reports, Marquess of Salisbury XI, 288.
31. *Calendar of State Papers James I 1857*, p. 301.
32. From deposition of William Younge; see *Gentleman's Magazine*, XI, pp. 354–5 (original document in custody of the Portreeve of Laugharne, Carmarthenshire).
33. W. Hepworth Dixon *Her Majesty's Tower*, vol. 3 (1871), pp. 152–3.
34. *Calendar of State Papers*, 2 July 1610.
35. *Dictionary of National Biography*, vol. 55, pp. 122–3.
36. *Calendar of State Papers*, 25 August 1625.
37. Ibid.
38. Reported 26 April 1628 by Capt. R. Fogg of HMS *St James*.
39. J. Foster, *Sir John Elliot: A Biography* (John Murray, 1864), pp. 624–9.
40. John Stukely, *Sir Bevill Grenville and his Times* (1983).
41. HMS *Assurance*, Capt. Richd. Plumleigh, sent to Lundy to capture Smith.
42. *Calendar of State Papers*, 30 July 1633, item 48.
43. Ibid., 14 September 1633, item 31.
44. Ibid., 28 January 1633/4.
45. Ibid., 24 February 1633/4.
46. *Notes and Queries*, 10th Series, Vol. 3 (Jan–June 1905), p. 469 quoting *Calendar of State Papers*, 30 July 1633.
47. M. Hervey *The Life of Thomas Howard* (1921), p. 383.

Chapter 5 The Civil War

1. Duncan Fielder, *A History of Bideford* (1985), p. 26.
2. 'Petitionary Remonstrance'. Lord Bath says Bushell 'rebuilt the Castle from the ground' which seems unlikely, and Meyrick's introduction in his *History of the County of Cardigan* (1810, p. 219), says Bushell 'constructed a harbour at Lundy where his vessels might lie in safety' which is also unlikely.
3. By August 1646 all the mainland had fallen and only the off-lying islands remained in royalist hands.
4. Southgate's saleroom No. 1436 F.10 (21 June 1852) and Warburton, *Memoirs of Prince Rupert and the Cavaliers* (1849).
5. T. Bushell, 'Brief Declaration . . .' pp. 3–4.
6. Ibid., p. 5.
7. Ibid.
8. A.C. Miller, *Sir Richard Grenville of the Civil War* (1979), p. 140.
9. Bushell, op. cit., p. 9.
10. Ibid., pp. 12–14.
11. Ibid., pp. 18–20.
12. J.W. Gough, *The Superlative Prodigal* (1932) pp. 78–9.
13. 'Mercurius Politicus'. *Annales Republicae Anglicae II* (1651) p. 888. He was there in 1651 and 1653, see Dorothy Osborne's *Letters*, edited by Moore Smith, p. 91, and Hist. MSS Comm. 7th Report, p. 81.
14. The first of these booklets directed against the Quakers, *Folly and Madness made Manifest* was published in Oxford in 1659. This evoked a reply from one Mr Bray D'Oyly which was answered by Saye & Sele in a second booklet entitled *The Quaker's Reply manifest to be Railing*, published in Oxford in 1660. (Both now in Bodleian Library. Wood 645.) Although there is no indication in either that the author was then on Lundy, the dates suggest that this was so.
15. Naval Record Society 76. *The Letters of Robert Blake* (1937), pp. 71–2.
16. 'Mercurius Politicus', op. cit., pp. 888–9.
17. *The Depositon Books of Bristol* (II), 1650–4 (Bristol, 1948), pp. 122–3.
18. Ibid.
19. *Calendar of State Papers* XXIX, 2 February 1653 and 18 March 1653.
20. Ibid., XXXII, 13 March 1655–6.

21. F.M.L. Poynter (ed.), *The Journal of James Yonge* (Longmans), p. 37.
22. T. Bushell, 'Petitionary Remonstrance', 13 December 1664.

Chapter 6 From 1665 to 1754

1. *Calendar of State Papers*, 21 June 1667.
2. Originally quoted by Grose.
3. *Calendar of Treasury Papers* II (1871), 144.
4. *Calendar of State Papers*, 9 April 1700.
5. Treasury Papers 114,9. See Martin, *History of Devon*, p. 122.
6. Graham Smith, *Smuggling in the Bristol Channel 1700–1850* (Newbury, Countryside Books, 1989), p. 126.
7. Stanley Thomas, *Nightingale Scandal* (Bideford, 1959), pp. 51–2.
8. *An Apology for the Life of Bampfylde-Moore Carew* (London, 1749); edition of 1931, pp. 207–8.
9. 'Politics and the Port of Bristol', Bristol Record Society, XXIII, p. 56.
10. Anthony D. Hippisley Coxe, *A Book about Smuggling in the West County* (Tabb House, 1984), p. 3.
11. 'Benson, M.P. and Smuggler', *Hartland Chronicle* (1906).
12. HM Customs and Excise Library. Originals in Public Record Office, Kew.
13. Coxe, op. cit., pp. 57–8.
14. Smith, op. cit., pp. 125–6.
15. Lundy Field Society, 40th Annual Report (1989), p. 50.
16. 'Journal of the Time I spent on the Island of Lundy, in the years 1752 and 1787' by a Gentleman (Lt. Chrymes, RN), being Article 1 of Issue No. 2 of the *North Devon Magazine* (Barnstaple, W. Searle, 1824), pp. 51–62 quoting 'Journal of 1787'.
17. Graham Smith, *Something to Declare.* (Harrap, 1980), pp. 42–7.
18. *Gentleman's Magazine* (1754) pp. 278–9.
19. Believed by some to have taken holy orders. See Britton and Brayley, *Beauties of England and Wales*, vol. 4 (1803).

Chapter 7 From 1754 to 1834

1. 'Some Account of Biddeford', *Gentleman's Magazine* (1775), p. 448; *Gentleman's Magazine* (1789), p. 1070. (This was written before December 1754 when Lord Gower died.)
2. 'Notes from a Diary' by an Irish Gentleman, quoted by J.W. Powell, *Bristol Privateers and Ships of War* (Bristol, 1930), p. 222.
3. Graham Smith, *Smuggling in the Bristol Channel 1700–1850* (Newbury, Countryside Books, 1989).
4. *Exeter Flying Post*, 29 March 1765, p. 2.
5. W.V. Anson, *The Life of Admiral Sir John Borlase Warren* (1912), p. 18.
6. *Annual Biography & Obituary* VII (1823), p. 145.
7. 'Journal of 1787'.
8. Manuscript notes typed by William Warren Vernon (great-grandson of Admiral Sir John Borlase Warren) taken from the Admiral's notebooks to his agent. These MS notes were in the possession of the Harman family.
9. Anson, op. cit.
10. Smith, op. cit., p. 126.
11. G. Steinman Steinman, *Coll. Top. et Gen.*, vol. 4, p. 327.
12. F. Nesbitt, *Ilfracombe Parish Church*, quoting *Calendar of State Papers*.
13. HM Customs & Excise Library. Original in PRO, Kent.
14. Revd Jas. R. Powell in MS notes, vol. 11, p. 499. West Country Studies Library, Exeter.
15. Cardiff Records, vol. 2, p. 385.
16. At Bristol the eggs were used to refine sugar and the egg whites, when mixed with sugar crystals, were used to form the 'Sugar Loaf' used by cooks of that period.
17. 'Journal of 1787'.
18. MS letters dated 2 August 1795 in North Devon Record Office, Barnstaple.
19. John Kinross, *Fishguard Fiasco* (Tenby, 1974), p. 45.
20. Undated newspaper cutting inside a copy of Chanter in the North Devon Athenaeum; see also *North Devon Herald*, 27 September 1906; also J. Green, 'History of the Marsh Family' (*c.* 1896).
21. Sir Aubrey de Vere Hunt (b. 1788, d. 1846), baronet. He succeeded to the baronetcy in 1818, took the name of De Vere in 1832: 'A quiet country gentleman and poet.'

22. Mrs M.C.H. Heaven; 'This was the account given by Stiffe to Wm. H. Heaven.'
23. Mrs M.C.H. Heaven.
24. *Gentleman's Magazine*, May 1832, pt 2, p. 640.

Chapter 8 From 1834 to the Present

1. Mrs M.C.H. Heaven.
2. Dr Kyan devised a method of preserving timber using mercury bichloride.
3. Memoirs of the Earl of Malmesbury (1884); entry of 22 October 1852.
4. P.H. Gosse writing anonymously in *The Home Friend* (1853).
5. J.H. Barrett, *A History of the Maritime Forts in the Bristol Channel* (1978), p. 28.
6. W.H. Norman, *Tales of Watchet Harbour* (1985), pp. 147–8.
7. *Weekly Mercury*, 2 September 1908. Similar rumours were current in 1856, 1916, 1936 and 1954.
8. *Hansard*, 16 March 1915.
9. Wilfrid Blunt, *John Christie of Glyndebourne* (1968), p. 51.
10. F.W. Gade, *My Life on Lundy* (1978); and in correspondence and conversation with the author.

Chapter 9 From Beach to Plateau

1. W. Camden, *Britannia* (1637 edn).
2. Mrs M.C.H. Heaven.
3. William Younge's deposition, in *Gentleman's Magazine*, vol. XI, pp. 354–5.

Chapter 11 The East Side

1. L.R.W. Loyd, *Lundy, Its History & Natural History* (Longmans, Green & Co., 1925) p. 12.
2. Rex Wailes, *The English Windmill* (1954) mentions that the first English windmill was built as early as 1191.
3. 'Journal of 1787'; entry dated 10 July 1781. This journey was almost certainly made on what is now the East Side path as the West Side path does not even appear on Chanter's map of 1877 and probably did not come into use until after the erection of the telegraph poles.
4. Lundy Field Society, 8th Annual Report (1954).
5. One is that they were sold to a salvage company and duly raised; another that they were taken to Cardiff Castle (a story refuted by the late Marquess of Bute); and lastly that they were salvaged by a tenant farmer and sold to Mr F.R. Crawshaw about 1865 and mounted by him on his 39 ton yacht *Querida*, a 54 ft schooner built in 1857.
6. Queen Mab is the fairy in Celtic folklore who presides over dreams. Originally a legendary Queen Maev of Connaught, she is mentioned in Shakespeare's *Romeo and Juliet*. The name was almost certainly given by the Heaven family as Shelley wrote 'Queen Mab' while on his honeymoon at nearby Lynmouth in 1813.
7. Mrs M.C.H. Heaven.
8. Notes in a copy of Chanter in the author's possession.
9. Lundy Field Society, 13th Annual Report (1959).
10. Notes in a copy of Chanter in the author's possession.

Chapter 12 The West Side

1. Mrs M.C.H. Heaven: 'So called by the Heaven Family – mis-named Long Ruse on O.S. Map.'
2. Throughout the country large works of nature are ascribed to the devil. Following the discovery of the Giants' Graves the Heaven family called this feature 'The Giants' Slide'.
3. P.H. Gosse, *Land and Sea*, p. 100.
4. Mrs M.C.H. Heaven.
5. Percy Russell, 'Fire Beacons in Devon' in *Transactions of the Devon Association*, LXXXVII (1955), p. 269.
6. J. & C. Bord, *Mysterious Britain* (Granada Publishing Ltd, 1983 edn.), p. 115.
7. Duke of Somerset's Papers, Hist. MSS Comm. 15th Report, App. VII.
8. The Heaven papers.

9. 'Journal of 1787'; entry dated 4 July 1787.
10. Gosse, op. cit., pp. 67–8.
11. *The Home Friend*, III (1853) no. 54.
12. Ibid.
13. Chanter, op. cit., p. 126.

Chapter 13 The Archaeology of Lundy
1. Keith S. Gardner, *Lundy, An Archaeological Field Guide* (2nd edn, 1978).
2. Douglas B. Hague, *The Early Christian Memorials, Lundy* (Aberystwyth, 1982).
3. Caroline Thackray, *The National Trust Archaeological Survey, Lundy Island, Devon* (April 1989).
4. Ibid., p. 25.
5. Ibid., pp. 30–2.

Chapter 14 The Castle
1. Stephen Dunmore, 'The Castle in the Isle of Lundy', Report for Department of the Environment (1981).
2. Alfred Harvey, *Castles and Walled Towns of England* (Methuen, 1911), p. 67.
3. T. Bushell, 'Petitionary Remonstrance', 13 December 1664.
4. Dunmore, op. cit.
5. Chanter, op. cit., p. 44.
6. G. Steinman Steinman, *Coll. Top., & Gen.*, vol. 4, p. 328.
7. *The Home Friend*, vol. 2, no. 47 (1853): 'The Cave is now used as an occasional stable.'
8. 'The De Vere Papers 1822–1827' (unpublished), p. 69; Michael Mannix writing to Sir Aubrey de Vere Hunt dated 'Lundy Is. 20 January 1824'.
9. Public Record Office, Admiralty Documents: ADM 116/957, /958, /959, /982.

Chapter 15 Ecclesiastical History
1. Charles Thomas, 'Beacon Hill Re-visited, a Reassessment of the 1969 Excavations' in Lundy Field Society, 42nd Annual Report (1991), pp. 43–54.
2. Ibid.
3. Exeter Diocesan Archives. Letter from county archivist to author, 26 March 1993.
4. *Liberate Rolls*, 15 April 1244.
5. E. St John Brooks, *Notes and Queries*, 4 April 1942, p. 190.
6. *Patent Rolls*. (An apparent error as this is the only reference to the chapel as St Mary's.)
7. Register of the Bishops of Exeter.
8. Britain, like Germany, may have established 'plural benefices' or brought about the 'closure of many Monasteries and Churches'. Cleeve was one of the severely affected houses 'so reduced that the Refectory and Dormatory had to be cut down in size accordingly'; see Philip Ziegler, *The Black Death* (1982), pp. 86–7 and p. 273. (Burnet Morris's card index in the West Country Studies Library, Exeter, lists 'de Griffin, priest, (1332)' under 'Lundy'. No source is given, but de Griffin may fill the gap between 30 November 1332 and 6 March 1333.)
9. *The Victoria History of the County of Somerset*.
10. Hugh Peskett, 'Guide to Registers of Devon and Cornwall 1538–1837'. Devon and Cornwall Record Society (1979).
11. *The Times*, 19 May 1856, p. 9.
12. Chanter, op. cit., p. 99.
13. 'Journal of 1787', p. 57.
14. Chanter, op. cit.
15. Heaven family history MS.
16. *Devon and Exeter Gazette*, 16 July 1895.
17. Revd F.E. Robinson, *Among the Bells*, (1909).
18. *The Times*, 9 August 1954; and *Ringing World*, 27 August 1954, 10 September 1954, 8 October 1954 and 29 October 1954.
19. Exeter Diocesan Register. Letter from deputy registrar to author, 13 September 1958.

Chapter 16 Communications

1. *Once a Week*, 25 January 1862.
2. Lundy Field Society, 12th Annual Report (1958).
3. History of the Heaven family, MS.
4. Ward's, *North Devon* (1885).
5. *Western Morning News*, 12 August 1863.
6. *North Devon Journal*, 28 June 1888.
7. *Hartland Chronicle*, 15 June 1919.

Chapter 17 Shipwrecks

1. Graheme E. Farr, *Chepstow Ships* (Chepstow Society).
2. John Keay, *The Honourable Company* (Harper Collins, 1991), pp. 246–8.
3. *Western Luminary*, 1 February 1820 and *Exeter Flying Post*, 3 February 1820.
4. G. Steinman Steinman *Col. Top. & Gen.*, vol. 4, pp. 328–9.
5. John Purdy, *New Sailing Directions for the English Channel* (1842, 9th edn).
6. Royal Commission on Harbours of Refuge (1859), p. 291.
7. *Exeter Flying Post*, 7 July 1842, p. 3.
8. Wreck Register in Parl. Accounts and Papers (1850–1918). See also Michael Bouquet, 'Lundy Shipwrecks' in Lundy Field Society, 18th Annual Report (1967), pp. 19–23.
9. *North Devon Journal*, 25 May 1856.
10. Ibid., 17 July 1856.
11. Ibid., 6 June 1861.
12. Ibid., 23 April 1868.
13. Ibid., 25 January 1866.

Chapter 18 Lighthouses

1. *Exeter Flying Post*, 22 February 1787, p. 1.
2. 'Journal of 1787'.
3. *North Devon Journal*, 20 June 1861.
4. *Western Morning News*, 28 April 1928.
5. Trinity House Records, 1856.
6. *The Home Friend*, vol. 3, no. 58 (1853), p. 128.

Chapter 19 Geology

1. A.T.J. Dollar, 'The Lundy Complex, Petrology and Tectonics' in *Quarterly Journal of the Geological Society* (Sept. 1941).
2. A.G. Tindle and R.S. Thorpe, 'Lundy – Site of Tertiary Volcano?', and C.L. Roberts, 'Magnetic Consideration of the Volcanic Dykes on Lundy Island' in Lundy Field Society, 42nd Annual Report (1991).
3. G.F. Mitchell, 'Glacial Gravel on Lundy Island' in *Transactions of the Royal Geological Society of Cornwall*, vol. 20, pt 1, 1965–6 (1968).
4. C.S. Taylor, 'Some Notes on the Pleistocene Geomorphology of Lundy' in Lundy Field Society, 25th Annual Report (1974), pp. 66–8.
5. K.S. Gardner, 'Lundy – A Mesolithic Peninsula?' in Lundy Field Society, 18th Annual Report (1967), pp. 24–5.
6. D. & F. Lysons, *Magna Britannia* (Thomas Cadwell, 1822), vol. 6, p. 581: 'Several unsuccessful searches have been made in the island for copper ore.'

Chapter 20 The Granite Quarries

1. Heaven papers; original lease.
2. Revd H.G. Heaven in *Western Mail*, 9 August 1906.
3. Medal now in possession of Christie family at Tapeley, Instow, Devon.

4. Letter from London County Council's Surveyor's Office in reply to enquiry by late A.E. Blackwell.
5. H.G. Heaven, op. cit.
6. Michael Bouquet, 'Lundy Granite Boom' in *Western Morning News*, 3 September 1963.
7. *Bideford and North Devon Gazette*, 22 February 1927.
8. J.L.W. Page, *The Coasts of Devon and Lundy Island*, pp. 239–40.
9. Mrs M.C.H. Heaven.
10. Rear Admiral Sir Matthew Slattery, 'Troubled Times' in *Three Banks Review* (Sept. 1972), pp. 42–5.
11. *The Times*, 9 November 1870, p. 7.
12. Law Reports, Chancery Appeal Cases 1870–1, vol. 6, p. 463.

Chapter 21 Climate and Cultivation

1. Mrs M.C.H. Heaven in a letter dated 15 July 1936.
2. W.G. Hall (ed.), *Man and the Mendips* (Mendip Society, 1971), p. 26.
3. England was then at war with Scotland, though the attack was most probably made by sympathizers of Isabella from Wales.
4. Geoffrey Baker, *Life and Death of Edward II* (c. 1350), p. 599. Wrongly attributed to Sir Thos. de la More.
5. *The Times*, 10 November 1992.
6. A.J. Loomie, 'An Armada Pilot's Survey on the English Coastline, October 1597' in *Mariners Mirror*, vol. 49 (1963), p. 293.
7. Devon and Cornwall, *Notes and Queries*, vol. 31, pt 4 (1969), p. 140.
8. Letter from Bevill Grenville to Eliot in Eliot MS, p. 181, published by Roger Granville (original letter held by Lord Bath at Longleat).
9. Notes by W. Warren Vernon from the notebooks of his greatgrandfather, Sir John Borlase Warren, sent to his agents. (Typescript dated 1897 formerly in possession of the Harman family.)
10. 'Journal of 1787'.
11. *Western Times*; letter from Lundy dated 29 June 1792.
12. G. Steinman Steinman quoting Feltham MSS. (Chanter wrongly dates this as 1802.)
13. 'Letters sent and received by the Barrack Master of the Cavalry Barracks, Barnstaple. 1794–1807', Report in North Devon Record Office, Barnstaple.
14. W.S.M. D'Urban and R.A. Mathew, *Birds of Devon* (R. Porter, 1892), Introduction, p. xli; quoting *Yarrells British Birds* 4th edn, p. 653.
15. W. White, *History of Devonshire* (1850), p. 565.
16. Chanter, op. cit., p. 109.
17. *The Home Friend*, vol. 3, No. 57, (1853), p. 98.
18. Chanter, op. cit., p. 111.
19. Mrs M.C.H. Heaven.
20. F.W. Gade, *My Life on Lundy* (1978).

Chapter 22 Lundy's Uniqueness

1. *North Devon Journal*, 28 July 1870.
2. Ibid., 18 January 1866.
3. Ibid., 3 July 1866.
4. Ibid., 12 December 1867.
5. Ibid., 21 December 1871 and *Ilfracombe Chronicle*, 19 December 1871.
6. Boundary Commission for England; Report (Dec. 1950) HMSO.
7. Lundy Field Society, 4th Annual Report (1950).
8. Correspondence held in the office on Lundy.

Chapter 23 Coinage, Mail Service and Stamps

1. *British Numismatic Journal*, XIX (1927–8), (2nd ser. IX).
2. *Post Office Magazine*, August 1953, p. 228.
3. The 'missing' rolls may have been supplied to and used at Plymouth, Jersey, Cardiff, or other airports served by Atlantic Coast Air Services.
4. Stanley Newman, *Stamps of Lundy Island* (Hove, 1984).
5. Stanley Newman, *Postal History, Postmarks and Cachets of Lundy Island* (Brighton, 1991).

Chapter 24 Flora and Fauna

1.   F.R. Elliston Wright, 'The Lundy Brassica with some Additions' in *Journal of Botany* (1936).
2.   Mervyn G. Palmer, *The Fauna and Flora of the Ilfracombe District* (Exeter, 1946).
3.   E.M. Hubbard, 'A Survey of Trees on Lundy' in Lundy Field Society, 21st Annual Report (1971), pp. 14–19.
4.   E.M. Hubbard, 'A Contribution to the Study of the Lundy Flora' in Lundy Field Society, 22nd Annual Report (1972), pp. 13–24.
5.   Lundy Field Society, 37th Annual Report (1986).
6.   Ibid., 13th Ann. Report (1959/60); 23rd Ann. Repot (1972).
7.   Ibid., 26th Ann. Report (1975).
8.   Ibid., 21st Ann. Report (1970); 22nd Ann. Report (1971); 23rd Ann. Report (1972); 38th Ann. Report (1987).
9.   J.N. Dymond, *The Birds of Lundy* (Devon Bird-Watching and Preservation Society, 1980).
10. Richard Perry, *Lundy, Isle of Puffins* (Lindsay Drummond, 1940), p. 266.
11. Lundy Field Society Annual Reports, 21st (1970); 28th (1977); 32nd (1981); 34th (1983); 37th (1986); 38th (1987); 40th (1989); 41st (1990); 42nd (1991).
12. Ibid., 5th (1951); 19th (1968); 23rd (1972); 24th (1973); 30th (1979); 32nd (1981); 36th (1985); 37th (1986); 38th (1987); 39th (1988); 40th (1989); 41st (1990); 42nd (1991); 43rd (1992).
13. Ibid., 36th (1985); 38th (1987); 39th (1988); 40th (1989); 41st (1990); 42nd (1991).
14. Ibid., 20th (1969); 26th (1975); 28th (1977).
15. Ibid., 27th (1976); 28th (1977); 29th (1978); 32nd (1981); 40th (1989); 42nd (1991).

Select Bibliography

Mention of Lundy is widespread. It occurs dozens of times daily in radio and television weather forecasts, it will be found in every guidebook to the West County, and it appears briefly in many books on speciality subjects and in magazine articles.

A select bibliography should include:

Works devoted entirely, or mainly, to Lundy

Places of publication are given only if outside London:

Boundy, W.S., *Bushell and Harman of Lundy*. Bideford, Grenville, 1961.
Chanter, J.R., *Lundy Island*. Cassell, Petter & Galpin, 1887.
Davis, G.M. and R.C., *The Loss of HMS Montagu*. Atworth, privately published, 1981.
——, *Trial of Error*. Atworth, privately published, 1983.
Dymond, J.N., *The Birds of Lundy*. Devon Bird-watching & Preservation Society, 1980.
Etherton, P.T., and Barlow, V., *Tempestuous Isle*. Lutterworth Press, 1950.
Gade, F.W., *My Life on Lundy*. Reigate, privately published (M.S. Langham), 1978.
Gardner, K.S., *Lundy, An Archaeological Field Guide*. The Landmark Trust, nd.
Lamplugh, L., *Lundy, Island without Equal*. Barnstaple, Robert Young, 1993.
Langham, A.F., *The Pirates of Lundy*. Reigate, privatelt published, 1985.
——, *The Shipwrecks of Lundy*, Reigate, privately published, 1985.
Langham, A. and M., *Lundy, Bristol Channel*. Reigate, privately published, 1959.
——, *Lundy*. Island Series, Newton Abbot, David & Charles, 1970.
Lauder, R., *Lundy, Puffin Island*. Bideford, Badger Books, 1984.
Loyd, L.R.W., *Lundy, Its History & Natural History*. Longmans, Green & Co., 1925.
Lundy, The official guide, no publisher, nd.
The National Trust Archaeological Survey, Lundy Island, Devon. 2 vols., 1989.
Newman, S.A., *Stamps of Lundy Island*. Hove, IPPA Publications, 1984.
——, *Postal History, Postmarks & Cachets of Lundy Island*. Brighton, CILA Publications, 1990.
——, *Mailboats to Lundy*. Brighton, CILA Publications, 1993.
'Journal of the time I spent on the island of Lundy in the years 1752 and 1787' in *North Devon Magazine*, Vol. 2. Barnstaple, 1824.
Page, J.L.W., *The Coasts of Devon & Lundy Island*. Horace Cox, 1895.
Perry, R., *Lundy, Island of Puffins*. Lindsay Drummond, 1940.
Rogers, I., *Lundy Island*. Bideford, no publisher, nd.
Studdy, r., *Lundy, Bristol Channel*. Bideford, no publisher, nd.
Watt-Smyrk, J., *Lundy*. Privately published, 1936.

Books or Pamphlets containing unique or useful references to Lundy

These have all been fully identified in the notes.

Index